MY TWENTY YEARS IN ITALY

How Opera and Skiing Changed My Life

DAVID SCOTT

outskirts
press

My Twenty Years in Italy
How Opera and Skiing Changed My Life
All Rights Reserved.
Copyright © 2023 David Scott
v2.0

The opinions expressed in this manuscript are solely the opinions of the author and do not represent the opinions or thoughts of the publisher. The author has represented and warranted full ownership and/or legal right to publish all the materials in this book.

This book may not be reproduced, transmitted, or stored in whole or in part by any means, including graphic, electronic, or mechanical without the express written consent of the publisher except in the case of brief quotations embodied in critical articles and reviews.

Outskirts Press, Inc.
http://www.outskirtspress.com

ISBN: 978-1-9772-5777-2

Cover Photo © 2023 David Scott. All rights reserved - used with permission.

Outskirts Press and the "OP" logo are trademarks belonging to Outskirts Press, Inc.

PRINTED IN THE UNITED STATES OF AMERICA

Table of Contents

Acknowledgements — i

Introduction: How it all began in an Italian neighborhood — ii

One: 1961: Luca Pacioli Accounting, The Tax Audit, and the Merlin Law/Berlin Wall Misunderstanding — 1

Two: 1962: My Lucky Day and Our Honeymoon in Greece and Turkey — 18

Three: 1963: Paris, Spain, Amalfi Coast, and a tour of the Alps — 35

Four: 1964: Sardinia, the Palio, and the Venetian Regatta — 44

Five: 1965: East Africa — 55

Six: 1966: A Change in Status and A Visit to Naples — 75

Seven: 1967: Gary arrives - Complete with dual American and Italian Citizenship Papers — 85

Eight: 1968: Labor problems in the Naples factory and business in Israel ... 100

Nine: 1969: Valeria arrives, Gary starts school, travels from Capri to Hong Kong ... 116

Ten: 1970: Exploring Russia ... 131

Eleven: 1971: Gary's first day of school, Sicilian Fish Soup, and doing business in communist countries ... 157

Twelve: 1972: Visit to Orsara Di Puglia and Pickpockets in Naples ... 178

Thirteen: 1973: Au Pair troubles and more adventures in Sardinia ... 183

Fourteen: 1974: Robin arrives and a trip to Nigeria ... 200

Fifteen: 1975: Nigeria and the Two-Step Viper ... 221

Sixteen: 1976: Jordan to Timbuktu ... 251

Seventeen: 1977 - Business in Saudi Arabia, Vacation in Sardinia, and the Houseboat Adventure ... 277

Acknowledgements

This book is dedicated to my beautiful and talented wife Lydia Vergani whom I was fortunate to meet and marry 60 years ago. She is as beautiful today as she was when I first met her at the early morning bus stop in the Piazza of the Sforza Castello of Milan.

I am grateful to my older daughter, Valeria Scott Laitinen for her editing and organizational help in completing this book and sorting through our photo albums to locate the images that support my story. I also appreciate the editing work of my younger daughter, Robin Scott in the early versions of the book.

Also, I extend my thanks to my friend and teacher of computer technology Nancy Little. Without her help in understanding the rapid growth of computer technology I would have not been able to complete this project.

Last but not least my thanks to Maia Laitinen, my granddaughter, for her expertise in proofreading the final manuscript.

David Scott

Introduction: How it all began in an Italian neighborhood

This book is a collection of twenty annual Christmas letters written from 1961 through 1980 for relatives, friends and classmates from my Harvard College class of 1951 and Harvard Business School class of 1953. It covers a great romance, three children and a fascinating career in international business.

The story of my exciting twenty years of living and working in Italy as an adult has its origin in the first 7 years of my life. We lived in an Italian neighborhood on the north side of Chicago, half a block from the beach on Lake Michigan and about a half a mile south from the Edgewater Beach Hotel. This area was not far from the headquarters of the famous Italian American gangster, Al Capone. In our apartment building lived several families of Italian descent who had recently escaped from the dictatorship of Benito Mussolini.

Our Italian neighbors were proud of their Italian heritage and believed Mussolini to be a disaster. They were pleased that in World War I Italy had been allied with Great Britain and America. They were impressed that my father had driven an ambulance as a soldier in the English army, allied with the Italian army at the Battle of Caporetto. That famous battle was on the Austrian-Italian front, south of the Brenner Pass. My father had been wounded when an Austrian shell hit his ambulance. An Italian soldier, Corporal Dante Fiorelli, had pulled him out of his burning vehicle and carried him to an Italian field hospital saving his life. My dad honored Mr. Fiorelli by naming his second son (my brother) Dante.

Young Dave (standing) with his mother, Eva, and brother, Dante

Because of that episode, I was welcomed as part of the Italian gang of kids in our neighborhood. Most of them were very musical and the boys had no inhibitions on singing anywhere they happened to be, whether walking on the streets or in their apartments. From time to time they, and their fathers, would burst out singing Italian songs at the top of their lungs. I learned some of their beautiful songs. One of the songs I particularly liked was *Funiculì Funiculà*, about going up in a funicular ski lift to the top of a mountain. I also liked the song about the Bay of Naples and fishing near Sorrento.

We moved out of that jolly neighborhood when I was seven and I missed my enthusiastic Italian playmates with their lack of inhibitions. On one wall in our Chicago apartment, we had large poster of the Sestriere ski area in the Alps between Italy and France. It was a beautiful picture of the mountain ski area and its famous 15-story round cylinder hotel. In the foreground was an attractive smiling couple on their skis. The girl had beautiful blue eyes and blond hair who looked very happy. She was smiling at her handsome escort. In the background was a funicular cab on its way to the top of the mountain crowded with skiers. When we moved out of Chicago to the northern suburb of Winnetka, we took that poster with us and pinned it onto the wall in our staircase landing. I looked at it every day.

My father was a professional musician, a concert soloist, and later became a piano and voice teacher. There was classical music constantly in our house, from Mozart to Donizetti to Verdi to Beethoven and Puccini. I started taking violin lessons when I was 4 years old. I was particularly fond of Vivaldi and his compositions about the four seasons. Because of those early music lessons, and competence with the violin I was offered a scholarship to the private school in our suburb - North Shore Country Day School. They needed a violinist in their orchestra and my complete fully paid scholarship was from the 8th grade through High School.

When I got to college as a freshman, my musical background resulted in a lucrative part time job. First tenors were in low supply for the Church Choir. My voice hadn't changed yet and, while still a first soprano, I was hired by the church to sing tenor at the Sunday morning services in the Harvard Chapel. The pay was excellent and covered the cost of my annual college room rent for each of the four years of college. This job exposed me to early Italian church music which I enjoyed as much as the later Italian opera. With the help of an English student, Arthur Shurcliffe, and Herb Lobl as stage director, I co-founded the Winthrop House Gilbert and Sullivan Society, producing *Trial by Jury*, *H.M.S. Pinafore*, and *Yeoman of the Garde*. We used the Winthrop common room and rented folding chairs for the performances to packed houses. The G & S club later moved to Agassiz Hall and still draws full houses for its performances.

At that time World War II had ended with the defeat of Germany and Japan but the war continued with the Chinese Communists under Mao advancing into Korea. I volunteered to join the Regular Army in October of 1946. My Army unit was stationed at Fort Dix, New Jersey. Half of the unit was sent to Korea and half was kept in reserve at Fort Dix. I was in the half that was trained as part of the reserve and experienced no battle action. After a year and a half at Fort Dix, I was discharged as a Staff Sergeant with a sharpshooter designation. My score at the rifle range was so high I thought the soldier to my left was shooting at my target.

After finishing my formal education, a bachelor's degree in Philosophy in 1951, and a master's degree in Business from Harvard in 1953, I decided to accept the challenge of Horace Greely who said in 1865 "Go west young man to seek your fortune." Following his advice, I purchased a 1938 Plymouth Coupe with a rumble seat for fifty dollars and headed west to Denver, Colorado. The motor of the car could start with either an electric starter as well as a crank, which was a useful as a back-up for cold weather. I realized what a wonderful climate Denver had with 300 days of sun. In just two hours one could be in the Rocky Mountains with good hiking, antelope hunting and skiing. A Sunday lift ticket at Winter Park was $3.00. If you had the time and money, a lift ticket at the excelent slopes of Aspen was $5.00 a day. There were also several rivers with rapids for canoeing within 2 to 4 hours of Denver, and with a group of friends we had fun running the rapids of Colorado.

To satisfy my musical interests I was delighted to find in Denver a semipro Grand Opera Company. It was founded by several businessmen who hired Dr. Antonia Brico, a talented musician and orchestra conductor, to produce full costumed and trained grand opera for the Denver public. This group hired one professional opera singer each year that increased the quality level of our enthusiastic volunteer local talent. The first year, Dr. Brico hired Soprano Lucia Albanese from La Scala Opera House in Milan for the lead role of La Traviata. The next year she hired the beautiful and talented Peggy Bonini, a professional opera singer from the San Francisco Opera company, for the lead role of Susana in "the Marriage of Figaro." I enjoyed singing in the chorus and was given minor tenor roles for these opera productions.

My interest in Italian opera led me to enroll in a night course in the Italian language in Denver, so I could understand what we were singing about. After a year I had picked up enough of the Italian language to carry on a modest conversation. In the textbook were gorgeous pictures of Italy.

I particularly liked the pictures of the Italian Alps on the French, Swiss, and Austrian alpine borders, which formed a half circle of mountains around Milan.

In the textbook, I also loved the beautiful pictures of the medieval cities of Florence, Siena, Venice, Verona, and Mantua as well as the three beautiful northern lakes of Como, Maggiore and Garda. Seeing pictures of the extraordinary scenery I was convinced I must spend a few years in Italy to be able to visit these beautiful sights as well as hear the exciting Italian operas in the theaters of the many towns where these great operas were written and produced. An added incentive to visit Italy was a recent movie starring the beautiful Sophia Lauren making pizza in Naples. As a young bachelor, Sophia fascinated me, and increased my desire to visit Italy. With my brother, Dante, an Officer in the US Navy whose battleship was docked in the bay of Naples, and with his high school classmate Tim Boudreau, we decided to meet in Milan over the Christmas holidays (1960) and ski together at the Sestriere area on the French-Italian alpine border.

At the same time, I noticed an article in the newspaper about Jack Arnold, a former World War II naval officer, radar specialist, and graduate of telecom engineering from Rensselaer Polytechnic Institute. Jack was appointed as the General Manager of a joint venture being formed in Milan, Italy between General Telephone (GTE) and Magnetti Marelli, a large Italian company making electric and electronic parts for Fiat and Alfa Romeo.

When I saw the word Milan, Italy in that article, I sent a letter to Jack Arnold, and mentioned that I would like to meet him to discuss whether I had some of the skills he may find useful in setting up the new Italo-American joint venture. I mentioned that I could speak some Italian and I was planning a ski vacation trip to Italy in December of 1960. Since I had already paid for the air fare to Italy and back, there would be no travel expense to his company for my visit to Italy for a meeting. This point drew his attention and Jack answered that he would like to meet me. He suggested that on my way from Denver to Italy I stop at the GTE manufacturing factory in Chicago and meet Vice President Bob McMichael who was coordinating production between the Chicago factory of GTE and the new joint venture company in Milan. I called Bob McMichael and arranged to visit him and see the factory and assembly lines making telephones and telephone equipment in the Chicago plant.

Lydia's painting of the Sforza Castle in Milan

My interview with Bob was good and he asked me if I knew any Italian. I responded in Italian with a few of the phrases from the Verdi opera I had been working on, plus a few phrases I remembered from the boys on my street in Chicago when I was seven. While my pronunciation was a combination of operatic Italian and street Italian of my 7-year-old Italian friends, it must have been convincing. Fortunately, Mr. McMichael did not ask me to take a test in Italian.

Jack Arnold welcomed me to Italy and was pleased I had made the trip. He was interested in my background in manufacturing and accounting. He introduced me to Al Vercillo, the Vice President of Finance of the European operation of GTE. Al was fluent in Italian and French and was a very intelligent and enthusiastic person with a good sense of humor, necessary in the difficult Italian business environment. We had a very positive meeting.

He asked me to take a train to Geneva, Switzerland to meet the European Director of GTE, Count Julian Dobrski, who had been a Colonel in the British Intelligence during World War II. Colonel Dobrski had been engaged in dangerous underground activities between the Allies and the underground Polish Army just under the nose of the Nazis occupation. He was an impressive and stately person and an excellent businessman. Colonel Dobrski was fully aware of the future enormous potential market using microwave transmission of telephone voice signals based on the patent of Gulielmo Marconi. Marconi was an Italian scientist and the inventor of wireless transmission who sent the first transatlantic signal from England to Canada in 1901. Another stunning Marconi achievement was sending microwave signals around the world, traveling at the speed of light and following the curve of the earth to turn on the light at a world exhibition Sydney Australia from the laboratory in his yacht, Electra, moored in Genoa Italy in 1930. Effective application of that technology, applied to sending private voice conversations from place A to point B, would replace thousands of telephone poles and millions of miles of copper wires currently used for long distance voice communication. Both Al Vercillo and Count Dobrski were excited about the future growth of that area of business.

When my brother Dante and our friend Tim Boudreaux arrived in Milan, we drove to Sestriere and arrived when there was still full sunlight. The 15-story cylindrical hotel, built by Mussolini in 1925, looked exactly like the beautiful poster we had on the wall in our home in the Chicago during my early years.

We had a room for three in this famous 15 story round hotel where the food was superb. The Italian girls we met at the hotel and on the slopes were beautiful, sporty, friendly, and beautifully dressed. The week we spent on the slopes of Sestriere added to my excitement about spending more time in Italy, exploring the charming medieval towns, castles, and mountains, and as a bachelor having the opportunity of meeting a beautiful Italian woman.

While I was in my bed at Sestriere I thought I heard Sophie Lauren, whispering in my ear, "Go east young man and there you will meet a beautiful Italian woman who will become your wife and a fine Italian mother. She will make you very happy and both of you together will raise intelligent, well-behaved children and grandchildren who will be respectful and helpful and make you proud. Your wife will be skilled in our Italian cuisine and prepare for you and your offspring wonderful Italian meals. Your grandchildren will be intelligent and well-disciplined and should keep both of you amused and proud parents and grandparents." I woke up with a smile.

The next week I discovered I had passed the rigorous screening for a GTE expatriate executive in Europe. A job offer was extended, and I started work in Milan on May 1, 1961 with the title of Controller for the American company interests of the newly formed company Marelli-Lenkurt, a 50/50 joint venture between Magnetti-Morelli and General Telephone International. The size of the new company at that time was 1,000 Italians and 2 Americans, Jack Arnold and me. Al Vercillo the GTE Financial Officer for Europe spent part time in Pavia (Milan), where GTE had a joint venture making Sylvania television tubes along with a German company making Sylvania fluorescent bulbs. They also had a company in Antwerp which was making telecom products and zippers for clothing. What the sales volume and problems of these diverse companies in its first year of its operation was to be discovered.

ONE

1961: Luca Pacioli Accounting, The Tax Audit, and the Merlin Law/ Berlin Wall Misunderstanding

I started work in Milan Italy on May 1, 1961. My employer was the newly formed joint venture company named Marelli–Lenkurt. That company was a 50%-50% partnership between the Italian industrial company Magnetti Marelli, specializing in making electric and electronic components for Fiat and other Italian auto companies, and the American company General Telephone and Electronics (GTE), which owned telephone operating companies with about 3 million telephone subscribers. GTE had recently purchased the Sylvania company that was making radio and television tubes and other electronic products. GTE had also purchased the Lenkurt company of San Francisco formed by telecom engineers, Lennart Erickson and Curt Appert.

These two engineers had improved on the work of Guglielmo Marconi in the transmission of voice by microwave signals. Erickson and Appert's development of Marconi's transatlantic signals was a major step forward in high quality distant telephone voice transmission by virtually instantaneous speech. This Italian American joint venture company was one of several companies engaged in this project.

Magnetti Marelli had an employment of about 25,000 people distributed in many factories in the Milan area. They were engaged in making electric and electronic parts for the Italian auto industry, including Fiat, Alfa Romeo, and other smaller Italian car companies. When I arrived in 1961 the new joint venture already had projects in Norway, Greece, Tunisia, Australia, and Argentina, and was bidding on a large project in Nigeria. The objective of this joint venture company was to sell equipment for improved long distance voice transmission of telephone. The current system of telephone traffic was carried on thousands of miles of coaxial copper wires strung on hundreds of thousands of telephone poles. The cost of this construction activity was very high.

I was the second American on the payroll at Marelli-Lenkurt after Jack Arnold, the American President. In addition to the two of us, the company has 1,000 Italians, primarily skilled telecom design engineers and a skilled and a large installation department.

Before starting work as a member of this joint venture company I had several days to explore my new city and then continued to use my weekends for further visits. Milan is very well located from a tourist standpoint, being 3 hours from Venice to the east, and less than two hours from Genoa and the Italian Riviera to the West. To the north, from my 15th floor apartment, I could see the mountains of the Italian and Swiss Alps. The snow covered 15,000-foot Mount Rosa is a very impressive sight on a clear day. Unfortunately, during parts of the autumn and winter, Milan and the Po Valley is famous for pea soup dense fogs, which many say are worse and more dense than those of London. Traffic becomes very slow, and one can barely see a car distance ahead. One evening in January, five cars drove into a small lake on the outskirts of Milan.

The Scala opera house is 10 minutes away from my apartment with public transportation and is only one of many nearby theatres and concert halls. The musical programs are excellent, and, except for opening night, the prices are reasonable.

Outside Milan, there is much beautiful architecture and natural scenery. Weekend trips have been made to visit Pisa with its famous leaning tower, and Florence. The lakes region to the north and east of Milan include Lago di Garda with its charming well preserved 14th century castle and the ruins of a 1st century Roman Villa.

One of the best weekends was spent in Venice. The September weather was gorgeous, and it was the weekend of the regatta. The boats in the parade were painted solid colors with bow sprints of prancing horses, tigers, lions, dragons, and eagles. The boats looked like a cross between a Roman Galley and a Viking long boat. Most of them had 8 or 10 gondoliers providing propulsion. Some of the larger boats resembled the boats of Columbus with 30 gondoliers at the Oars, and colorful red and gold shirts. On the front bridge of the large boats there was a brass band to keep the stroke. Following the larger galleys were small gondolas carrying people dressed as noblemen of the 14th and 15th century and others dressed as their noble visitors from Africa, Turkey, China, Arabia, and other Mid-East and Asian countries. Following the procession there were numerous gondola races between sections of Venice, each dressed in their 14th and 15th century costumes.

The streets of Venice are only for pedestrians. There are no cars in the amazing city. In many of the narrow streets one can touch the walls on both sides of the street, and two people can't pass unless they turn sideways. One of the best trips in Venice is to rent a Gondola for two hours and tell the gondolier to take you on a trip in the side canals. Otherwise, a trip on the Vaporetto, a public and crowded bus boat, from one end of Venice to the other. It is best to start at the place which has a garage and wait for an empty Vaporetto so you can get a seat in the very front of the boat.

The Ducal Palace with its grand council rooms, enormous pictures of battles with the Turks, the Museum of Medieval Armor, Bridge of Sighs, and dungeons were interesting to see. A 30-minute ferry boat ride takes one to the Lido of Venice and the very nice beaches on the Adriatic. I was surprised to see how clean the beaches and water were at the Lido, since the canals in the city of Venice have numerous floating objects of dubious origin. However, the tide clears out the canals twice a day without any human assistance. This cleaning is helped by an army of little crabs that line the walls of the buildings just below the water line. In spite of the crabs and their dinner, the city is charming.

Perhaps one of the most startling things about this area of Italy is the great difference of purchasing power of equivalent jobs here and in the US. The take home pay for an average factory or office person in the US will allow the US person to purchase about twice as much as his Italian counterpart. And yet in spite of this mathematical difference the people here are better dressed and eat quite a bit more than the average American. The cost to the company is about twice as much.

Back in Milan, I also toured the Sforza castle in the center of Milan, built about 1400, had a museum of science containing a display of the many inventions of Leonardo DaVinci. He had been hired and given an apartment in Milan by Duke Sforza, the ruler of Milan at that time, to design and build military machines for the duke. The museum has many fascinating models made by Leonardo, including an airplane he designed. His airplane design was unable to get off the ground, but it was a clever design. He made many designs of impressive looking military tanks.

Also given an apartment in the Sforza castle in Milan was Luca Pacioli, a monk from Florence who was a mathematician and published a book in 1494 on a new double entry bookkeeping and accounting systems. He was good friends with Leonardo and shared with him his ideas about the math of an orderly bookkeeping system which was used by Florentine bankers and businessmen.

1961: LUCA PACIOLI ACCOUNTING, THE TAX AUDIT, AND THE MERLIN LAW/BERLIN WALL MISUNDERSTANDING

It was difficult doing business in a language that was not my primary language. Although I knew some Italian before arriving and my facility with the language improved over time, it was frustrating to be involved in discussions of systems, procedures, accruals, budgets, and other words whose meaning was not entirely clear. Misunderstandings occur frequently when both parties use the same language. I am making progress, but am still far from fluent, and exhausted at the end of the day.

I was hired by the company to bring an American accounting system, which was based on the book written by Luca Pacioli, the 15th century Florentine monk who invented the double entry accounting system. Luca Pacioli's system of debits and credits (*dare* and *avere* in Italian) helped skilled builders, bankers, and businessmen in the leather and cloth business become very wealthy. They understood the concept of net worth and growth of money and the definition of a profit and loss statement. The Florentines became the bankers of the Middle Ages lending large sums of money to the royalty of other countries.

Unfortunately, Italians of later periods up until 1960 used the math concepts of Mr. Pacioli as a basis for fooling the tax officials and the Italian accounting system became "now you see it, and now you don't.".

When I arrived at the company, I asked to see the accounting books and was surprised to find that there was not a single set of books but three sets of books. The first set of books was created to fool the tax officials. This book portrayed a sad state of affairs and a loss of money for the prior year. Therefore, the company was unable to pay any taxes on company profits because this set of the company was losing money.

The second set of books was prepared for the banks and showed a profitable operation to reassure the banks that their loans to the company were protected and that the company would be able to repay their bank loans. The 3rd set of books was a confusing collection of data indicating a large number of adjustments, to accounts payable, accounts receivable, reserves for bad debts, adjustments to inventory for obsolescence and a verity of other adjustments. The managers couldn't remember which were the actual accounting numbers and which were the adjustments made for the banks and for the tax authorities. Therefore, there was no complete nor accurate set of books indicating whether in this period there had been an actual profit or loss.

My job was to create a single set of books that could tell the whole story of the company's economic progress. Without this accounting clarity it was not possible to understand the net worth and the problems of cost and revenue that the company faced nor what was the current net worth of the company. The clear and accurate double entry accounting system invented by Lucca Pacioli in 1494 was what was needed to provide the management of the company with consistent and accurate accounting. With the existing three accounting book system, it was impossible to untangle the mess and really know what was going on.

This problem was resolved two years later at a stockholder meeting in Milan where we told our Italian partners that the Italian and American systems of managing companies are so different that it would be better for one of our companies to purchase the 50% share of the other. It was agreed that we purchase their 50% share, and we parted friends. At that point I was finally able to follow the path of Brother Pacioli's double entry bookkeeping system. It became easier to understand where the financial problems were, and the company started to make a valid profit.

Three months after arriving in Italy, I had my first experience of an Italian Tax Audit. I was in my office at 8:30 one morning when four officers from the Italian Fiscal Police entered the factory with pistols drawn. They went to the reception desk and put their hand on the phone of the receptionist and told her, "Don't tell anyone we are here."

1961: LUCA PACIOLI ACCOUNTING, THE TAX AUDIT, AND THE MERLIN LAW/BERLIN WALL MISUNDERSTANDING

The door of my office was open, and I could hear the receptionist as she pointed to my office and said, "The office of the Finance Director is there and just behind his office is the office of the President." Following her instructions two officers of the Fiscal Police burst into my office, with pistols still drawn and said, "Hands up!" followed by "Put your hands on your desk."

I complied. Then one of the officers applied sticky fiscal tape to cover and shut all the drawers of my desk and files. On the fiscal tape was printed a large warning in red stating "Anyone who breaks this tape may suffer jail penalties."

After applying the tape, they asked, "Where is the President's office?" I took my hands off my desk and pointed to his office. They arrived at the President's door and burst into his office with an expression that said, "We gotcha!" They didn't point their pistols at him but just said "Hands up," again followed by the phrase "Put your hands on your desk." He had had this experience before, and he got up from his chair to make it easier for the Fiscal Police officer to tape the drawers of his desk shut.

The police said they would be back the next morning to review the evidence and said, "Please show us where the vault is where you keep all company accounting documents." The vault was a large brick room with a heavy steel door just behind the desk of the receptionist. The two police officers applied their fiscal tape to all corners of the door. Then they told me "This is step one. We will be back tomorrow morning to start our thorough review" and they left.

After they left, I went to the office of Count Quintevalle, the President of Magnetti Marelli who had an office in this factory. I told him that I was concerned that there may be some documents in the vault that pertained to the "black payroll" which could be compromising. The black payroll was the amount paid under the table and not registered in the books as payroll. This was an extra compensation to some of the most valuable company employees and the amount they received was not declared to the tax authorities and therefore not taxed.

I had not yet had time to review these payroll records so was not aware of the number of employees nor the amounts of their compensation not reported to the Tax Authority. It was my understanding that unreported wages could be a large percent of the company's actual payroll meaning there could be a major underpayment of payroll earnings and taxes. The Count replied to my alert by saying, "Don't worry. It will be taken care of."

That evening four masons arrived at the factory after normal closing time. They went to the back of the accounting vault and broke through the bricks of the back wall, making an opening wide enough for a person to enter and exit, carrying boxes of documents. Then two of the company accountants went into the vault through the broken back wall, identified 4 large bins of records which they thought might be compromising and removed them through the back hole in the wall. In the process they didn't touch the fiscal tape on the front door to the vault.

The masons then bricked up the hole they had made in the back wall, taking care to erase any evidence of new mortar on the bricks that might indicate the back wall had been broken into and bricked it back up. They finished their work long before dawn.

When the Fiscal Police returned the next morning, they came to my office, and carefully examined the fiscal tape that they had taped to the drawers of my desk. Then they carefully removed the tape. They looked through the papers that were in the drawers without asking any questions. They took none of my work sheets and said I was free to start work at my desk again.

Then two members of the Fiscal Police, still armed with their pistols,

1961: LUCA PACIOLI ACCOUNTING, THE TAX AUDIT, AND THE MERLIN LAW/BERLIN WALL MISUNDERSTANDING

went to our document vault. The officers removed the fiscal tape that had been placed on the steel door of the vault and entered. They spent about two hours in the vault going through baskets of documents and files. They found a few documents which they put into a box and prepared a document which indicated which papers they were taking to the Fiscal Police office for review and that they were obligated to return them after going over them. I had to sign the document as a witness on behalf of the company and they placed the documents in the back seat of their car.

The officers' final stop was to the Count's office. They removed the tape from the drawers of his desk, opened them, and shuffled through some of his papers. Then they said, "Thank you, we will get back to you in two weeks with the results of our audit" and they left. The Count said that he had taken care of the tax auditors' questions. I never heard anything more from the Count about the outcome of this tax inspection.

When I arrived in Italy in May of 1961 there was a visible battle between the free market nations of the newly formed Common Market, Great Britain, France, Italy, Belgium, West Germany, and Luxembourg, and the communist bloc, led by Communist Russia, East Germany, and the East European communist satellites.

The countries of the west and the Common Market that had been newly created were thriving with free enterprise systems, while the Eastern European block of countries, under the heel of communist Moscow, were suffering economic stagnation, lack of freedom of speech and restricted. The large differences in living standards and freedom of speech between East and West Berlin was not good advertisement for the German Communist war lord Walter Ulbricht, who was running East Germany under the thumb of Khrushchev.

After World War II ended, the Russia army occupied Eastern Germany, which was about one third of the former land area of the former German nation. The city of Berlin was also divided with between East Berlin and the island of West Berlin.

The East German Communist chief, Walter Ulbricht, was appointed by Stalin to be the leader of Communist East Germany. After Stalin died Walter Ulbricht reported to Nikita Khrushchev. The tight communist collar on those living in East Berlin produced a stagnating economy and an exodus of its skilled manpower.

The people living in western Germany and West Berlin, had freedom of speech and press. With their free enterprise system their economy was thriving with full employment and good wages. West Berlin companies were even importing skilled factory workers from Turkey. The contrast with their East Berlin neighbors and relatives, living next door under Communist dictator Walter Ulbricht was stark.

Up until August 13, 1961, a German living in East Berlin could take a subway and get off at the first stop in West Berlin and walk out of the West Berlin station to freedom. If he had a skill, he could easily obtain employment in West Berlin.

At the time there were 2 million people living and working in West Berlin and one million in East Berlin. The population of West Berlin was increasing and that of East Berlin decreasing at an accelerating rate. The West Berlin newspapers were reporting that in June of 1960 five hundred Germans per day were entering West Berlin and in June of 1961 that number increased to 1,000 per day. What was of more concern to Walter Ulbricht than the absolute numbers, were that the people escaping to the west were the highly skilled scientists, medical doctors, dentists, nurses, lab technicians, accountants, engineers, skilled machinists, and factory workers.

The Russians and East Germans realized that a free West Berlin was a large hole in their Iron Curtain. Private industrial companies located in

1961: LUCA PACIOLI ACCOUNTING, THE TAX AUDIT, AND THE MERLIN LAW/BERLIN WALL MISUNDERSTANDING

West Berlin and their employees were protected from Russian domination by the World War II treaty signed between Russia and the allied powers at the end of the World War II. That treaty protected Germans living in West Berlin and the Western zone of Germany. President John Kennedy went to Berlin and reminded the Russians and the world of our international treaty at the end of WW II. He warned the Russians that the US would enforce that treaty.

It was not surprising that private businesses, operating in West Berlin were thriving, and needed additional skilled manpower. The managers of German companies located there welcomed German speaking workers. Other Germans living in East Germany used this Berlin hole in the Iron Curtain to escape Communism to the west. Once an East German arrived in West Berlin, he or she could find a good paying job there or fly to other towns in West German from the small Tempelhof Berlin airport.

Exactly a full year before I started my Italian employment by GTE International, on May 1, 1960, Gary Powers piloting a U2 high altitude reconnaissance flight over the Urals, Gary's plane was shot down and captured by the Russians. I had a minor and indirect role in that international episode. Prior to moving to Italy, I had been working for two high tech companies in Denver, Glen Martin, and Stanley Aviation, both of which had been providers of crucial equipment used in that mission to verify whether the Russians were following their treaty with the NATO. They were not.

The first company involved was the Glen Martin company that designed and built a high-altitude reconnaissance airplane. The Russian MIGS in 1960 had an altitude of 60,000 feet. The Martin plane had an altitude of 70,000, theoretically beyond the capability of the MIGS. The second company with crucial equipment was Stanley Aviation with designed and manufacture the ejection seat.

Apparently, there was sign language between the US and Russian plane MIGS and Powers plane. The Russian plane indicated the US plane must leave Russian Air space. Gary Powers thought he had made himself clear with his sign language reply, that he had two more pictures to take and after that he would leave Russian air space. The Russians must have misunderstood or ignored Powers' communication, because one of the MIGS shot a missile at the Gary's plane. It was a lucky shot which hit and disabled his plane.

Fortunately, Gary was sitting on Stanley Ejection seat and pushed the button. The seat with Gary to it was shot up and out of the cockpit and after a long free fall its parachute opened and he floated down to ground. As he landed a Russian patrol welcomed him to their beautiful Ural Mountains and offered him a bowl of borsch. He was taken to a Russian prison and later returned to the United States in a prisoner transfer.

In spite of his capture Gary Powers had been able to send picture verification to the US that Russia had been violating its international treaty with the West. The result of his reconnaissance trip was that Russia pulled their missiles out of that area of the Ural Mountains, and Gary was returned to the US in a prisoner exchange with Russia.

This event of May of 1960 was followed by a Russian response at a meeting of the UN in New York, On September 23, of 1960. The NY Times reported that Nikita Khrushchev made a speech at that UN meeting in New York with the quote "we with communism will bury you," and he emphasized his point by taking off his shoe and banging it on the table.

Walter Ulbricht, the Communist leader of East Germany, was even more aggressive than Khrushchev and asked permission from Moscow to block the escape of East Germans through the East Berlin escape route though Checkpoint Charlie. Khrushchev refused that request.

1961: LUCA PACIOLI ACCOUNTING, THE TAX AUDIT, AND THE MERLIN LAW/BERLIN WALL MISUNDERSTANDING

The escape of skilled manpower from Communist Germany to free West Germany and to free West Berlin continued at an increasing rate.

The next step in this unfolding drama between the communist East and the capitalistic West, was that Russia sent several battalions of Russian troops to East Berlin, with orders to shoot anyone trying to escape their communist paradise. To make certain the escape hole between the East to the West was shut tight, the Berlin Subway between East and West Berlin was closed, and Check Point Charlie was also shut. That was still not enough to stop the escape of skilled people. A few swam the canal between East and West Berlin and one person built a balloon and floated over at night. Others were shot as they tried to swim to freedom, and a few succeeded.

On July 25 of 1961, President Kennedy gave a speech in West Berlin indicating that the United States had made a commitment to the 2 million Germans living in West Berlin at the end of the war. He said that the troops of NATO would protect them and their homes from invasion. Kennedy added that any attempt by Russia to unilaterally disregard the NATO treaty was unacceptable, and if Khrushchev took any aggressive actions the US would activate the mutual defense clause in the UN treaty, to defend the rights of each of the NATO countries. Walter Ulbricht the communist leader of East Germany urged Nikita Khrushchev to give him permission to build a wall. Nikita still withheld his permission.

Finally, Khrushchev relented and gave the order to Walter Ulbricht to build the wall. The last subway from East Berlin to West Berlin was stopped on August 13, 1961, and the construction of a double wall began.

It followed the ancient Greek design of a double wall with a corridor of about 20 feet between walls, an area in Berlin patrolled by police dogs with sharp teeth and who run much faster than people. The dogs were more effective than soldiers with rifles. No person trying to escape was able to run faster than these furious dogs once in the corridor between the two walls. Once the escapee had been cornered by one of the dogs, he would be fortunate if the East German police arrived to call off the dogs.

The NATO response to the Berlin Crisis was to initiate a massive air lift from Western Germany to the Templehof airport in West Berlin to supply the city with food, fuel and materials. Templehof was the oldest airport in Berlin. It had a short runway that limited the weight each plane could carry. This air lift brought food, coal, raw materials, and spare parts needed to maintain and heat the factories, and residences of the people living in West Berlin. This very expensive operation kept the city of West Berlin with materials allowing it not only to survive but to prosper, as Russia and the German communists tried to choke it into submission. During the air lift allied planes bringing an enormous amount of food, coal, and supplies to West Berlin and landing and taking off every 30 seconds – a truly amazing organization.

When the Italian city states became a country in 1865, there was no city or state in the Italian peninsula that prohibited prostitution. Back in 1358, the City-State of Venice indicated prostitution was not only legal but desirable. In one of their documents, it was declared that "Courtesans were indispensable to society."

In addition, when Napoleon conquered the Netherlands in 1795, he was concerned that his soldiers could be absent because of venereal diseases. He initiated medical exams in the Netherlands and the doctors provided a red or white passport to the individual tested. A red passport indicated the individual had no venereal disease and a white passport indicated the individual was infected. If a woman that appeared to be a prostitute and had a wrong color passport, she was taken off the street and taken to prison. There she received medical care and released when she was cured and then given a red passport.

1961: LUCA PACIOLI ACCOUNTING, THE TAX AUDIT, AND THE MERLIN LAW/BERLIN WALL MISUNDERSTANDING

Apparently, Napoleon's system reduced venereal disease in the French army in Holland. In 1861 Italy became a nation and made their own laws, many of which were adapted from Napoleonic law.

In 1958, the Merlin Law which made prostitution illegal in Italy, was filed by Senator Lina Merlin, a member of the Italian Socialist party from Padova. Senator Merlin was very popular in her city of Padova partly because she opposed Mussolini and protected residents of her district from being sent to Poland and Germany to make parts for the Nazi war machine.

The passage of the Merlin law in Italy created many new problems not anticipated by the Senator. The incidence of venereal disease in Milan increased after 1959 because the ladies were no longer required to be examined periodically by state paid doctors so those infected were no longer cured. Another negative was the decrease in safety for the ladies because state police protection was eliminated, and the Italian state protection was replaced by struggle between Mafia gangs.

Furthermore, as the marketing of their services was taken over by the Mafia the ladies were no longer entrepreneurs with a direct business relation to the client and their perception and status as business professionals was diminished. Unfortunately, under the Merlin law, they became slaves of the Mafia bosses.

The other result was that their business location in the Milan area was transferred from their warm and private residences to fields along the highways at the outskirts of the city. Advertising for this drive-in business included bonfires consisting of old, used tires and logs to keep people warm and dry during rainy or cold winter nights. Tents provided partial shelter from the elements.

As could be expected, the lack of municipal oversight resulted in wars between rival Mafia gangs in the Milan area and resulted in slavery and death of many of the courtesans. It was reported in Milan papers that the known incidents of venereal disease were increasing rapidly, likely due to the ladies no longer being required to have frequent medical exams paid for by the city.

Concurrently, the crisis that was brewing in Berlin resulted in a growing number of people escaping from East Germany to West Germany through the free city of West Berlin. Their motives were political freedom and better paying jobs.

In June of 1961 there was a large amount of newspaper publicity in the Milan press about the negative impact of the Merlin Law, as well the dangers of an outbreak of war between Western allies and the Soviet Union resulting from the Berlin Crisis. The standard of living of inhabitants of West Berlin was much higher than in East Berlin and in East Germany. In West Berlin and West Germany there was a strong demand for skilled labor and many doctors, nurse's dentists, accountants, teachers, and skilled factory workers crossed from East into West Berlin and then onto Germany reaching 1,000 per day in June of 1961.

Nikita Khrushchev gave the order, "Build the wall" on August 13, 1961. It was erected with Germanic precision. The Berlin subway which traveled through both East and West Berlin was closed at the communist border. A double wall was built with a 15-foot corridor between the double walls. Within that corridor East German soldiers, with large German Shepard dogs, patrolled during the day and at night. Many believed a war between East and West was imminent.

The American, Al Vercillo, the financial director of many GTE companies in Europe, with his offices in Milan, dictated to his 20-year-old, partially bilingual Italian secretary, a letter to all Americans working in Europe of the pending crisis. His young secretary aware of the many newspaper articles that gave as much space to the Merlin Crisis as to the pending Berlin crisis, thought Mr. Vercillo was referring to the "Merlin Crisis" rather than to the Berlin Crisis.

1961: LUCA PACIOLI ACCOUNTING, THE TAX AUDIT, AND THE MERLIN LAW/BERLIN WALL MISUNDERSTANDING

Al's message to all the GTE employees in Europe was "with respect to the Merlin crisis, stay calm and carry on. More instructions will follow. The advice coming from GTE European headquarters will be based on what action the Russians take in this crisis." Al signed the letter without reading it and it went out to all American and English employees in the GTE Europe organization. The reaction of some of the GTE employees was curiosity. What advice would there be the next instructions from Al Vercillo?

TWO

1962: My Lucky Day and Our Honeymoon in Greece and Turkey

The luckiest and most important date of my life was Sunday, February 11, of 1962. On this day, I met Lydia Vergani.

I had planned to take a bus from the center of Milan at Piazza Castello to go skiing in the Alps with some fellows from the factory. My alarm was set for 5:00 am on Sunday morning. The alarm went off and I looked at it and said to myself, "it's time to get up, it's time to get up, it's time to get up." By the third time I said to myself "it's time to get up," an hour already passed.

I bolted up in bed, looked at my watch and said "damn it, I have missed the bus. I hope my friends have gone ahead." I had no way to notify them. I got dressed quickly and drove the mile to Piazza Castello where there were many ski buses parked with people boarding. There were also a number of beautiful well-dressed young women waiting on the sidewalk holding their skis.

The many ski buses parked at Piazza Castello were going to a wide variety of ski areas within a 3-hour bus ride from Milan. To the north,

1962: MY LUCKY DAY AND OUR HONEYMOON IN GREECE AND TURKEY

their destinations were ski areas on the Swiss-Italian border - to the west, buses were going to the many ski areas on the French-Italian border and to the east, to the areas on the Austrian-Italian border. I assumed my friends had already gone ahead and I decided I would find a bus at random and go alone to its ski area destination.

I went up to one group of three nice looking girls that were standing waiting to board a bus. I asked, in as good Italian as I could muster. "Could you please tell me where this bus is going?" I got a cold shoulder from all three of them. I am certain it was because I never took much interest in clothes and was not properly dressed for the occasion. I was wearing a pair of army fatigue pants and must have given the appearance of being scruffy.

There was another beautiful girl with blue eyes and auburn hair standing alone nearby, holding skis and poles. I asked her where she was going. She responded with a big smile and said in discrete English, "I am waiting for the bus hired by the Lever Gibbs soap company in Milan. The bus should be boarding in about 10 minutes and if there is space, I am certain you would be welcome." I thought, "What an attractive and friendly young woman." Five minutes later the driver stepped out and said "All aboard," including me.

The lovely woman handed her skis to the driver, who put them in the rack. Then she got on the bus and went to the back. She took a seat next to a young man, whom I thought was probably her date waiting for her. "What a shame," I thought, "she may be already taken." I took the front row seat opposite the driver and beside the front steps. As the bus started out of Milan, I had a perfect front seat to see the Po valley below and the snow-covered mountains ahead.

After a while, I looked to the back of the bus and there was the auburn-haired, blue-eyed beauty walking towards the front. There was an empty seat in the row behind me. She took the seat and leaned forward and spoke to me and told me her name was Lydia. She explained that she gets sick sitting in the back of the bus as it goes around curves on its way up the mountain side. She explained that the young man at the back of the bus was new to Milan and had been hired by her father and this was his first ski trip. She also said that she came to the front of the bus to practice her English with me. She had a beautiful smile, and I was captivated by her charming Italian accent. We had a series of amusing linguistic misunderstandings, and the 3-hour bus trip was over too soon.

When we arrived at the ski area of "Passo Tonale" south of the Italian-Austrian border, we picked up our skis and went to the start of a two-person bucket ski lift. One has to be awake and agile to get into the swiftly moving bucket which sweeps around a large wheel at the bottom of the lift where two skiers must jump aboard it rapidly, one after the other. Luckily, we both made into the bucket and enjoyed the ride up the mountain.

When we got to the top the mountain view was splendid. Lydia quickly put on her skis, pointed them down-hill and away she went at top speed with excellent balance and form. I followed as best I could, trying to keep my balance, first with all my weight on the left ski then on the right ski as both arms made circles in the air. Lydia led the way all morning, stopping every once in a while to let me catch up.

When it was lunch time we went to the restaurant at the top of the mountain. There were tables of 10 places and we joined one table where there were two empty seats. At the table was a noisy and laughing group of men and women. My objective at this point was to figure out how I could obtain the telephone number of this beautiful girl with the blue eyes and the auburn hair.

I said to the other 9 people at the table, maybe we could get together to ski again another day. They all answered "certainly" prompting me

1962: MY LUCKY DAY AND OUR HONEYMOON IN GREECE AND TURKEY

to pull out a piece of paper and a pen from my pocket. To get a subtle start and not make it look too obvious, I asked the person to my left if he would give me his name and telephone number. He did and fortunately he passed the paper and pencil to the person on his left. The paper and pen made a complete circle of our table until it arrived to where Lydia was sitting. I held my breath. Lydia took the pencil and paper and added her name and telephone number to the bottom of the list. Success, mission accomplished.

I carefully put that paper into my wallet. Monday after work I pulled out the precious piece of payer and dialed her number. After a few words that sounded like "Chi è?" - Italian for "Who is this?" she finally said, "Oh yes I remember you." She politely didn't add in the scruffy ski outfit.

I replied, "We skied together at Passo Tonale on Sunday, and I would like to see you. I have two tickets to a performance on Friday evening at the Piccolo Scala for a performance of a Pergolesi operetta, 'La Serva di Due Padroni' and I hope you would be free and would join me."

Lydia answered, "I love opera and would be pleased to join you."

My heart skipped a beat.

Then I added "But I can't wait until Friday to see you."

Lydia responded, "Wednesday evening, I am having some friends over at my parent's apartment at Via Tazzoli for a dinner party. I would be pleased if you would join."

"That would be delightful," was my reply.

For that dinner party Lydia's mother had ordered a cake from the bakery. It arrived with a small porcelain statue of "the Two Lovers" by the famous French sculptor - Pernaia. When Lydia saw the small statue on the cake, she told her mother that it would be embarrassing and premature to serve that cake with the statue of the two lovers. "I've just met the young man yesterday" she told her mother. Her grandmother came to the rescue and said, "Just remove the statue." Problem resolved.

At the Wednesday evening dinner, all of her friends spoke good English. One of them volunteered that in 10 days they were going for the weekend trip at the Dolomite ski area, Madonna di Campiglio, and I would be welcomed if I would like to join them. I signed up.

Then just two days later I called at her house, and we went to the opera at La Scala for Pergolesi's 'La Serva di Due Padroni'. The Vergani family, knowing I was a bachelor and probably not a good cook, invited me for dinner every evening thereafter.

At the Friday evening performance at the Piccolo Scala, shortly after the lights went out, I reached over and took Lydia's hand and held it during the entire performance, interrupted only when we applauded at the end of each scene.

The second Saturday after we had met on the Italian – Austrian border we took the weekend to ski the ragged Alps of the Brento region at a ski area called Madonna Di Campiglio. On those steep and challenging slopes Lydia displayed her skill as an expert skier with the balance of a ballet dancer and the speed of the French Olympic champion John Claude Killy.

On the first morning of our weekend at Madonna Di Campiglio, Lydia and I stopped on a slope. We were the only two skiers on that part of the slope. Overcome with her beauty, I told her I loved her and wanted to marry her.

She said "yes." I felt myself lifted up through the clouds to Heaven with the angels singing, "Hallelujah." I had never felt so happy in my entire life.

1962: MY LUCKY DAY AND OUR HONEYMOON IN GREECE AND TURKEY

Proposed to Lydia in the Dolomites

My mother living in Chicago had given me one of her Danish rings when I left America for Italy. She said it was an engagement ring and had been in the family for many generations. She had been saving it for me, hoping I would find a nice girl to marry. I gave Lydia that ring. She put it on her finger, smiled and kissed me.

She didn't want to wear it before she told her parents of my proposal, so she kept it in her purse, and took it out and wore it when we went out alone together.

After two weeks of being invited to her house for dinner every evening after I finished work, Lydia thought it best that I follow the Italian tradition and formally ask her father for his permission to propose to his daughter. Lydia coached both me and her father separately before our meeting. She told me what her father was likely to ask, and I felt fully prepared for the crucial encounter. She also briefed her father on what she anticipated I would ask. I was well prepared for the important meeting of joining our families. When the time came for the private meeting between myself and Lydia's father, I understand from Lydia that Mario Vergani was as nervous as me. This was his first and only daughter. Fortunately, we had both been well prepared by Lydia and our conversation went well.

New coat of arms, as painted by Lydia, combining both families

Although it was necessary that I speak Italian during the day at the factory, I was only partially fluent in the Italian language. Now that I am more fluent in Italian, I would love to see a transcript of the conversation between the suitor and the future father-in-law. With hand gestures and a few words, we understood each other. At the end of the interview, we shook hands and he said, "You have my permission to present your proposal to my daughter. The decision is now up to her alone."

To arrange the wedding ceremony, Lydia went to the priest of her local church and informed him that she was going to marry a Protestant and would like to have the wedding in her favorite chapel in his neighborhood church. The priest said he could not marry a person who was not a Catholic in that particular chapel and he offered another less attractive chapel.

When she told her father the answer of the local priest, he became furious. He went to see the priest and told him, "I know you have married Communists in our church, and I could provide you with their names. In addition, my daughter wants to marry a Protestant which is a cousin to our Catholic religion. As know the Communists have no religion."

Mr. Vergani related that the priest said "Calma, Calma, Mr Vergani, I will marry your daughter in the chapel she wants. But please don't mention to anyone that you know that I have married a Communist in our church. That was my unforgivable sin."

Then Lydia and I had separate private interviews with her Parish Priest. Lydia was required to sign a pledge that she would try to persuade me to become a Catholic. She said she would try. I was asked to sign a pledge that I would not try to persuade Lydia to become a Protestant. I signed willingly. So the legal threads were wrapped up to the agreement of all and the date for the marriage was set at September 3, 1962 and invitations were sent out.

The next step for me was to order a wedding suit. The first stop was to decide the suit fabric. There was a shop in the very center of Milan at Piazza Duomo that had a wide variety of bolts of fine Italian woven cloth that could be used to make a stylish tailor-made suit.

Lydia has excellent taste in clothes, and she chose a dark wool pattern for a skilled tailor to make a marriage suit. We purchased a bolt of three yards of a beautiful wool pattern. We took the bolt of material to the apartment of Lydia's parents. There we were met by two small and short tailors Lydia's mother had hired to turn the fine cloth we bought into a luxurious wedding suit.

Tailor-made wedding suits

The miniature tailors, who looked like they just stepped out of a Grimm fairy tale, measured my body from more directions than I thought possible and came up with a wonderful looking suit in the fine pattern that Lydia had selected. In reviewing the almost finished suit the two tailors could not understand why the crease on the left leg did not fall straight. I was unable to understand it either. We and the two small tailors scratched our collective heads but could not come up with a reasonable answer. They volunteered that one of my legs may not be straight. But if that is the problem, is it possible to cure that problem with cloth rather than doing something with my left leg. Or walking leaning slightly to the left. The tailors made adjustments and there was no anatomy that had be modified.

At the ceremony, when we were in the church kneeling before the alter, the priest made the sign of the cross with many bold strokes. Out of the side of my eye I looked to see what Lydia was doing. She made the sign of the cross correctly with medium strokes. I felt I should do

1962: MY LUCKY DAY AND OUR HONEYMOON IN GREECE AND TURKEY

something similar to avoid the risk that our marriage would become void because I omitted an important part of the ceremony. At the same time, since I was not a Catholic, I didn't want to be a hypocrite. So, I made the sign of the cross with my right hand on my chest with the index finger making the sign of the cross with small finger movements. I heard no one object to my miniscule sign of respect to the church. We received a telegram from the Pope congratulating us on our wedding and there was representative from the Vatican at our wedding and reception.

For Lydia's relatives it was a proper and official wedding followed by a reception on the sunny terrace of the top floor roof apartment of Lydia's parents in via Tazzoli. My mother, who came over from Chicago for the wedding, enjoyed seeing her sisters and cousins that came from Denmark for the occasion. After sharing toasts with members of both families Lydia and I left for our honeymoon.

Our honeymoon was to Greece and Turkey and was full of interesting places and fascinating archeological sites. We started with Athens, where we enjoyed visiting the Acropolis and the old blacksmith section of the city at the foot of the Acropolis. The blacksmiths have been at this location since the time of Plato. We purchased a fine old samovar from this shop.

As Greece is very hot in the afternoon, even in September, we adopted the Greek habit of a two-hour nap after lunch. Lunch starts late, usually about 1; 30 and then after lunch the whole city slumbers. At 5 o'clock in the afternoon the stores open again and remain open until 8.

One afternoon we took a drive to Cape Sounion where the Temple of Poseidon, the god of sea still stands. It was built about 500 B.C. on a high bluff about 50 miles southeast of Athens and is the first sight seen by ships as they approach Athens. This is the place where Aegeus, the King of Athens and father of Theseus, threw himself into the sea when he saw his son's ship returning from Crete with black sails. Theseus who had killed the Minotaur in Crete, had forgotten to change the sails to white, as he had promised, if he was successful in his mission. The king, seeing the black sales assumed his son had been killed, and threw himself into the sea in despair. Thus, we have the Sea named Aegean.

Our next stop was the seaside resort of Glyfada. This was a picturesque place but too close to the airport. In fact, it was on the approach leg of the jets as they land in Athens. We were so close to the runway it seemed that the planes were flying into one end of our balcony and flying out the other end.

The next day we boarded a ship which took us to the coast of Turkey and stopped at a small town at the entrance to the Dardanelles. The name of the village was Chanak Kale. As Lydia and I stepped off the small ship it was the first step for both of us onto Asian land. What we saw as we walked off the boat was mostly men with neatly clipped moustaches of many styles. They wore baggy pants and there were many small boys playing around the dock. It was startling to see the few women on the street in their black clothing whose faces were covered with veils.

Even though Mr. Ataturk became the ruler of Turkey in 1924 and his many changes caused the country of Turkey to move towards the West in their use of metric weights and measures, and align their clocks with European time, his attempts to modernize the dress of Turkish women in the small towns had not yet taken place. In this small town on the western coast of Turkey, women were covered in a black gown reaching to their ankles and a full facial covering. One could only guess how attractive the woman underneath all this heavy protection was, which I am certain was uncomfortable in the full summer sun.

We were told by our guide that this village was the place that the Trojan Wars took place in 1300 BC. It was the location of the battles

1962: MY LUCKY DAY AND OUR HONEYMOON IN GREECE AND TURKEY

of Achille and Agamemnon. He said that it was here where Cassandra tried to warn the combatants that disaster was on the way. She was correct but no one listened to her. Our guide took the position that it was the Greeks, with their ships full of soldiers who were the pirates and not the Trojans who were the good guys.

The excavations had been going on for many decades, particularly by German archeologists who tried to determine what was really the truth and what was mythology. The archaeologists had found 7 levels of walls of different ancient cities each built upon the walls of the city that had been conquered earlier and the occupants slaughtered by each wave of invaders. At several of the levels of excavation, the archeologists found bags of gold and silver coins that had been dropped by inhabitants of the city as they were running away trying to avoid the swords of the invaders of the month. It was a tough life to live on the shore of the coast of Turkey for the past 15,000 years. One would be wise to expect a new invader every 200 or 300 years. All of them come to your city to rob you of your gold and silver coins and destroy your city and extinguish your life.

Leaving Troy our ship entered the Marmara Sea and the Bosporus River with Istanbul ahead. It was about 6 in the morning when Istanbul came into view and there was a light fog over the city. All that was visible were the tops of the taller needlelike minarets and the domes of a few of the higher mosques on the hill in the old part of the town. As we came nearer the fog lifted and the many mosques which dominate the skyline gave the city the appearance of an unreal mural of the 17th century. We felt as if we were sliding into a page of the Arabian Nights.

At Istanbul, the Bosporus narrows to a distance of about 3 football fields and our ship continued upstream to the enter the Black Sea. In addition to the many Turkish ships with their colorful flags of red with the black Crescent, there were a large number of Russian ships, probably on their way to Cuba full of who knows what mischief.

About 10 miles east of Istanbul we passed a 15th century fort built by Sultan Fatih Mehmet when he swept in from the east to conquer Istanbul. Our cruise ship went along the Turkish north shore of the entrance to the Black Sea where many beautiful shoreline villas had been built. Our ship returned to the main part of the city, and we landed near the Galatea Bridge. There, waiting on the dock for the tourists to embark, were a number of Turkish guides offering their services to show us the palaces of the kings and queens.

We hired an excellent guide, and he showed us the old part of the city including the Blue Mosque, Hagia Sofia, and the Sultan's palace, along with various charming structures which looked like they came straight out of the Arabian Nights. Then we toured the large, covered bazar, which at one time was the stables of the Sultan. We found an old Turkish cavalry sword from about the 1850 period and purchased it for a wall ornament. I also purchased an oriental ring for the hand of my lady.

We saw many very husky men carrying great loads on their backs. One who passed us on the street, walking faster than us, was carrying a large refrigerator on his back which must have weighed over 100 pounds. He was walking bent over at a 45-degree angle and was handling his burden proudly without any complaints. This person, built like Sampson, walked ahead of us for about half a mile before turning down a side street. He never put his heavy refrigerator down to rest while we were watching.

Crossing the Golden Horn over the Galatea Bridge one passes from the old city to the new city. It is like passing from the past to the future. In new Istanbul we found modern apartment buildings, streets full of automobiles, and a clean and prosperous atmosphere.

The next day our ship sailed to the city of Pergamum, a Greek colony prior to the Roman times, which became one of the most famous and

1962: MY LUCKY DAY AND OUR HONEYMOON IN GREECE AND TURKEY

prosperous cities on the coast of Asia Minor. It was built on the top of a hill dominating the countryside with high stone walls.

The following day we landed at Ephesus, which used to be a famous Greek and Roman trading port. The annual rainfall had been much greater in the Greek and Roman periods, and we understood it had been a fertile area growing tomatoes, peppers, and wheat along with cotton. With an increase of rain, it could again become a very prosperous agricultural area.

At Ephesus there was the Roman prison where St. Paul was held by the governor to protect him from irate citizens of the city, who felt his continued preaching would be harmful to their sales of religious trinkets, idols, and sacrificial hardware. In the past few years further excavations at Ephesus have unearthed a large well-preserved complete Roman city with wide paved streets one layer under the present level. On the sides of this street stand large stone slabs with parts of Roman law chiseled in Greek and Latin into the stone slabs. There are also several temples still standing.

The next stop of our ship was the Greek Island of Patmos, a 3-hour cruise from Ephesus. All the houses of Patmos are white and built like steps going up the side of the hill. The only fresh water for the town comes from rain. All the houses have flat roofs to catch the precious liquid which drains into large cisterns. If the water does not last until the next rain, the people drink wine. There were donkeys that took us up to the fortress and sanctuary. We stopped at a local tavern where the men were doing a Greek style circle dance. Lydia and I got pulled into the circle by some of the local residents and Lydia picked up the steps quickly.

After Patmos we visited Rhodes. In the old city there is the fortress built by the knights of Cyprus. This is near the site of the exciting movie "The Guns of Nazarene." Then came a visit to Crete. It has a Minoan palace built in 1400 BC. This civilization was known for bull jumping worshipers and earthquakes. There are still clear pictures on the walls of scenes of the acrobatics with bulls. The athlete bull jumper would grab the horns of a charging bull. They would then do a somersault over the horns and land on their feet upright, on the back of a very surprised bull. The frescoes did not show what happened to the athlete after he completed this acrobatic jump, but I assume the somersaulting athletes ran as fast as he could to get out of field of vision to an angry 2,000-pound bull.

Judging from the low ceilings of the palace, the Minoans who lived in Crete in 1500 BC we could see that the tall ones reached not much over 5 feet. The ceilings were supported by heavy wooden pillars painted red with a large black band at the top. In the palace room of the queen were clay pipes through which fresh water had flowed during hot summer days to keep the queen cool. There was also an elaborate sewer system under the streets of the city, similar to Athens.

Crete was a bridge between Egypt and Greece, and the Cretans were good sailors. They reached as far as the English coast. In a few English towns where the Romans lived the model of the Minoan dagger was chiseled in the walls of pre-Roman excavations in England.

Our tour of the Greek Islands included a stop at the beautiful island of Santorini. This island is shaped like the sliver of a new moon. The town sits on one side of a sheer cliff about 700 feet directly above the bay. There is a narrow zig zag path cut into the side of the cliff from the shore to the top. Brave tourists ride donkeys up a narrow path cut into the rock of the sheer cliff wall.

1962: MY LUCKY DAY AND OUR HONEYMOON IN GREECE AND TURKEY

We were told the donkeys have excellent balance. You must not lean in towards the cliff wall believing you have better balance than your donkey. You don't. If you try to compensate by leaning your body toward the wall of the cliff your donkey will lean out on the narrow ledge path cut into the rock wall to offset your shifting of your weight. We were told the donkeys have a better sense of balance than humans, without the same fear of heights. One last warning as you get on your donkey, "Don't look down!"

The view from the top of the cliff, once back 6 feet from the edge of the cliff is impressive and worth the frightening donkey ride up the face of the narrow ledge.

The last part of the trip was a tour through classical Greece towns with Delphi, Olympia, Nauplius, Mycenae, and Corinth. At Mycenae we saw the Cyclopean walls built by Agamemnon. When one sees the size of the large stone blocks used to build the walls, and each weighing many tons, one wonders what kind of machinery they had to lift these enormous heavy boulders into place.

At Nauplius we climbed the 999 steps to the top of the cliff where there is a fortress built by the Venetians. There is also another fortress on a large rock island in the bay. When you honk your horn, a porter gets in a motor launch and brings you to the front door of the small island hotel.

The food market at the port of Piraeus had a most amazing large butcher area where there were about 30 butchers, each with a large block of wood as their worktable. At the side of the table were places for holding a large number of sharp knives and hatchets. Watching from a safe distance, we saw a continuous motion of flashing steel as the butchers rapidly chopped and cut various sizes of meat on their wooden blocks, accompanied by a continuous shouting of their products and prices to the public.

Many of butcher blocks had a small boy in front of their stand who added to the salesmanship of the butcher, yelling at those that walked by at a high pitch. With all the knives and hatchets moving rapidly and at such close quarters, along with shouting and distractions I would not be surprised if a finger gets chopped off and wrapped up in a neat meat package for sale.

In the fish section were a wide variety of all strange sorts of creatures of the sea. Some of the octopuses seemed to look right at you as they read your mind. We were told they were smarter than humans. The lobsters were also very much alive. If you did not lose a finger at the butcher section of the market, you might find an arm of an octopuses reaching out for your wrist.

Prior to leaving Athens we spent one evening at Dafni where the annual wine festival takes place. For an entrance fee of 30 drachmas (about 1 dollar) we received a glass and a pint flask. We then walked around the fair grounds and tested some of the 116 different wines from all parts of Greece, served out of large barrels by girls dressed in the local costumes of each region. We learned that after you have decided which of the many different wines you liked best, if you could remember, you would stagger back to the place where you were offered the best tasting wine. There you would fill your empty flask without paying extra and take it to one of the outdoor restaurants and order your dinner. I am sorry to say we were able to taste only 20 of the 116 different wines offered.

On our return to Milan, we had trouble getting the Turkish sword past the customs official. There was a law on the books in Italy which states one must not bring weapons into the country. I assume that the Spanish, French, Austrians, Germans, and Attila the Hun crossed into Italy before that law was passed.

THREE

1963: Paris, Spain, Amalfi Coast, and a tour of the Alps

This was a year of two major events. The first event was our first wedding anniversary and the completion of two years of overseas service as an expatriate with General Telephone which carries with it an excellent prize - a five-week vacation titled "Home Leave".

The second important event was the move to our newly constructed factory which comfortably housed our 1,200 employees. The factory address was Cassina Di' Peccei, which means the farm of Mr. Peccei, and was located about 12 miles from the center of Milan to the southwest of the city. The closest town was Gorgonzola, which is where the famous cheese of that name is made.

In 1963 there was a general movement of factories to the outskirts of Milan which generated an unusual commuting pattern. Unlike the U.S. where a large number of people live in the suburbs and commute to the city for their work, the opposite occurred in Milan where people lived in the city and commuted to the outskirts. This created commuting problems in a reverse direction than that of the U.S. My commute was 40 minutes to an hour each way depending on the traffic. In spite of that inconvenience for work, it was nice that our apartment was only a 15-minute walk from the very center of Milan.

Lydia and I used the "Home Leave Vacation" time to explore Paris, several cities in Spain, and an ancient Greek settlement in the south of Italy. We assumed that within the last 4,000 years at least a few of our ancestors probably had called one of those ancient cities "Home."

We enjoyed Paris very much. We had one big night on the town which included Apache dancers, a small cabaret on Mont Maître, and the Lido. We also saw the Folies Bergères another evening. At the Folies, I was particularly impressed by the acrobatic mostly naked women lowered from the ceiling on a large chandelier. Lydia thought the dancing was good.

Our visit to Pigalle quarter left quite a lasting impression on us. Five minutes after we had arrived, we passed in front of one of the small bars. There was a crowd out in the street and the bar was empty, except for the bartender who was wiping off the top of the bar. A second glance revealed a shoe on the floor which was attached to a body stretched out in a wild west saloon fashion. His shirt was covered with blood. There had been a stabbing or shooting just 5 minutes before we arrived. Two minutes later we heard the cling clang of the French police wagon, and the body was taken away. This catchy cling clang was a tune we heard many times while we were in Paris and we couldn't decide whether this is evidence of efficient law and order or of a substantial disorder, but either way the police were omnipresent and responded rapidly.

The Isle De France with Notre Dame, the prison of Marie Antoinette during the Revolution, and the Seine River front were among the more impressive things we saw. The broad boulevards of Paris were very attractive. One of the things that we particularly enjoyed about Paris was all the green and the many parks in the city. The view from the Eiffel tower increased our awareness of all the shrubbery. Of particular interest to Lydia was the museum of French impressionists. The palaces of Versailles and Fontainebleau were also awe-inspiring though the opulence of Versailles and Fontainebleau paled in comparison with the palace of the royal Spanish Kings in Madrid.

David and Lydia in Paris

Our first wedding anniversary dinner celebration took place in Granada, Spain on the terrace of a hotel adjacent to the Alhambra. It was a fine view overlooking that beautiful city. On the second day we obtained tickets to a bullfight. One of the Toreadors was voted by the crowd as "very good" and received several Bulls' ears as recognition. As he was walking proudly around the ring after his fight, showing the crowd his collection of ears, he threw one of them in our direction. I caught it and assumed it was a gesture of good will. Unfortunately, we didn't have anything to throw back. The enthusiastic fans surrounding us were throwing several objects back at him, mostly goat skin wine flasks filled with wine. He caught one of these flasks, tipped his head back, and took a long dramatic swig. Then he passed the flask to his second, who threw the flask back into the crowd, and the stands exploded with applause.

It is quite fascinating to watch the Toreador dodge a 1,200-pound bull that comes angrily at him at top speed with his head down and its horns aimed at the slender Toreador in his tightly fitting pants. With graceful steps our hero Toreador, stepped to one side and the sharp horns passed two inches to his left without touching him. The bull did catch one edge of his cape and tossed it up into the air.

In Seville such an opportunity presented itself. There was a small rink which was open to the public. For 50 cents you could get into the ring with a small bull and try your skill at dodging. These bulls were smaller than the big ones used in the official bull rings and their horns were blunted. There was also a ring master in the ring with the novice whose mission was to divert the bull if the novice lost his nerve or his footing as the bull charged. We went to watch the amateurs who were mostly teen-aged boys trying to outdo each. One of them lost his nerve and ran for the exit with the bull close behind. He made it to a wooden barrier and the bull stopped. The crowd roared with laughter.

Although I was tempted to try my luck, I thought "next time." My suit had a thin red pin strip in its weave. I decided that even a small amount of red might enrage the bull, so I decided to pass. Lydia had no red, but also decided to skip the opportunity to poke or challenge the bull.

We saw the old section of Seville which is charming. The streets were wide enough for only one car at a time. Most of the ancient houses had wrought iron balconies on the second floor and a collection of flowers and plants overflowing these balconies.

The old section of Cordoba is even more charming than Seville. One evening we took a very scenic carriage ride through the old section of the city. Cordoba had a most impressive Mosque with a forest of columns. A Catholic Church had been constructed in the very center of this very large Mosque immediately after Cordoba was captured by the Christian army. The church diminished the architectural beauty of this Mosque, but its presence in the church did prevent it from being destroyed by the Kings of Castile when the Moors were defeated there.

The Alhambra in Granada was a beautiful structure which is still virtually intact. We learned that the gardens and fountains were as they were in the 14th Century. The combination of the formal gardens, pools and fountains, and Arabic arches provided magnificent views of the city of Granada below. It was one of the many lovely places we saw in Spain.

There were a number of gypsies living in Granada. We were told these gypsies come not from Egypt where most gypsies originate, but from Pakistan. They were mercenary soldiers who were imported to assist the kings of Castille in their fight against the Moors. In gratitude they were given a section of the city along one steep hill. Their houses were built into the sides of a hill and many gypsy families still live in this section of Granada.

We went to see the gypsy dances in Granada. Accompanying the guitarist were two aged women clapping their hands half chanting and half singing in loud voices as background for the dancers. Included in the admissions was a small glass of wine. We thought it was sherry, but we had doubts. Not everyone finished their glass of wine, and I am quite certain the wine remaining in the glasses, was recycled into the large flask, to be used for the next group.

The gypsies that weren't dancing or clapping were out in the street selling trinkets or begging. After some sharp bargaining Lydia purchased a pair of castanets for 25 pesetas (50 cents). The first price started at that price. When she showed interest, the price suddenly increased to

50 pesetas. She was told she was mistaken if she thought she could purchase such a fine pair for less than 50 pesetas. Lydia offered 25 pesetas and walked away with the pair.

Our drive through southern Spain included a stop off at Gibraltar. Being a free customs port without taxes of any sort, Gibraltar presents great temptations to the traveler. We found ourselves seduced by attractive prices of objects from North Africa and the Near East and came away with our arms full of packages. There were many monkeys living in the upper rocky areas of the great Rock of Gibraltar as well as many chattering monkeys looking at and purchasing things for sale.

We visited Toledo, a charming medieval city standing at the top of a hill, surrounded on three sides by deep canyons cut by the Tajo River. This steep natural moat surrounded on three sides, plus the stout walls of the ancient city still standing must have made the city virtually impregnable to passing armies. Toledo was famous for its steel, and we purchased a fine Toledo sword.

In our drive through southern Spain, and despite the donkey carts on the roads, we had the impression it was a prosperous area. My former negative impression of Dictator Franco was modified by this trip. It had been my impression that Franco had upset a democratic elected government when he came to power. In talking to a number of Spaniards, we were led to believe that the pre-Franco government was only democratic in name. It was suppressing its opposition and a coup from the communist left was imminent supported by Stalin. Franco was considered by many people with whom we spoke as a dictator but the lesser of two evils, the greater evil being a Communist regime as in Russia. Certainly, many of the freedoms we take for granted in America or Italy did not exist in Spain. However, under Franco's regime there has been economic stability and growth of Spain's private sector and employment.

In Italy, the political struggle was between the socialist and communist parties on the left balanced by the Christian Democrat Party plus a few minor parties on the right. At the end of World War II, Italy elected an excellent Prime Minister, De Gasperi, who was responsible for producing the "Italian Economic Miracle." We were hopeful that his middle road would continue to be followed.

Returning to scenic Italy we had some wonderful ski trips during the past winter and were impressed with a place called Selva in the Val Gardena. It is an area in the Dolomites about 30 miles southeast of the Brenner Pass. The scenery was magnificent with massive rocks rising straight up out of the snow fields. The area had an extremely large variety of trails and lifts of many kinds. It was possible to ski in that area for a week and not repeat the same trail.

One day we took the trip of the Four Passes, which circles one of the large mountains in a one-day trip. The changing panorama circling the mountains was magnificent. We took a first ski lift from Selva, on the Italian speaking side, which took us to the first pass. From there, we skied down to the village in the German-speaking valley below. From there we took another lift to the second mountain pass and skied down to its valley below. We repeated that sequence to reach four different mountain tops and four valleys, switching from German to Italian, though in most of the towns the residents spoke both Italian and German.

We also had a trip to ski Mont Blanc, a ski area at the center of the Alps with one of the steepest runs we had ever been on. In good weather the ski run goes from a vertical drop of 12,000 feet to 5,000 feet. About a third of the way down we passed some large spooky ice caves and the ice inside had a sinister light blue color. It was not possible to see the back of the ice cave and it seemed as if the cave led right into the center of the mountain. Other winter ski excursions took us to Zermatt, St Moritz, Courmayeur and back again to Madonna Di Campiglio.

As members of a Milan Ski Club, we travelled to and climbed the Torre di Venezia and to the Stelvio area which used to be the old Italian–Austrian border before the first World War. The peaks in this area were named Gran Zebru, Piccolo Zebru, Koinigspitts and Thurwieser. We stayed at mountain refuge called the Quinto Alpini which was the headquarters of the 5th Italian Alpine regiment during World War One. It was not difficult to see why the war in that area was inconclusive as the mountains were so difficult to breach by the enemy. Ropes were needed to go across the terrain from one side to the other with several large glaciers.

David & Lydia mountain climbing in the Alps

1963: PARIS, SPAIN, AMALFI COAST, AND A TOUR OF THE ALPS

Turning to warmer weather we took a wonderful trip in the spring to the Amalfi Coast which had a most spectacular view. The little town of Ravello was breathtaking, sitting on a plateau 3,000 feet above the town of Amalfi.

We also visited the nearby former Greek walled city of Paestum. Many parts of the walls of that great Greek city were still standing., enclosing an area 2 miles by 2 miles. The walls were 15 feet high, but we understood from the guide that they were, at one time, 50 feet high. The main gate, built right at the sea, was built the same way as the gates of the city of Troy. The angles of the walls gave the defending archers an advantage over the attackers. An earthquake blocked the exit of the nearby Sila River in about 100 BC and produced a swampy malaria zone and the city was abandoned. Silt covered the town completely and excavation started in 1950. Only 5% of the city had yet been uncovered. Its three massive Greek temples, dating back to the 5th century BC, were among the best preserved, missing only their wooden roof. Recent discoveries were housed in a nearby museum overflowing with tools, jewelry, pottery, and sculptures.

FOUR

1964: Sardinia, the Palio, and the Venetian Regatta

Life in Italy continues to be very enjoyable. My job as Controller of Marelli Lenkurt has taken a different complexion as we purchased the other 50% interest of our Italian partners at the beginning of the year and are now in the process of merging with another manufacturing subsidiary of General Telephone in Milan. The merger of the two companies should provide us with more flexibility to weather some of the problems connected with the present state of the Italian political and economic environment. It is hoped that the present government can take the necessary steps that are needed to restore the degree of prosperity that existed prior to Premier Fanfani.

Fanfani's experiment to achieve prosperity by the nationalization of all the electrical power companies has been bad for the economy. Other policies of his Center Left government discouraged investments which, in turn, have had severe repercussions on the general economic health of the country. He was not returned as the leader of the Christian Democrat party and was replaced by Aldo Moro.

In contrast to the depressed economic environment, the rich musical

1964: SARDINIA, THE PALIO, AND THE VENETIAN REGATTA

environment of Milan has provided us with many pleasant days and evenings. We continue to enjoy the proximity of Milan to the Alps with its good skiing and to many other places of interest.

The island of Sardinia has held a fascination for both of us, and in September we had the pleasure of spending 9 days there. The trip started with the two-hour drive from Milan to the port of Genoa. There, our car was hoisted aboard a ship. After dinner on board and a moonlit walk around the deck at night, plus a deep sleep in our cabin, we awoke to find the island of Corsica on our left and Sardinia ahead.

Sardinia is very dry, and in some areas, it reminds me of Wyoming. If Wyoming were surrounded by an emerald sea in which you could find octopuses, the comparison would be extremely close. While Wyoming was famous for its bandits, Sardinia not only was and still is a haven for outlaws. A month before we left for our trip, three separate episodes were reported in the Milan newspapers. In one of these, large boulders had been placed in the middle of one of the roads. When the driver of a lone car stopped to clear away the stones, three bandits emerged from behind other large boulders and took his money.

The bandits harvested the money from two other cars before they vanished into the hills. A week later, three bandits armed with rifles stopped a local bus going between towns in the mountainous Gennargentu area. In this episode the bandits were not looking for money but for a person. The person they were looking for was invited to step down from the bus and was never heard from again. Apparently, that person was also a bandit and had not respected the bandit law of Silence (Omerta) and was punished.

Eight days later, near the large town of Alghero, 6 bandits held up a night club. The real loser of this episode was the bar owner. The bandit stayed for three hours, kept the music playing and invited all the bar guests to drink with them. In contrast to the damaging effect of this publicity on tourist travel in Sardinia, the Italian Tourist Bureau reimbursed the foreigners that were in the night club to the full extent of their loss. Unfortunately, the bartender, whose wares were pillaged in the episode, did not receive such generous government consideration.

Our awareness of recent banditry added some spice to our trip through the interior of the island. We were almost disappointed not to see desperados emerging from behind large rocks, with their weapons. Lydia felt it was the worn condition of our car which was responsible for our passage through the dangerous areas untouched. In spite of the attempts of an occasional shepherd to try his hand at a more lucrative profession, we found the people we met to be very honest.

The scenery of Sardinia deserves the attention which it is now beginning to receive. It combines a very clear transparent Mediterranean Sea in which the bottom is clearly visible 30 feet deep, with a coast that has a combination of large sand beaches and rocky coves. In many places cliffs rise straight up from the sea and contain interesting grottos to visit. The interior is mountainous and wild boar are still hunted. The population is sparse, and you can drive for miles both in the interior and along the coast, and not encounter another person in September even though the weather is still very good.

Sardinia has an interesting historical background. In the 7th century B.C., the Phoenicians established settlements along the coasts of this large island. They were followed by the Carthaginians and Romans. On the southern tip below the small city of Cagliari and four feet below the current level of the sea is the ancient city of Nora, built first by the Carthaginians and later enlarged by the Romans. Part of this ancient city has been excavated and much of it is now below the current surface of the sea. Lydia and I put on our masks and snorkel to see it.

It is possible to make out the outlines of some of the houses below the surface of the sea, at the depth of about 30 feet. Twenty miles north of Nora there are many coves and beaches that we had completely to ourselves. We learned that our hotel was the site of the large Roman city of Bithia. Two years earlier, they told us, a group of 50 Swedes with shovels, had been working on our private beach excavating without getting permission from Rome. Had we known that our deserted beach covered part of an ancient Roman city we should also have brough shovels with us. In any case in one of my shallow dives I come up with part of a clay amphora in about 6 feet of water with one handle that is now resting at one side of our current fireplace.

While the Romans occupied much of the coast of Sardinia, they were never too successful in subjugating the people living in the interior of the island. These early inhabitants can be traced to the Bronze Age. One recent discovery is near the town of Alghero. It is a construction consisting of a series of connecting rooms cut into the side of a hill, which we understood had been used as tombs for the local chiefs.

Following the Bronze Age was the Nuragic civilizations which ran from about 1600 B.C. to 500 B.C. Throughout the interior of this large island there are remains of Nuragic structures, towers in the shape of a wasp hive made of very large stones, piled one on top of the other. The unusual thing about these structures is that the stones are of irregular shape, and yet the structures stand without the aid of cement.

Of great interest for us was a visit to the Nuragic village near Barumini, about an hour drive north of Cagliari. Excavations at the foot of one of these towers have brough to light a complete village in which approximately 2,000 people were considered to have lived. Although this tower today reaches 15 feet above ground level, the excavations have exposed the balance of it and the structure is now measured to be 45 feet tall. Surrounding the central tower are 4 towers, each about 30 feet high. Surrounding these shorter towers are a number of two room houses. Enclosing the houses there is another group of 7 towers each about 15 feet high connected by walls. Outside of these walls were a larger number of single room houses.

Inside the four main towers is a large courtyard and a deep well. A very spooky and steep stone staircase spirals up inside the wall of the main tower. The distance between the steps is uneven and required using our hands in some places. These main towers have three inside levels and ports for shooting arrows. A rope ladder which could be pulled up allowed the defenders to retreat to the upper stories in case of attack. Rolling back a large chest high stone at the ground floor of one of the main towers must have been a small prison room.

Entrance into these towers as well as into all of the houses was by a narrow entranceway. To enter one had to bend over with hands touching the ground. This leaves the back of one's head at the mercy of anyone standing to one side of the entrance with a big club. With this difficult entrance, doors were probably unnecessary since one man could undoubtedly defend his house and, in the process, accumulate a pile of unwelcome guests in his vestibule. Such a town would be a wonderful site for a slapstick movie, 1920 style.

This town dates back to about 1500 B.C. and we were quite impressed with the similarity between it and the tomb of Agamemnon which we saw at Mycenae in Greece on our honeymoon. The tomb of Agamemnon also has this wasp hive shape and made with the same type of heavy stones without cement. Many Nuragic towers can be found throughout Sardinia. It is extremely likely that if additional excavations were made, many Nuragic villages similar to this one could be uncovered.

The type of accommodations that can be found in Sardinia ranges from the beautiful and luxurious Moorish style hotels built by the Aga Khan on the Emerald Coast where room and meals will run $50 per day per couple, to the small "pensione" that can be found in the villages of the interior where a room without meals will cost a dollar per day. The interior of this large island is not yet ready to handle a large flood of tourists. In the town of Barumini, the hotel listed in the guidebook is described as having four rooms and one bath. It is also the only restaurant in the town and after visiting the Nuragic village we went there for lunch.

In the restaurant there were two tables that could accommodate 6 people at each table. We were the first ones for lunch and after 10 minutes three tourists from Ravenna arrived. They were seated at our table, and we were served family style. The service, plus ample quantities of the excellent local wine, soon made us all great friends. Four quarts of wine later we parted company with reluctance and continued on our way.

Many of the small towns of Sardinia are known for their local products. With large quantities of cork trees growing in Sardinia, many attractive art pieces made of cork and large quantities of wine corks are produced. The Sardinian carpets are very full of color. We visited a small shop and carpet workshop in the town of Isili (pronounced "easily"), where 10 women were working on hand looms.

It was obvious to us that a tourism had not yet reached Sardinia. We wanted to order one of the carpets but were running short of cash and asked if we could pay with a check drawn on a major Italian bank. This was the first check anyone had ever tried to offer to this small business, and we encountered some resistance. After explaining how the banking system works, the check was accepted, and we left the shop with a colorful tapestry of "The Hunt for Wild Boars" for our bedroom wall and another carpet with the traditional black and red Sardinian design will be sent to us in a few months.

The Sardinian dialect is virtually another language than Italian, and Lydia could understand only an occasional word when Sardinians replied to us in their dialect. On the west coast of the island the dialect has a Spanish flavor, and quite understandably so. While the city states of Pisa and Genoa were at war with each other for control of the island in the 13th and 14th century, the Aragonese from the east coast of Spain landed on the west coast of Sardinia and finally captured the entire island. The large town of Alghero with its towers and heavy wall protecting it from invasion from the sea the town looks much more Spanish than Italian.

Alghero is famous for its sea food and octopus is included among its specialty. While we were snorkeling in of one of the bays, we came upon two boys diving for octopus. In this bay the octopuses were quite small with tentacles up to 20 inches. My curiosity led me to test the suction of the small cups on their tenacles. They held on impressively even when the octopus was out of the sea. We watched the boys pulling the octopus off of the rocks at the bottom of the bay and then attaching them to their bathing suits. Then they swam to shore and sold them to the restaurants.

It was quite a scene to see the boys emerge from the sea with 5 writhing octopuses around their waists. The thought that one or more of these arms might reach out and grab onto a rock and pull the boy under water and keep him from breathing was frightening. We were told that if these creatures were any larger, they could keep the boy under the surface of the water and drown him. For this reason, they had to let the larger ones go. In conclusion Sardinia is a wonderful place for a summer vacation.

Moving back the mainland, we attended two different historical pageants this year, each with a different medieval flavor. One of these was the Palio of Siena and the other was the historic regatta in Venice.

More impressive than the race in Siena is the parade preceding the race. In Sienna the various sections of the city, called contrada, compete for honors in the flag twirling prior to the race. There are 17 contrade and each have their own distinctive flag with colorful costumes. Page boys lead each group, and they are followed by the flag twirlers, knights, archers, and spearmen in medieval costumes.

The horse that is to race representing the contrada is led by a groom followed by the jockey. The flag twirling, which apparently takes years of practice, fills the main square with a swishing sound as the large flags at least 7 feet large are whirled about and thrown into the air and caught.

Lots are drawn to determine which 10 horses which will race on the first day and the others race at a later date. In addition to the 17 contrade there are other contrade who have been prohibited from racing because of terrible crimes that were committed as many as 500 years ago. Representatives of these evil sections are dressed in black with the visor down. It is not clear to how many years, decades or centuries ago those evil contrade must remain in purgatory.

The crowd is fiercely partisan, and some fights break out even before the race begins. While the representatives of each contrada are parading around the square, their supporters in the center of the square seem to be having contests to see how high they can toss one of their members. This combination of flags twirling, and bodies being hurled in the air adds to the excitement which sets the stage for the bareback race.

Just prior to the race, a troop of mounted "carabinieri" take two turns around the ring. They are dressed in colorful red and blue uniforms of the late Napoleonic period, complete with Napoleon-type hats. The race consists of three laps around the large square and there are no rules which prevent the jockeys from hitting or even trying to unseat their opponents. Two jockeys fell off their horses by the first turn and a third on the second turn. Although we could not distinguish clearly what happened during the first frantic start, it is most likely that these three unhorsings were not entirely accidental.

The main square of Siena was not originally planned as a racetrack and therefore the sharp curves at the four corners are not banked to the benefit of the racers. In fact, two of the corners are slightly banked in the opposite direction. As the horses come skittering around these corners at virtually full speed, it seems as if the horses and rider are so tilted that the jockey could drag one of their knuckles on the ground.

Visit to Palio at Siena

Immediately after the race, the supporters of the various contrade break out onto the track and pummel the horsemen of the opposing contrada, who may have been guilty of hitting their horseman, or perhaps they do not need a reason. The members of the contrada whose horse appears to be winning run onto the racetrack to form a bodyguard around their hero to protect him from other members of the crowd. These fights last only a few minutes as the "carabinieri" quickly restore order. The winning contrada then parades through the town twirling their flags and singing. The celebration continues far into the night.

Within an hour the stands are dismantled, and the racetrack is transformed again into the main square of Siena and the restaurant owners set up their tables on the former racetrack for those who wish to eat outside. As it grows dark, torches are lit on top of many of the buildings that surround the square, some of which resemble battlements and the scene seems more appropriate to the 14th century rather than the 20th century.

While the Palio at Siena takes you back to the 14th century, the historic regatta of Venice has a 15th century flavor. The parade preceding the race of the gondoliers takes place on the main canal and anchored barges covered with collapsible chairs provide good views for the spectators. The really lucky ones watch the "regatta" from balconies of the mansions that are on the main canal.

The boats used for the guest of honor, dressed in their 14th century costumes and the many ships on which they watch the regatta looking like Roman Galleys and Viking ships with bowsprits of eagles, lions, dragons, winged horses, and mermaids. Each boat is of a different solid color. The gondoliers that row these boats from their customary standing position, wear loose fitting pants and shirts with large sashes around their waist.

The parade on the grand canal is led by gondoliers with heralds standing in their gondolas. There is a herald in one of the larger gondolas that announce the location and name of the dignitaries who come from such locations as Cyprus, Istanbul, Syria, Egypt, Tunisia, Spain, France, Russia, and China, each dressed in the appropriate dress of their country and accompanied by their wives.

Following the ambassadors are brightly colored galleys with up to 40 men at the oars, carrying the Doge, the chief executive of medieval Venice, and his various advisors. On either side of these official vessels are large gondolas carrying archers and spearmen who provide protection for this august group. The gondola races which follow are less exciting than the horse race at Siena, probably because there is more gallantry on the water. It may be that the Venetians of the 15th century were more civilized than the Sienese of the 14th century. However, the fact that the fans would have to swim to get close enough to molest the participants probably also has its influence.

FIVE

1965: East Africa

The big event in our lives this year was our trip to East Africa, and we had the pleasure of spending three weeks touring Kenya, Uganda, and Tanzania. Our touring never took us farther than three hundred miles from the Equator and we crossed it six times.

Lydia's painting of our trip to Uganda on elephants, protected by the Lion

The airport of Entebbe, Uganda was our first contact with East Africa and as we looked out from the window of our airplane, we expected our initial concern of equatorial heat in August to be confirmed. The airline ground personnel, customs officials and police were all wearing shorts and shirts with short sleeves. A few bearded Sikhs were wearing turbans along with their shorts, and we saw two people with pith helmets and shorts. However, we were pleasantly surprised by the wonderfully comfortable golf and tennis weather which we found throughout our trip.

The second pleasant surprise was the lack of insects. We had come quite prepared for our stay on the Equator with numerous jars of insect repellent. However, except for an occasional mosquito and a Tse-Tse fly now and then, we were not bothered at all by insects.

The topography of East Africa is extremely interesting and varied. The coastal area is tropical with dense unusual vegetation. Moving inland you rise slowly to the central plains. Here are wide expanses of grassland and rolling country at an altitude of 3,000 to 4,000 feet. In the middle of this grassland area, and straddling the Kenya and Tanzania border, rise the beautiful cone of Mt Meru (14,980 feet) and the majestic snowcapped Mt Kilimanjaro (19,300 feet). Much of this area is now a national park and contains great quantities of wild game. Continuing west you come to the Great Rift Valley which has provided water, grass, and hospitality to wild beasts (including man) for hundreds of thousands of years. Proceeding west you come to Lake Victoria which is only slightly smaller than Lake Superior. The area between the Great Rift Valley and the eastern shore of Lake Victoria is very dry. However, from the western shore in Uganda to the mountains which mark the border of the Congo, there is very fertile and profuse vegetation.

In Kenya, where we spent most of our time, there is a vast area of dry rolling grassland to the south of Nairobi. To the north, between Nairobi and Mt. Kenya, there is very beautiful high country, extremely green and covered with heavy forestation interspersed with tea and coffee plantations. In this area, about 50 miles north of Nairobi, there is the town of Thiki with its famous waterfall and pool from which many of the scenes from the Tarzan movies have been filmed. The vines that hang down from the trees look very strong and we were tempted to swing from one side of the pool to the other.

Still farther north are the Aberdare mountains which many of the English settlers compare to the Scottish Highlands. In the Aberdare Mountains there are also thick bamboo forests with bamboo stalks up to forty feet tall. Dominating the landscape to the east of the Aberdare and astride the Equator is Mt. Kenya which exceeds a height of 17,000 feet. Mt, Kenya is of volcanic origin and contains several living glaciers, one of which is cut by the Equator. The area to the north and east of Mt, Kenya and up to the Ethiopian and Somalian border is a desert. However, the sparse grass that can be found here supports an animal population and a number of tribes.

While we think of the United States as a melting pot, East Africa seemed to us to be a much greater melting pot. First, in East Africa there are many tribes which are quite different. The major tribes include the Buganda, Kikuyu, Masai, Tabora, and Boran, but there are also many others. In addition, there is a wide mixture of Asians which includes Indians, Goans, Pakistanis, turbaned Sikhs, Persians, and Arabs from various Arab States. To this add a sprinkling of European stock including British, German, Dutch, French and Italian, plus a few Americans and Canadians, and you have quite a mixture.

From a religious standpoint the same diversity can be found. Muslim, Hindu, Sikh, Christian, and Jewish plus the many tribal religions. The major representation among the Christians includes Catholic, Episcopal, and Seventh Day Adventists.

However, in spite of all the diversity, the newly independent country seems to be making good progress. English and Swahili are the two languages which tie this assorted population together and almost everyone speaks both to some extent. The government of Kenyatta has been able to find workable compromises between the various groups and is presently respected by all.

One of the most encouraging aspects of this new country is the great interest the Africans have in sending their children to school. This was particularly apparent in Uganda. We were aware of a very large number of schools, all filled with children. Schools are not cheap, and the parents must pay a monthly school tax for each child they send to school. This school tax averages 3 to 5% of the average monthly earnings of an average African and has become the most important family expense.

The Masai tribe is the only one that does not share the enthusiasm of the other tribes about education and has been very slow in sending their children to school. The Masai is the fierce warrior tribe that keeps great flocks of cattle. They are the ones that take blood from the neck of their cattle, mix the blood with fresh milk, and this lovely cocktail then becomes their main course. Fortunately, we did not receive any invitation to dine with a Masai. The Masai are also the ones that paint their faces with a combination of red earth and animal fat. Apparently, the aesthetics and visual benefits of this face cream overcome the rather unaesthetic odor of rancid animal fat, which becomes very obvious as you draw close.

The story of the Masai is perhaps analogous to the story of the Mohicans in the U.S. For centuries, the Masai have had the reputation of creating terror in the other tribes. Physically they do not seem too imposing. Although quite tall, they are rather thin and almost scrawny. However, they have great courage and are fierce warriors. Even today you will rarely see a Masai adult male without his spear.

Their tactics have been to completely exterminate the groups they go to war against. They would kill all of the enemy warriors with spears during the battle and at night they would kill the women and children of the defeated tribe with clubs. This warfare against other tribes continued up until about 60 years ago when the British stepped in and prevented the massacres which used to be quite commonplace.

One of the Masai traditions apparently kept the weaker and less courageous warriors from reproducing weak and uncourageous offspring. This tradition, which is still practiced by perhaps a third of the Masai who live away from urban centers, is that of having to kill a lion singlehandedly before getting married. The thought of having to face a charging lion alone and with only a spear probably keeps a certain group of males resigned to bachelorhood. Those that have the courage but not the strength get killed by the lion and only those with both courage and skill, plus probably a little luck, survive to get married and reproduce the race.

In the combat against the lion, a large towel or blanket is wrapped around the left arm, which is then thrust in the lion's mouth as he springs, this is supposed to protect the throat of the Masai and also give the lion something to chew on while the right hand is trying to push the spear into the lion's body. However, when you think that the spring of a 400-pound lion would probably knock over a 170-pound Masai, towel or no towel, the advantage seems to be definitely with the lion.

While the Masai is the only tribe that paint their faces with animal fat, other tribes have different traditions involving changing body parts. One such tradition involves creating a large hole in the earlobe, resulting in earlobes that hang down in a great loop two to three inches below where it would normally be. It is quite startling to see many of the older people with a hole in their ear lobe the size of a silver dollar. Sometimes you will find one ear thru which you can see a large area of daylight, and the other ear will have this flap wrapped up and over the top in a manner that almost closes the ear. This practice is now dying out among the present generation and, based on a discussion we had with one of our drivers who was a Kikuyu, we got the impression that the present generation has discontinued this practice.

With the great mixture of races and religions one would expect to find considerable antipathy between the groups. And as whites in a predominately black country, we rather expected to find some antagonism towards our white skin. Quite on the contrary the Africans were extremely friendly and in areas where we went, we felt very welcome. Their attitude seemed to be: "This is my country, welcome to it. I hope you enjoy it. We are very proud of our country, and I hope you will like it too."

The interest in schools plus an awakening political awareness on the part of the population, combined with the great pride of the African that this is now his country is the basis for considerable optimism for the future. In addition, the population seems to be very sparse in comparison to the potential of the country. For example, Kenya and Uganda together are about the size of France and Italy and have 15 million people rather than the 100 million of these two European countries. Tanzania compares in area with the rest of the common market, plus Great Britain, Ireland, East Germany, Austria, and Switzerland. This European area has a population of 150 million people as opposed to the 10 million of Tanzania. Therefore, Kenya, Uganda and Tanzania together have only 25 million people as opposed to 250 million people in an equivalent area in Western Europe.

The agricultural potential of East Africa is very great, and they are able to get normally two to three harvests per year and, for some crops, even more. Lack of rain can sometimes be a problem as it was this year, but over a 5-year period, yields of grains and vegetables are much higher than in Europe. The European farmers in

Kenya are responsible for a very large percentage of export and foreign exchange of the country and it is hoped that the Africans can get away from their subsistence farming and start producing crops on an equally large efficient scale for export.

It was our impression that the country could support a much larger cattle population. Many of the grasslands have abundant growth, much more luxuriant that the vast cattle ranges of Wyoming, Nebraska, and Colorado.

One factor which has inhibited the growth of the cattle industry in Kenya has been a rather high rate of cattle rustling. Although progress has been made in apprehending the rustlers, the problem is far from under control. For centuries one of the main pastimes of several tribes was stealing cattle from the next tribe, avenging the stealing of the cattle, and then stealing them back. The roots of this accepted behavior are difficult to eradicate.

Our trip started in Kampala, Uganda, which is at an altitude of 4,000 feet and 20 miles from the Equator. The climate is pleasant and constant throughout most of the year. Kampala is built on seven hills and gives the appearance of a very green suburb rather than a city. It is very clean, and the parks, parkways, shrubs, and private lawns are neat and well kept. The soil is extremely fertile and most everything grows quickly. Almost every family has a small plot of land on which you will find a number of banana trees. These bananas are green when ripe and are cooked like a vegetable. They are the staple diet of a large part of the population. Pineapples, mangoes, breadfruit, yellow bananas, coconuts, and corn also grow in great profusion,

Western marketing had started to make inroads into this area, and we found quite a battle going on between Coca Cola and Pepsi Cola. It seems that Pepsi Cola had the slight edge. The first advertisement we saw coming in from the airport was simple and to the point, "Pepsi is the big one". We found this theme repeated throughout East Africa.

From Kampala we drove north to Murchison National Park which is on the border of the Congo and not far from the Sudan. The Park straddles the Nile virtually at its source and contains the very impressive Murchison Falls. The rapids above Murchison Falls are breathtaking and are surpassed only by the falls themselves. This great mass of water, draining from Lake Victoria funnels through a cleft which is but 20 feet wide and drops 130 feet with a tremendous roar accompanied by great clouds of mist. If someone had the misfortune of being swept over the falls and managed to survive the pounding, his troubles would not be over, because just below the falls you can see large numbers of crocodiles who are facing downstream with their mouths open hoping that something or someone will drop in for lunch. Since they prefer a meat diet to fish, they would certainly make short work of any swimming human, and very often do.

The Nile just below Murchison Falls is very rich in fish and Nile trout that weigh up to 300 pounds are often caught. Since many of the boats which go out to catch these big fish are quite flimsy, the crocodiles could also report that fishermen are often caught that weigh 200 pounds,

We stayed for two days at a lodge about 10 miles below Murchison Falls and at this point the Nile is about half a mile wide. One of the high spots of our trip was the ride in a launch up the Nile to the upper falls. We saw a lot of wildlife on the banks and in the river including great numbers of hippo eyes and snouts. If the launch approaches too close they raise their heads above the water, open their large mouths and most often lumber away pushing their young ahead of them.

On the banks of the river were large quantities of crocodiles taking the sun. Very often as we passed, these ugly but magnificent creatures would open their mouths rather than retreat. Others, however, slithered into the water and disappeared. We saw no signs warning that swimming in the area is not recommended. Elephants, rhinos, water buffaloes, baboons and numerous quantities and varieties of the deer family could be seen through the trees on the bank, on top of the bluffs, and in the gullies that lead down to the river. Hovering overhead or sitting on the very top of an occasional dead tree were vultures of various sizes. From the launch we witnessed an interesting exchange between a rhino and a family of elephants. We could not tell whether it was the desire for companionship or just plain mischief that motivated the rhino, but it seemed that he wanted to approach the female elephant. Regardless of his motivation, the large male elephant did not appreciate the attentions of this nosy fellow behind his back and several times turned to chase him off. At one point the rhino faced the elephant's charge and we thought we would witness a fight. The elephant stopped and both looked at each other for a few seconds. The elephant then charged ahead at the rhino, who turned and trotted off.

Perhaps an elephant is one of the only animals a rhino will not attack. However, an automobile does not enjoy the same immunity. When we were at Tsavo National Park a week later, we were following a rhino with our Land Rover. The rhino stopped, looked at us, started snorting and pawing the ground, and then lowered his horn and started coming towards us. We thought our guide was overly prudent in speeding away so soon, particularly because I was getting a good movie sequence of the beast. Despite my pleading our guide continued to drive away. He explained afterwards, that within a few steps, a determined rhino can charge at a speed of 40 miles an hour. Although this one did not seem too determined yet, he could become so from one second to the next. Our driver also explained that a week earlier in the same park, a rhino had charged a car and had pierced the door of the car with his horn and in the process had gored the driver very badly.

In so far as the rhino is not very agile and charges only in a straight line, it is possible for someone on foot to dodge this charge. Their eyesight is also very bad so if you stay motionless, they may forget where you are, provided you are downwind from them. Nevertheless, many people are killed by rhino every year. The majority of these are poachers who hunt the rhino illegally for their horns. The horn is smuggled out of the country from Mombasa in Arab dhows and taken to India and Arabia where it commands a very high price. The horn is ground into a powder and is sold to older men to increase their potency. Regardless of the validity of this supposition, a lot of people believe it and as a result the East African rhino is threatened with extinction.

In the Serengeti National Park, we had a wonderful time watching a lion family. We managed to get within about 10 yards of one group who had already eaten and who were stretched out asleep on the grass. However, our guide was very careful not to get too close to lions who had not eaten for a couple of days. We came upon one group of three lions who were watching a herd of impala. At one point, one of them started to stalk the closest impala. The movement of the lion was beautiful, very similar to that of a cat stalking a bird and, in spite of being 400 rather than 4 pounds, the same grace, coordination and attentive patience was displayed. The impala caught sight of the lion as it moved from one crouching position to another and ran off.

The lion came sauntering back towards us and her two companions and we were extremely disappointed as the driver put the car into gear and drove away. It is true that the lion was coming more towards us than towards her companions, but she did not seem to display any aggressive tendencies in our direction. I was getting some wonderful movies from the top hatch and pleaded with the driver to wait a few more seconds. "This is no zoo" he replied sharply as he put the car in gear and lurched off. Despite the protection afforded by a sturdy LandRover it is apparently best to give a hungry hunting lion as well as any other of the large beasts plenty of room,

Several weeks earlier, a couple of tourists in a Volkswagen without a guide got too close to a large bull elephant, The elephant put his trunk in through the open window, picked up the car and threw it down on its side, The occupants although unhurt were, needless to say, a bit shaken up.

We came upon another group of lions later in the day, and this group included 7 adults and 5 cubs of about 6 months old. The adults were all sleeping but the cubs were restless and walking about. A large female lion, who had apparently been out scouting, came walking towards the sleeping group and all the lions got up to greet her. This greeting of the lions was amazing to see. All of the lions trotted out to the newcomer who was apparently part of the pack and they actually seemed to be talking with their grunts and meows. This female must have been the mother of the cubs as they also came running over to mommy. Apparently, the female had found some prey because they all walked off together.

They were successful and managed to kill an impala about half a mile away, but unfortunately, we missed the attack because our guide stopped for a souvenir, After the lions had left, he got out of the car, took his handkerchief out of his pocket, and picked up one of the fresh droppings of one of the lions. When we asked him what he was going to do with it, he answered that he was going to give it to the "old man" of his village who would make medicine out of it. Within a few minutes of the kill, we saw vultures hovering overhead and a jackal appeared, waiting patiently in the distance until the lions had finished.

At the Ngoro Ngoro crater we saw another pack of lions just after they had killed a zebra. The zebra was about half eaten and was hosting the female and her cubs when we drove up. These cubs were about 10 months old and were making purring sounds as they were pulling off pieces of meat and licking the bones clean with their sandpaper tongues. The mother had apparently already had her fill as she was laying close by, though she seemed to be watching rather than sleeping. Every now and then the cubs would leave the zebra and lie down with the mother. Apparently, this was to be dinner as well as lunch as the mother lion watched closely to keep the vultures and jackals away. At one point a vulture landed on the ground about 10 yards from the carcass and the lioness was off like a flash to chase it away. We saw jackals again in the background and they remained about 50 yards away, walking back and forth in a semicircle, and straining their necks to see if the lion had left the meat.

While it is fairly easy to see lions in the national parks, leopards are quite a bit more difficult. They usually hunt alone and stay away from humans, whereas the lions do not seem to have any concern at all for humans. We did see one leopard in the Serengeti National Park sleeping in a tree with a tail and one leg hanging down limply from a large branch. Another had pulled the carcass of a gazelle it had recently killed up into the tree with it and was eating it.

In the Nairobi National Park, we managed to get quite a bit closer to a leopard. We met the curator of the animal orphanage there and he showed us a leopard which had just been recently caught by a farmer about 50 miles from Nairobi. The leopard had been killing livestock and he was going to be shipped off to one of the national parks in the hope that he would leave domestic livestock alone and be   satisfied with gazelle and impala. However, before being shipped off, they wanted to find out a little more about the habits of leopards, they planned to put a marking on its ear so that in case it was caught again or killed, they would have a better idea of the amount of territory a leopard covers. They also wanted a sample of its blood.

As we entered the room in which the leopard was caged, we were greeted with a vicious and angry roar which was enough to make your hair curl. Although the leopard weighed no more than 150 pounds, were he to have gotten out of his cage, I think he could have killed the five of us within just a few minutes, His paw struck out with lighting speed at the bars of the cage, accompanied by snarls. I wondered how they were going to get the hypodermic needle into him, which the vet was preparing. It was obvious that the leopard was not going to cooperate and give us his paw.

A cover was put over the top of the cage and one man went in front of the leopard to attract his attention while three men plus the vet went to the back of the cage. As the leopard began to get angry and excited at the man in front, he began swishing his tail. The three people at the back of the cage watched attentively and as his tail flicked out between the bars of the cage, three pairs of hands grabbed for the tail and pulled it. Quick as a flash the vet stuck the needle into the tail, squirted in the fluid and then jumped back,

Within about ten minutes the leopard began to droop and within 15 minutes he seemed to be sleeping. The brave vet put his fingers thru the cage to touch him to see if there was a reaction. Even though the leopard did not stir, he felt it prudent to let the leopard have still another 5 minutes to be sure it was fully unconscious. As the gate of the cage was being pulled up, the vet said he hoped the leopard had not been through this before and was just "playing possum."

Lydia and I got ahold of its tail and helped pull the leopard out of the cage and onto a piece of burlap on the floor. The leopard was then carried to the scale for weighing. We then lifted it up and put it on a table and the vet began to work quickly. Although the leopard seemed to be asleep his mouth was twitching. I asked the vet how long the leopard would be under the effect of the hypodermic and his answer was a bit alarming. He said he did not yet have enough experience with leopards to know how long he would remain sleeping, but he thought it would be for at least half an hour. He reassured us, however, that it was unlikely that the leopard would wake up suddenly. If we saw him starting to twitch a little more violently, he thought there would be time to put him back into his cage before he was again in full command of his senses.

While watching the work we forgot that there was another leopard in a cage in the same room behind us. Just at the time the leopard on the table made a twitch with his mouth, the other leopard in the cage behind us made a frightful roar, and Lydia and I jumped a foot off the ground.

In addition to the ear tag and a blood sample, the vet also took the leopard's temperature, which was 103 degrees Fahrenheit, a normal temperature for leopards. Fortunately, we managed to get the beautiful animal back into its cage in plenty of time. The person that got into the cage with the leopard to help pull him in deserves a medal for courage.

Our trip continued with a visit to the three hundred mile stretch of coast Kenya has on the Indian Ocean. The towns of Mombasa, Malindi, and Lamu which we visited were also supposedly visited by Sindbad the sailor. Mombasa is a main port on the African coast and carries on considerable traffic between Arabia and India. During the monsoon season large fleets of dhows come westward with the wind and crowd the old harbor. They return with the winds in the other direction carrying mango poles, coke, ivory, bananas, and passengers.

We visited two dhows in the harbor and the thought of crossing the Indian Ocean on one of those small boats is quite sobering. They will take up to seventy passengers who must sleep on the deck. The price of a passage from Mombasa to India is fifty dollars and this covers a place to sleep on the deck and drinking water only. The passengers must bring their own food and cook it on the deck. Since the dhows are entirely made of wood, this must create a fire hazard.

With a good wind the trip to India takes about twenty days. Even though some of the dhows are getting motorized, they are only able to cut three or four days off their time using both motor and sails. As can be imagined, the sanitary facilities on the dhow are rather rudimentary and consist of two wooden baskets that hang out over the stern of the boat. It looks like no place to be during stormy weather since the abrupt motion of the waves might send the inhabitant flying out.

A young boy of 18 offered to take us out to a dhow in the harbor. In discussing the various dhows that come into Mombasa, he explained that the best dhows come from Persia with nice carpets on the deck that are superior to dhows from Aden, Muscat, and other parts of Arabia.

The old part of Mombasa is a mixture of African, Arabian, Portuguese, English, and Pakistanis. The promontory of the old city is dominated by a Portuguese fort, built in or about the 1500's, which was alternately occupied by the Portuguese and the Arabs up until the late 1800's when the English gained control. Even when the Arabs had control under the rule of the Sultans of Zanzibar, everything was not peaceful because the Sultans were often opposed by relatives from the coast of Arabia and interfamily warfare and intrigue kept the place in constant turmoil.

In the old town we found a varied mixture of races. Passing in front of us in quick succession we saw African women carrying baskets on their heads, Indian women in saris with thumb print of gray ash on their foreheads. The Muslim women were dressed in black with a veil covering their faces and no skin appearing from anywhere. Several Indian temples can be found in the old city along with a number of mosques, a Catholic chapel built by the Portuguese, and a 19th century Episcopal church built by the British.

Mombasa has some marvelous curio shops, and Lydia and I lost our heads (and our savings) in one that specialized in ivory carvings. We watched the craftsman who worked in the back of the shop as he turned ivory tusks and hippo teeth into beautiful, sculptured pieces. He was a 76-year-old man from India who makes many of the tools he uses. The shopkeeper told us that he is having a hard time finding and keeping young apprentices to learn to carve ivory.

Sadly, the art is dying out. Watching the old master work, we became very appreciative of how difficult it is to carve ivory. For many of the cuts he would rest the chisel against his shoulder to get added leverage. We bought a beautiful ivory tusk that he had carved into a series of jungle scenes. The elephants gave away his nationality as they had the smaller ears of the Indian elephant while the African Elephants have very large ears.

Our hotel in Mombasa, situated on a lovely spot overlooking the ocean, was of a very attractive tropical style. However, we found certain inconveniences with this tropical style with the many permanent openings in the rooms and walls of the building. The construction supposedly takes full advantage of whatever breeze happens to be blowing. However, when we were there, there was a little more than a gentle breeze and the construction seemed to amplify the currents. Because the hall door of our room had slats which could not be closed, it became impossible for us to leave the door of our balcony open. Therefore, we were faced with the choice of no fresh sea breezes or very fresh sea breezes sweeping through our room accompanied by a vigorous howling wind, which blew the curtains out into the room horizontally, virtually touching the ceiling.

Apart from amplifying the breezes, these many openings make you very quickly aware of the private lives and habits of your neighbors on either side of you. This can be both amusing as well as disturbing. Usually, conversations are overheard only the first day of a guest's visit before they get wise to the fact that they are virtually broadcasting endearments (or insults) meant only for the immediate family. However other noises by necessity cannot be dampened out. The poor chap next door to us apparently had a big night and we heard him as he came in quite late, but he (and we) paid for his sins shortly afterwards, as we were awakened half an hour later by the sound of someone vomiting who seemed to be no more than three feet away from us. He must have had a particularly big night as this went on for a full half hour. Unfortunately, he must have had another big night as we became unwilling auditors to a repeat performance at 6:00 o'clock the following morning.

Apparently, this porous building style is the rule rather than the exception because our hotel at Malindi was of the same construction. We were lucky that in Malindi our neighbors did not include a big party boy and we had relative quiet.

The last coastal town we visited was the ancient slave trading port of Lamu. Lamu is not far from the Somali border and experiences occasional raids of Shifta tribe. They kidnap people and release them only after a ransom is paid. It is necessary to get a special permit to fly into the town, but the danger of an attack from the Shiftas is apparently not very great. It takes about 40 minutes to fly to Lamu from Malindi, and if you go by road it takes about six hours.

Lamu is another town which has changed hands many times, going from the Portuguese to the Arabs and back again. A row of about 50 old Portuguese cannons is stretched out in front of the main colonial type buildings along the waterfront. The houses in back are largely of white stucco with thick walls and are of Arabian style. The town has no cars or bicycles, and its streets are more like passageways and somewhat spooky.

The town dates back before the entry of the Portuguese into East Africa and has some Turkish influence, including a minaret built in about 900 AD. Legends also trace the origins of the town back to the queen of Sheba, but no archaeological evidence has yet been found to support these stories. On the outskirts of this Arabic town is the African quarter with grass covered houses. Most of the Africans in this area are Muslims and the town has several attractive mosques. The town used to be a very large slave trading center and was also an exporter of heavy carved wooden doors. It still exports carved wooden doors.

Our trip finished with a climb up Mt. Kenya. The climb takes four days, and you go a good part of the way on horseback. We met our guide at the starting point and were very surprised to find that two of the pack horses were zebroids. Our guide had bred them, and they are a cross between a horse and a zebra, with the body and shape of a horse but the coloring and stripes of a zebra. We were even more surprised to find that such a large party, which included our guide, three African porters, five horses, two mules and two zebroids, were there to take only us up the mountain.

In spite of the luxury of having nine animals and three porters to take care of the tents, cook the meals and tend the animals, plus a European guide for the mountain climbing itself, the cost of the trip was about what we would have paid had we stayed at a luxury hotel for the same period of time including meals in a mountain area in the Italian Dolomite mountains.

The equatorial alpine scenery of Mt. Kenya is very unusual, and this was the first mountain climb we have ever taken where we have seen a family of baboons at the 7,000-foot level. The dense forest begins to open to a sparser vegetation at about 9,000-foot and then you move into alpine meadows. At about 12,000 feet you come upon a strange mushroom type of tree ten to fifteen feet tall, and these remain with you almost up to the 15,000 feet level. From there on up it is quite barren and rugged. Whereas a climb up to the very top of Mt. Kenya involves considerable skill and equipment, the climb to Point Lenana at 16,400 feet, which is where we arrived, is primarily a steep walk up a glacier. The altitude is what makes it particularly difficult. However, we both made it and it was certainly well worth the effort. After gasping for breath above 16,000 feet for a few hours, getting back to our top camp at 14,000 feet was almost like returning to sea level. Even though we have only seen a little bit of East Africa, we can easily understand the nostalgia that the early explorers had for this area. It is a fascinating frontier with great potential.

Back in Milan, my work with General Telephone & Electronics International continues but in a somewhat different direction. I have recently left my job as controller of the Italian operations and have been promoted to plant manager for the manufacturing of the Switching Division of GTE International in the Italian operations. With this promotion I have in my area of responsibility the startup of the new factory we are building in the south of Italy near Naples. This factory should employ about 1,000 factory workers, manufacturing telephone switching equipment and the Sylvania flash cube, developed by the Sylvania branch of General Telephone to be sold in the Common Market. This should provide the two of us the opportunity to get to know the beautiful area of the south of Italy which is much different than northern Italy.

Lydia still finds time to prepare illustrations for some of the local book publishers. We continue to enjoy the skiing areas of Italy, France, and Switzerland and, with the opening of the tunnel under Mt. Blanc, the beautiful French ski area of Chamonix can be reached from Milan in under four hours if you go under the mountains through the tunnel.

The alternate route is between the Italian ski area of Cervinia over the Mont Blank pass into France crossing the glacier on the French side. We have also had the opportunity to ski the magnificent Zermatt area with the Matterhorn.

SIX

1966: A Change in Status and A Visit to Naples

This year brought with it a substantial change for both of us. The shopkeepers in our area have finally stopped calling Lydia "Signorina" (Miss) and now call her "Signora" (Mrs.), though it took the 6th month of pregnancy to bring their old habits to an end. The little stranger should arrive about the third week of December for which we should receive some credit for excellent planning from a fiscal standpoint. Not only do we get a full year of deduction for less than two weeks of presence in the year 1966, but we also may be able to get by combining future Christmas and birthday presents into one somewhat larger present to cover both holidays.

Because of the change of Lydia from Miss to Mrs., our travels were somewhat subdued. I was involved in overseeing a fascinating project as GTE opened a new manufacturing factory in the South of Italy, about 20 miles from Naples, near Caserta where there is a famous palace of Italian, Spanish, and French nobility.

Naples is fascinating. In addition to chaotic taxicab drivers, an occasional pickpocket, and some areas that are very dirty, Naples has a marvelous charm. Apparently speed limits, stop signs, and one-way streets do not apply to taxicabs in Naples, which makes for a very thrilling ride. The fee requested seems to be in proportion to the thrills provided rather than based on figures registered by the meter, provided you had the presence of mind to remind the driver to engage the meter as he starts. If he forgets to start the meter, a little friendly negotiation usually allows for a reasonable settlement of the fare, probably two-thirds of his original request.

On a subsequent visit to Naples, I was deprived of the thrill of a taxi ride because the taxi drivers were on strike. The strike was not for an increase in fare, but in protest to the growing number of unauthorized and unlicensed taxis that were operating clandestinely. Apparently, the Mayor and police force of Naples had done very little to eliminate this unauthorized competition and the taxi drivers had their noisy way of bringing attention to the avoided problem. More than half of the large municipal square, into which eight main streets converge, was blocked by parked horn-blowing taxicabs. Circling the square were several groups of taxicabs driving side by side very slowly with their horns blaring. Needless to say, the traffic leading into the main square was hopelessly tied up for several hundred yards in all directions.

Unfortunately, the Mayor was not there that evening, and the Assistant Mayor told the taxi drivers that the mayor would be glad to speak to them the next morning. He continued by saying that it was useless to continue this disturbance anymore that evening. This explanation was not sufficient to dissolve the strike and the congestion, and it continued past midnight. I never did hear the resolution of the problem, but the cabs were operating again on my next trip.

The street scenes of Naples either at night or during the day are quite a wonderful show. There is a heavy pushcart population, and a wide variety of delicacies are sold by these roving and operatic vendors, most of whom seem to be tenors. "Lattuga, fagioli e cavoli, raccolti questa mattina", (Lettuce, beans and cabbages picked this morning) has not yet made the Italian hit parade but it has a very nice melody. More accurately their sales song has a variety of enthusiastic melodies and the one with a long drawn out "raccolti" on a high C was the best of them. Neapolitan gelato is very tasty and to hear the vendor sing about each flavor makes it even more mouth-watering.

"Trippa fresca con limone" (Fresh tripe with lemon) also had a luring and haunting melody from afar, but as I neared this pushcart and got a better look at the product, I realized that the "stomach" he was selling was a little too much for my stomach. However, he was doing quite a brisk business, cutting off pieces of quivering tripe, squirting them with lemon, and giving the half alive looking pieces of spongy edibles to eager clients, who gobbled them down.

The car with roasted nuts and a steam engine whistle looked like old New York at the turn of the century, and the vendor with his large moustache completed the picture. Probably his cousin immigrated to New York with such a wagon in 1890. Apparently, this singing salesman had lost his voice because his only noise was an occasional pull on the steam whistle of his cart.

This exuberant and noisy salesmanship does not stop when night falls. In fact, the streets continue to resound with sellers of all kinds of products far after midnight. Leaving a restaurant in the old section of Naples at 10:45 pm we came upon a roving vegetable vendor carrying a large basket of peppers which he sang out with a piercing shout, loud enough to shake anyone from their slumber within a radius of a few blocks.

This nocturnal sales activity is not confined only to ambulatory vendors as numerous stores also stay open until very late. Continuing our walk through the narrow and winding streets we were brushed by a basket lowered on a rope from a 5th floor window. The empty flask of wine in the basket included a 100-lira bill. The clerk of the street below replaced the empty bottle with a full one and shouted back "Grazie!"

We were startled to see a small fruit and vegetable shop still open at 11:30 p.m. I stopped to chat with the shop owner who graciously offered me a bunch of grapes while we talked. I asked him what time he normally retires, and I was amazed to hear that he goes home at 1:30 a.m.

"But do you get any customers at this hour?" I asked.

He answered, "every now and then". At that moment a little boy of five or six, who in Milan would have been in bed by 8 pm, came up to purchase 20 Lire worth of grapes (about 5 U.S. cents). Thinking that the vendor would probably sleep late after working to 1:30 or 2:00 in the morning I asked what time he opened during the day. His reply of 7:00 am was unbelievable. Unlike the Athens vendors we saw during our honeymoon, he does not close for a long nap in the afternoon. This fellow must spend 110 hours per week on his feet working.

This willingness to work long hours coupled with enthusiasm and a high degree of inventiveness gives Italy a high potential for productivity. Unfortunately, this potential is not reflected in as high a standard of living as one would expect for a number of reasons. On one hand, the hard work of the Italian is also accompanied by substantial waste motion and the tendency to over express oneself. Economy of words is not one of the characteristics of the Italian. Although this volubility makes for pleasant and boisterous social activities, it detracts from productivity.

There is also in evidence a primary concern with the present at the expense of the future which becomes more accentuated as you travel south. I am quite sure that the repeated invasions since the breakup of the Roman Empire with the devastations that followed, have been a factor in forming this part of the character of the extraordinary people that live on this attractive but politically unstable peninsula. Nevertheless, this factor probably contributes to the inventiveness of the Italians. Too much concern with future planning, a characteristic more common to northern Europeans, probably acts as a brake upon inventiveness.

Two other factors that inhibit the rise of the living standard in Italy are an antiquated distribution system and an extremely complicated and burdensome tax superstructure. Substantial cost is added to products because of the above factors. This funnels substantial manpower into activities which do not add value to the gross national product.

In the food area, for example, the number of middlemen between the farmer and the consumer is unbelievable. The result is that everyone in the chain works very hard, but no one earns very much. The farmer gets very little for his produce, the consumer pays a high price and none of the many middlemen seem to get rich on the small segment of the distribution portion which each of them handles.

The final step of the distribution channel is also inefficient with many small family shops, each the size of a one car garage and each with a high degree of specialization. The shopper gets much individual attention in these shops, but it is expensive for the one being served.

Not only is it virtually impossible to find meat and fish in the same shop, but there are also four distinct and separate shops which sell meat. The Macelleria sells beef, veal, and lamb; the Polleria handles chicken, rabbits, other birds, both wild and domestic, along with eggs; the Salumeria handles pork products, ham, cold cuts and sausages; and, last but not least, there is the "Macelleria Equina" where horse and ass can be obtained. Another shop, the Drogheria sells canned goods and olive oil; the Latteria sells cheese, milk, butter, and eggs; the Ortolano handles fresh fruits and vegetables, and the Fornaio carries bakery goods and pasta.

This diversity and variety really blossom when it comes to different kinds of pasta products. With spaghetti there are at least 7 kinds, differing with respect to diameter. With maccheroni the differences involve both wall thickness as well as diameter while with other kinds of pasta variations involve egg content, color, and shape. In one small store near our apartment in Milan, I counted 38 different kinds of pasta, and I am sure their selection was modest. While perhaps inefficient, this variety does make for sociable shopping and pleasant eating.

A supermarket chain started in Milan about five years ago and now has about ten stores throughout the city. Their prices are at least 10% less than the mom-and-pop stores and they are always crowded. In fact, one of the supermarkets in Milan a year ago made a worldwide record regarding sales per square foot of floor space among supermarkets. What is surprising is that competitive super marketing has not grown faster in Italy.

The complicated and interwoven tangle of taxes is the other element that keeps the inventiveness, hard work and enthusiasm of the Italian from being reflected in a higher standard of living. Rather than increasing the general tax rate for additional revenue, one way around this unpopular move has been to establish a separate tax with a limited life for special purposes. However, as evidenced by past experience it is much easier to start a new tax than it is to remove an old one. For example, there is still a small contribution being collected for the flood victims of Calabria back in 1918. Although this tax is insignificant in amount, it still absorbs time on the part of numerous administrative levels. In addition, I doubt that there are very few survivors of that flood still living.

One of the taxes which are a carryover from the medieval times is the "Dazio" or what amounts to a city customs tax. This tax used to be collected at the gates of the walled towns for all goods entering and was originally intended as a major city revenue source. As industrialization

1966: A CHANGE IN STATUS AND A VISIT TO NAPLES

grew it also served as a protective tariff to guard the artisans of the city from the competition of the outlying districts or from rival towns.

One would have thought that this tax would have been eliminated when Italy was unified 100 years ago. At that time, the regional customs duties were removed while the city customs duties remained in place. Prior to that time, goods travelling from Milan to Naples by land would be taxed five times when travelling from Naples to Milan - each one by itself was small but overall, they added a burden to total costs. It was difficult to pick your way from Milan to Naples without passing at least three frontiers; it is easy to see how the industrialization of Italy and the free flow of commerce was delayed prior to its unification. You can imagine the waste there would be in the U.S. with a custom duty between individual counties plus a separate tax as products enter each city.

Nevertheless, the Dazio remains, and it is a tax system more in line with an oxcart rather than an automobile society. On each road into Milan there is still a Dazio station with a truck scale and a man on duty, supposedly 24 hours a day. I would estimate that there must be at least twenty Dazio stations surrounding Milan and it is my guess that the amount of money they collect is barely able to cover the salaries of those collecting these taxes. If the laws were enforced rigidly and they stopped all cars coming into the city as opposed to only some of the trucks, enormous traffic jams would be created.

The Dazio tax per se is more of a bother rather than a financial burden but when taken together with the other indirect taxes, the sum total takes on significance. For example, the Dazio tax we paid on some furniture purchased outside of Milan was about 3% of the value of the furniture. However, in addition to this, there was a 4% turnover or sales tax on the furniture. The price charged by the furniture maker took into consideration the turnover tax of 4% which he paid on all of the material he purchased and so on. Therefore, when you get the cascading effect of this tax plus the turnover taxes, the cumulative amount becomes a sizeable element of the price.

The heavy social taxes which are paid for by the employer, and which in part are also deducted from the pay of the employee, are another part of the unfortunate tax jungle. Under the mistaken impression that you can increase the standard of living by legislation and that the cost of new programs can be paid for by the employer without affecting the purchasing power of the employee, numerous social improvements have been enacted over the past years. One result has been that the burden of fringe benefits paid by the employer has been moving steadily upwards resulting in the factory worker getting in his pay envelope less than one half of his cost to the company. A small portion of the half which he does not see gets to him ultimately in the form of deferred compensation, but the balance is divided among several government agencies for redistribution.

While the benefits received by the worker could still be described by the word fringe, the cost of these benefits is substantially more than fringe. A small portion of these funds undoubtedly gets diverted into private pockets as evidenced by the numerous articles of scandal in the press, but a much greater portion of these funds are eaten up by the large number of state employees engaged in the administration of these funds. The net result equals high cost of manufacture, low disposable income, and a substantial part of the labor force siphoned off into unproductive government bureaucracy. The fact that the Italian economy had a brilliant upward movement in the ten years prior to 1962 and now seems to be recovering moderately from the depression of 1963 and 1964 is of great credit to the ability of the Italian to be able to compensate for these heavy burdens.

Were the taxes, both direct and indirect lumped into just a few general categories you would probably find that Italy has one of the higher tax structures in the western world and perhaps also one of the highest administrative costs for the collection of these taxes. However, such a bold move would probably be political suicide for the party in power. The paradox is that most of the Italians feel they are avoiding their taxes, because in partial compensation to heavy indirect taxes, the direct national income tax and the city family tax are somewhat lower than the federal and state taxes in the States and in neighboring countries. In effect, what they are not paying directly in income tax is reflected in a higher cost of goods than they would pay if the system were more straight forward and rational. While the statement of the problem is easy, the solution certainly is not.

Apart from the problems posed by the tax structure and the political instability plus the frequent strikes in all sectors of the economy, the charm of Italy more than compensates for these inconveniences. Not only is the countryside very attractive and varied, but also some of the personal characteristics of the people are very appealing.

One of the characteristics that are particularly appealing to me is the willingness of the Italian to recognize his defects. This honest self-appraisal is refreshing. Unlike his Anglo-Saxon counterpart who seldom admits to himself, much less to others, the existence of character defects, the Italian accepts the existence of his defects and lives happily, in spite of and with full knowledge of them. The use of psychiatry to try to erase personality disorders is rare in Italy.

Another noticeable Italian characteristic is the attention to being well groomed. I was surprised when I first arrived in Milan to find that the people on the street were extremely well dressed. This seemed in contradiction to what I would have assumed, being aware of the difference in living standards between the United States and Italy. The answer is that grooming and being properly dressed is very important, and rather than being an attempt to show off to others, I believe this emphasis comes from a personal sense of aesthetics and harmony which satisfies the artistic feelings of the Italian.

Still another characteristic of the Italian which I have come to appreciate is the attitude towards food. Italians believe that a meal is one of life's principal pleasures rather than a half hour interlude for nourishment. The fact that it may also be nourishing is incidental, and yet it invariably is. There is a long tradition that influences the preparation of meals in this area and within a 150-mile radius of Milan covering the Lombardy, Piedmont, Veneto, and Emilia regions almost all of the raw materials for the famous northern Italian dishes can be found.

In the Alps to the north there are seven or eight varieties of wild mushrooms, while in the rolling hills of Alba, to the south, there is one of the major zones in Europe where truffles are found. Wild birds of all sizes from quail to pheasant are obtained to the east towards Veneto, and some of the best beef and veal is raised in the Piedmont area to the west. Fresh fruits and vegetables are extremely flavorful and available most of the time, and within a 100-mile range some of the best Italian wines including Barbera, Gattinara, Valpolicella, Chiaretto, and Bardolino are produced. For 75 cents you can get a bottle of the best, and for less than half that amount, you can obtain good wine from the prior year.

SEVEN

1967: Gary arrives - Complete with dual American and Italian Citizenship Papers

Gary arrived on Christmas day in 1966. He was considerate enough to be born at a reasonably civil hour in the morning which allowed both the doctor and me to return home in time for a fine Christmas lunch. Lydia was not quite as fortunate. Needless to say, I was quite envious to see him born with a fine crop of hair, and more so as it did not fall off a few days after birth but continued to flourish and grow at a very fast rate. We now have the bushiest haired baby in the neighborhood. His round face, framed by his impressive head of blond hair, punctuated by two very blue eyes has made him quite an attraction in our neighborhood where children of this coloring are not common.

While the birth and recovery were remarkably smooth and uncomplicated for Lydia, our problems in getting Gary registered were quite the opposite. I received some papers at the hospital and was told to take them down to the City Hall for the registration. I had my first start when I discovered that window 51, to which I was directed by the porter, was for both births and deaths. Knowing what mistakes Italian bureaucracy can sometimes produce, I wondered as I waited, whether many mix ups resulted from this lugubrious combination of activity handled by the same desk. As I took my place at the window, I noticed that on the desk of the clerk was a request for permission to bury someone. I felt like a rejuvenator when I presented my papers.

Unfortunately, I was handed the papers quickly back because they lacked the necessary fiscal stamps. I felt somewhat sheepish about this oversight and the expression of the clerk, which was a mixture of contempt and patronizing comprehension, added to my feeling of apology. I should have known better. I have been in Italy long enough to know that no document is ever presented to the City Hall without the proper number and type of fiscal stamps. Since fiscal stamps are normally purchased at tobacco shops, I went outside looking for the nearest one. After taking my turn behind those buying cigarettes, matches, salt, and quinine (quinine is sold only at tobacco shops), I was told that that particular type of stamp I needed is not sold there but only at the post office.

I am not sure why, but I imagine there is a good reason for it which probably made sense 50 years ago. Fortunately, the nearest post office was less than half a mile away and, at a brisk walk, I arrived there just before the noon closing hour. There was a large mob gathering between windows 4 and 12, without any semblance of a line. I uttered an oath which could have been understood as a prayer. Fortunately, my prayer was answered, as fiscal stamps were dispensed at one of the empty windows. But there was no one present at that window. The nice lady at the next window was not allowed to sell fiscal stamps and she called the lemon faced teller whose responsibility this was.

That State employee did me a large favor in tearing out the necessary stamps from her sheet and I hoped my expression displayed sufficient gratitude. But apparently it didn't because when I handed her the equivalent of a 16-dollar bill for the 90-cent fiscal stamp, quick as a lizard's tongue, she snatched back the fiscal stamp, which I hadn't yet

1967: GARY ARRIVES - COMPLETE WITH DUAL AMERICAN AND ITALIAN CITIZENSHIP PAPERS

had the presence of mind to paste on my document. She returned my large bill with an almost smug satisfaction and said: "sorry no change". Before she had the opportunity to tell me to come back after lunch with the proper change, I encouraged the kind lady at the next window to break the bill into sufficient small pieces, and the transaction was completed.

With step one accomplished (of what I thought was at most a three-step operation) I walked briskly back to City Hall with the attractive fiscal stamp, which did add color to the rather bland hospital document. As I hurried up to window 51, the very superior clerk, who was filling out yet another burial permission, took my documents with a slight sneer, evidently remembering my faux pas of 30 minutes earlier and studied me for a moment with an expression that said, "You are not trying to pull a fast one, are you?".

Perhaps unconvinced, he gave the documents to a messenger who went to check the archives to see whether we really were registered as residents of Milan. Even though I pay the Milan family tax, I was not on the rolls, while Lydia, who does not pay the tax, was on the books. Fortunately, the appearance of one of us on the official books is sufficient for the registration of a newborn. This information was then stamped on the papers, and I was told to go up to the third floor.

Entering room 46 on the third floor, I came upon a Charles Dickens scene. Resting on top of two very heavy wooden desks were two enormous volumes and caring for these impressive tomes were two thin clerks eating sandwiches. I was told by one of them that I would first have to give the papers to the messenger outside. I was curious to know what the next task was, but there were no messengers outside. However, down the hall there was a cluster of five messengers, all in uniform. I managed to pick out the right one. He scolded me for coming in right before lunch but agreed to perform his task.

He first summoned his assistant to whom he gave the papers and we waited for about 10 minutes. My curiosity got the better of me and I asked him what his assistant was doing to or with the papers. I was told he was checking the data on them which had been printed 10 minutes before on a metal tag at window number 51, to verify Lydia's residence in Milan. When I asked why it was necessary to check this information so soon afterwards, he explained in a half whisper: "We have a duplicate file, just to make sure."

Since it was also getting close to lunch time, I didn't think it wise to continue the questioning, although I was puzzled as to what they would do if they found a difference in the information in the duplicate file. It would undoubtedly take a long time to resolve as I am sure there would be long arguments as to which of the two files was correct. Many of the administrative procedures in Milan date back to the Napoleon era and I am sure Mr. Buonaparte would be pleased to find that many things are still being done exactly as he established 150 years ago.

Then, sitting down to his desk, the uniformed messenger took on the expression of a king about to sign a peace treaty. With great ceremony and in slow motion he took an ink pad and a rubber stamp out of his desk and positioned them along with my documents on top of his desk. This required great care. Only after several studied adjustments which included slight changes in their angle and relationship to one another, did he leave this portion of the task to go on to the next step.

He was finally ready, but only after a slight pull at each sleeve and a straightening of his jacket. Then, picking up the large rubber stamp, with a majestic flourish he hit the ink pad and the fiscal stamp on my document, in one wide continuous motion, and bowed his head as he laid the rubber stamp gently back on the table. I felt like applauding.

With the papers properly cancelled and double-checked, I went back to room 46. At this point the man sitting behind the large books

1967: GARY ARRIVES - COMPLETE WITH DUAL AMERICAN AND ITALIAN CITIZENSHIP PAPERS

looked up at me and said: "Well, and where are your two witnesses?" Maddening as the Italian bureaucracy is, there always seem to be ways available to lighten the load just as it becomes unbearable. Two of the five messengers in the hall cluster agreed to act as my witnesses and we all three signed our names in the big book.

In signing the book, I went against my principles because the clerk had not yet entered all of the information above our signatures. He said he would do that as soon as the lunch period was over. Trusting to his good faith I went ahead and signed, hoping he would not register Gary as a girl.

David and his son, Gary at 3 months old

When it happens that a registrar mixes up the sex of a newborn on the official books, it is quite an ordeal to get it changed. A court order is required to get the mistake rectified and this can sometimes take years. There was recently a case in the newspapers of a poor Sicilian chap whose marriage was held up for three years because he had been registered as a girl, and the law here, as in most places, does not allow girls to marry girls. A doctor's certificate was not sufficient, but a court order was needed, to change him back officially from a girl to a boy. And while waiting they had a baby girl which further complicated matters. I can imagine the difficulty they had in registering the birth, as both parents were officially females.

Anyway, after signing the big book, I was given another piece of paper and with this I could go to room 42 and they would give me the birth certificate. Surprisingly, the clerk in room 42 had some fiscal stamps in his drawer so it was not necessary to make a second half mile walk to the post office. With this birth certificate I went to the American consulate in Milan and in 20 minutes I had an American passport for Gary.

Although it took quite a bit of red tape to get Gary Francesco registered as a legal person, he is now recognized as my legitimate male heir by the American government and presumably so by the Italian government, provided those two chaps behind the large books in room 46 filled in the blank spaces correctly after lunch. With Gary's legal well-being taken care of, we began thinking about his physical well-being, particularly for the summer. We understand that babies suffer from heat in the summertime in Milan.

In order to give Gary, the benefit of clean air and less heat for his first summer and also to give his neophyte parents the same benefits, we decided to rent a villa above Lake Como. The villa we found was in a little village called Brunate, which is way above Lake Como. In fact, we were 2,500 feet above the lake at almost a 45-degree angle.

1967: GARY ARRIVES - COMPLETE WITH DUAL AMERICAN AND ITALIAN CITIZENSHIP PAPERS

Lake Como: Lydia holding Gary at 7 months

While it takes 15 minutes to drive up from Como on a winding switch back, there is a funicular which travels on tracks straight up the mountain, and it makes the trip in seven minutes. At the time the funicular was built about 1890, there was a surge of construction in Brunate, and many Milanese bought land in this area and built large houses with gardens on the slopes and terraces of these mountains. The villa we rented was divided into two apartments with a very large terrace that looks directly down on to the town of Como and its long lake.

The entrance way is guarded by two white statues of Satyrs, each of which has an arm around a half-dressed girl and in the other hand a bunch of grapes, held out as incentive to come on in for a party. Although resisting, as all good girls should, when a Satyr tries to get too friendly, the expression of the two maidens as they look at the grape's registers curiosity and indecision. We discovered later that the villa had been occupied by Racheal Mussolini, Benito Mussolini's second wife, for a couple of summers in the 1930's. However, there were no signs posted that Mussolini slept here and the owner did not go out of his way to advertise that fact. Lydia and I were curious to know if the room and bed we used last summer were the same one used by Benito and Racheal.

Lydia telling Gary he will soon have a playmate

The villa came complete with a custodian who took care of the property, and he and his wife lived in an apartment on the ground floor of the villa. The custodian informed us of the prior ownership of the property. He had an extensive sense of history and said that between the Spaniards, the French, and the Austrians, this area of Italy has seen turmoil ever since Julius Caesar left to conquer Britain. The custodian said Mussolini was not all bad. At least he made the trains run on time in the decade of the 1920's. However, he also said Mussolini made an enormous error aligning with Hitler who caused the complete ruin of Italy.

1967: GARY ARRIVES - COMPLETE WITH DUAL AMERICAN AND ITALIAN CITIZENSHIP PAPERS

The wife of the custodian took care of the flowers and grew vegetables and chickens, and her husband took care of the grounds. He was a retired funicular driver and kept a "ferocious dog." We were told there was no need to worry at night because he let the dog run free on the grounds and no one would dare come in. We were a bit preoccupied going out one evening but discovered the dog could be bought with a lump of sugar.

Commuting time was a bit long, being almost one and a half hours from door to office each way. However, the view on a clear day was magnificent as you could see a large range of the Alps including 14,000-foot Mt. Rosa. The clear air and cool evenings more than compensated for the long commute. This location was also convenient on the weekends for trips around Lake Como, and we visited a number of the large old villas built on the shores of the lake. Nearby was Villa Plinio built about 1500 on the foundations of a villa occupied by Plinio the Elder. Some pillars of the Roman era are still visible and in use as part of the villa. There is a famous siphon at the villa which is fed by an underground spring which brings water from the mountains. It rises and falls at regular intervals. This siphon is the center of attraction of an internal patio of the villa. A small waterfall is the center of attraction of a second patio.

Farther up Lake Como at the town of Bellagio, is Villa Mali, famous for a lovely garden and large variety of trees. Also, at Bellagio is Villa Serbelloni, right at the tip of the peninsula which separates the two legs of Lake Como. There was a fortress here during the time of the Crusades occupied by the German king Barbarossa. Later it served as a stronghold for bandits in about 1600 at the time of the Spanish occupation of Lombardy. At that time, it became a home for the Spanish governor of this area. It then passed down thru various families until it was donated to the Rockefeller Foundation and is now used as a retreat for writers and for international conferences. The woods behind the villa are still part of the property and lead up to the ruins of a fortress at the top of the point. From there, looking north, is the steep alpine barrier that marks the border between Italy and Switzerland.

With two grandmothers and one grandfather staying with us, we decided to take advantage of the expert and free babysitting staff and have ourselves a separate vacation. We chose to go to one of the Mediterranean Club villages for a two-week stay and picked Palinuro on the west coast of Italy between Salerno and Reggio Calabria (the toe of Italy). Palinuro has a combination of beautiful sandy beaches and rocky coast. On the cliffs overlooking the sea there are many watch towers, some of them built over 800 years ago to warn of the approach of Turkish pirates.

The fame of Palinuro dates back to a time when the line between history and myth is fuzzy. It was here that Aeneas first landed on the western coast of Italy for the purpose of burying his helmsman named Palinuro, who had fallen asleep at the tiller, and fell into the sea and drowned. The cape juts out into the sea and resembles a large tiller reminding travelers of the boat of Aeneas.

The area occupied by the Mediterranean Club village is situated in an olive grove on a terrace that slopes gently down to the beach. The olive trees are very old and tall and provide good shade during the day. Even though the weather was hot, it was dry, and, in the evening, it was necessary to be covered with a blanket.

The village offers an informal camping environment. Each couple occupies their own Polynesian-type circular house with a straw roof. Two cots with mattresses and a wooden frame on which to hang your clothes complete your rustic living quarters. The dining area, which is among the olive trees, serves good food family-style at tables of eight. Being a French club in Italy there was also an abundance of wine and there was no limit to the amount you could drink with your meals with no additional charge.

1967: GARY ARRIVES - COMPLETE WITH DUAL AMERICAN AND ITALIAN CITIZENSHIP PAPERS

As is common in Latin countries, mealtime is an occasion for relaxation and conversation and with 75% of the villagers of French nationality, I picked up quite a bit of the language. Whereas I was able to understand almost all conversation by the time we left, speaking French was another story. I can better understand the frustration Gary must feel at times since it appears that he can understand most of what we say, but when it comes to expressing himself only a few gurgles and shrieks come out. However, Lydia spoke French fluently and translated my gurgles into French and by the time we left the village I was able to say a little more than Mama and Papa.

My lack of French did cause some problems during my course at their underwater diving school. The instructors are members of the French diving school and the explanations of what you are supposed to do are also given in French before you climb over the side of the boat with your heavy air bottles and sink below the surface.

My greatest problem was distinguishing between the suffixes and prefixes and a few times I inhaled when I should have exhaled. Also, I did not fully understand the part about clearing the water out of the breathing apparatus before making a dive. At one point when I was about 20 feet below the surface, I took a deep breath and found to my horror I was sucking in water rather than air. Apart from a few misunderstandings on the surface, under water it did not make much difference because the sign language was international with a Gallic flourish. The instructors were excellent.

Along the edge of the cliffs, which drop abruptly into the sea, is the zone where the deep divers explore, and in this area are numerous grottos and underwater passages that have been carved out of the porous rock by the action of the sea. The bottom is 40 meters down and within diving range of reasonably competent divers. With a bit of luck, you might come up with an ancient piece of pottery from an ancient wreck resting in the bottom half covered with sand.

In addition to scuba diving, this village caters to a large number of other sports and there are good instructors for all of them. Lydia reactivated her fencing talents and consistently beat the French fencing instructor. I tried Judo, but in spite of my rusty wrestling talents, did not come anywhere near beating the Judo instructor. Quite the contrary, and because I opened my big mouth about having wrestled once, I was paired with a black belt specialist who was also much bigger than me. He took serious pains to show me how to fall properly from a Judo slam and then gave me plenty of opportunity to practice what he had taught. The fact that I was not able to defeat him was undoubtedly due to my lack of fluency with the French language in fully understanding his instructions.

The club also ran several all-day picnics along with overnight trips to isolated beaches on the coast. In many places the only way to reach these beaches was by boat. However, being on an isolated beach doesn't assure that you will not have visitors and the day we went on the picnic two carabinieri came to tell us that fires are not permitted on the beach. The fire was necessary for the spaghetti the trip leader was cooking for lunch in a big pot for the 20 people in our group. However, since we were only 10 minutes from the completion of the spaghetti, we managed to prevail upon the two handsome young carabinieri to let us finish the meal before putting the fire out. The fact that there were a number of attractive girls in our group undoubtedly added to our persuasive ability. As it turned out we managed to convince them to stay for lunch and one of them was competent on the guitar and entertained us with Sicilian songs.

The organization of the club is very good and despite there being 1,200 people at this Palinuro location, we did not have the impression of a large crowd. The organization is silent, unobtrusive, and works efficiently, and everyone does what they want within the framework of the facilities offered by the club. The cost is also modest, being about 100 dollars per person for a two-week period, including meals and all

1967: GARY ARRIVES - COMPLETE WITH DUAL AMERICAN AND ITALIAN CITIZENSHIP PAPERS

the wine you can drink, as well as access to all sports equipment and coaches.

Low-cost transportation is also provided to the various locations either by air or train from central places as Paris, Brussels, Turin, Milan and Rome, and their volume allows for exceptional special charter rates. In fact, their volume is such that they are the largest single customer of the Italian railroads. The Mediterranean Club now has about 20 camps throughout the Mediterranean, with locations in Greece, Turkey, Israel, Tunisia, Morocco, Spain, Sicily, Corsica, and Sardinia, as well as the French Riviera and the Italian coast. Because of their size they can buy food in quantity which adds to the economy. In fact, I was told by the club manager that they also rent entire steamships that make trips once a week to Argentina.

On their return to Europe the ships bring back Argentina beef for their various clubs. Fruits and vegetables are purchased locally, but other food stuffs are purchased by a central office in Rome for the five camps in Italy. Pastries are made by the pastry chef at each club and most of the cheese is imported from France. The club also has about five winter locations for skiing and their St. Moritz club has taken over two of the very large Victorian hotels. In addition to providing good vacations, it is also a good business, and I understand the Rothschild family provided the initial capital investment. It has filled a very obvious void in Europe for low-cost sporty vacations. A similar vacation club is being formed in the Caribbean by a group of Texans and I understand they are following the general layout and organization of the Med Club.

While the watchtowers on the many hills along the coast at Palinuro remind one of the times when pirates from North Africa and Turkey raided the coast, the historical pageant at Arezzo, called "The Jousting of the Saracens" also remind one of those epochs. The jousting dates back to the time of the crusades when Arezzo sent a group of volunteers to help wrest the holy land from Saladin and his followers. For our fifth wedding anniversary we decided to go to Arezzo to see this yearly festival.

The costumes of this pageant are of the 12th and 13th century, and it seemed to us the costumes of the horses were even better than those of the knights. The horses had colorful drapes that reached down to their ankles. The games take place in the main piazza of Arezzo and consist of a series of jousting attacks against the Saracen dummy which has a large shield on one arm with a target over the shield. Three thongs hang from his other hand, each with a lead ball covered with leather. When the lance of the attacker hits the shield of the Saracen the impact swirls the dummy around and the unskillful horseman gets thumped on the back or head with one or more of the swinging lead balls. These balls are also covered with chalk so that the judges can easily tell if a horseman has been hit. In addition to the beating the competitor may have taken from the impact, he also loses points. As the scope of the jousting is accuracy, and as it is easier to hit the high numbers of the target riding at less than at full speed, these swinging balls act as the incentive to attack at full speed. The faster you go, the less chance there is of being socked.

The four quarters of the city compete for the highest score and there are numerous parades in full regalia before the competition starts. On the morning of the celebration there is a procession through the town. A herald, preceded by the heavy beat of the drummers and the call to attention by the long flag-draped trumpets of the trumpeters, stops at several of the main squares of the town and announces the call to all who would like to go to arms against the Saracen. The herald is accompanied by soldiers of the Commune di Arezzo carrying their crossbows and halberds.

We attached ourselves to the Santa Crucifer quarter and learnt quite a bit about the pageant and its history from them. There is a heavy participation of the people from this quarter, and all of the medieval

1967: GARY ARRIVES - COMPLETE WITH DUAL AMERICAN AND ITALIAN CITIZENSHIP PAPERS

costumes for both the people as well as for the horses are made by the women of the quarter. They are renewed continuously and work for the preparation of the festival goes on all year. Such importance is attached to the winning of the jousting tournament that very often, if there is not a capable jouster from the quarter to represent them, the Quarter will hire some, even from another town to ride for them.

In the early afternoon, the representatives of the four quarters with their armed guards accompanying the horsemen, parade through their own quarter, visiting the orphanage and hospital after receiving the blessing of their priest in front of the main church of their section of town. Then they all gather in the main park of Arezzo. With the forest of lances, banners, horsemen, colorful soldiers, and costumed officials with their consorts in long flowing gowns of the 12th century, it seemed as if we had been transported back 700 years and that we were out of place with our 20th century clothes.

Regarding the business area, production at our Milan plant is now about twice what it was when I moved into the newly created job as Director of Factory Operations two years ago, and production at our factory near Naples has tripled. While this substantial increase of production has involved a great deal of work, it has also been very much fun.

Now that we have a child, I have rediscovered the pleasure that can be had crawling around the room on all fours, playing with blocks and rolling a ball around. We will have to have another baby soon so that I will have the excuse to continue crawling around the floor after Gary outgrows this stage. Also, the home-made vegetable soup Lydia makes especially for Gary is extremely good and I get to finish what he does not, so this joy must be perpetuated.

EIGHT

1968: Labor problems in the Naples factory and business in Israel

The day you open your Christmas presents we will be celebrating the 2nd birthday of Gary. As could be expected, he is growing, and as most parents, we continue to be amazed at the phenomenal rate of growth and development of our particular child. We are convinced he is doing things at the age of two that we never did until much later. I certainly wasn't able to count to 10 in Italian at this age and neither was Lydia able to count in English. And Gary can do both.

While he can go from "uno" to "dieci" without a flaw, he occasionally gets side-tracked between one and ten. After one and two, "buckle my shoe" gets inserted in the series, quite often in place of three and four.

Early influences certainly have a lasting effect, and in fact, I have read in a learned book that the first words a baby uses indicates the general areas of interest the person will develop in the future. We are both curious, as well as somewhat concerned, to see whether this theory will materialize in Gary's case. His vocabulary started near the beginning of the alphabet with the three B's. The first words he learned and used with good knowledge and in the following sequence were "book, ball, and bottle". The "bottle" he refers to is our wine bottle and not milk.

Lately he has been moving up the alphabet and when I get home now greets me with "Car Dadda". The pleasure of sitting behind the wheel of the car, manipulating the clutch and signal lights, has now replaced the book, ball, and bottle trio. His interest in books is still very strong. I wonder if his interest in the wine bottle is lurking in the background. We had been concerned whether he would be slower in talking, hearing two different languages spoken, but this has not been the case. We took an inventory of words he uses, and his vocabulary is fairly evenly divided between English and Italian. However, Italian words, being regular and ending in vowels, seem to be easier for him to pronounce than English words.

In the last chapter, there was a brief description of the Italian bureaucratic steps that had to be followed in getting Gary legally recognized as a person. Some other aspects of the differences between the Italian and American business environment are equally fascinating. One of the differences is the high degree of political orientation of the unions. In Italy, there isn't one union of factory workers as there would be in an American automobile plant, for example the AF of L or the CIO. Instead, there are several unions representing some of the political parties. There is the union of the communist factory workers, and the union of the socialist factory workers and the union of the right-wing factory workers, referred to as the Misini or the crown.

Another difference between the American and Italian business environment is the effect and consequences of the more volatile Italian temperament. This is particularly noticeable in the south of Italy, where this difference is particularly pronounced. At our factory in the south of Italy, two of our employees have been murdered in the past year, and one of these murders took place in the factory itself. The first one had a Hatfield and McCoy flavor, the second one was within the framework of "Are you going to marry my sister?"

The first case can be called "A shoe, a threat, and a transfer". This combination of an object, a word, and a transfer would have gone largely unnoticed had all three events not happened in quick succession. In this particular case, the series of events came rapidly one on top of the other creating a tragedy which left two women, with seven children between them, without husbands and means of support.

The story starts many generations ago with some insignificant incident, seemingly long since forgotten, which became the irritant upon which a series of subsequent feuds were based. The two families concerned were distant relatives who lived next to each other in a small agricultural town not far from our factory. As fate would have it, they both moved to the larger town at the same time to seek their fortune and, unfortunately, they found living quarters in the same building adjacent to each other. As there was no running water in this building, they both used the same well. The proximity of the two families plus the common use of the well added to the friction between them, as each accused the other of contaminating the water.

The head of one of the families was fortunate to find himself a job as a driver with our company almost immediately as we opened the factory. The job also carried with it a certain amount of prestige, as the driver not only drove the Plant Manager to various appointments with the Mayor, Chief of Police, and other high officials, but also accompanied important guests to the airport, both from the Milan headquarters and from more distant prestigious locations, such as England, Switzerland, and the United States. The other head of family had considerable difficulty in finding a job. He finally went to work as a night guard for the local police department, who furnished the equivalent of Pinkerton's private protection service for many of the nearby companies.

1968: LABOR PROBLEMS IN THE NAPLES FACTORY AND BUSINESS IN ISRAEL

Our company is one of those that subcontracts the night guard service, and this person was unfortunately assigned to our company. One day, the wife of the driver found a shoe floating in a bucket full of water which she had just drawn from the well. She passed on her fury to her husband, who jumped to the conclusion that the obvious offender was their uncivilized country cousin. The driver marched over to the apartment of the guard and announced that he was completely fed up with their carelessness. The driver indicated that he was in frequent contact with important people, and unless the guard wanted to find himself without a job someday, he had just better watch his step. Although this guard scoffed at this bravado, the threat nevertheless had a very sobering effect on him and his family.

The very next day and without anything at all said by the driver, our Plant Manager noticed that this particular guard was a bit too friendly with one of our employees as the 3rd shift left and the first shift entered. He called the police chief and asked him to transfer this guard. While most events progress slowly in the south of Italy, the police chief responded to this request promptly, and as a consequence, the day after the threat, the guard found himself called by his police chief and told that he would be transferred immediately to another post.

As could be imagined, the guard was both enraged as well as panicked, and interpreted this as step one of a series of moves on the part of his vindictive cousin to make him lose his job. He decided that the town wasn't big enough for both of them.

The next morning the guard came to the factory gate, left his motorcycle running outside, walked into the guard house where the driver was sitting reading a newspaper, pulled out a pistol and fired three shots at him. He then ran out, jumped on his motorcycle, and rode off. The driver died after three hours, and the guard turned himself in after four hours with typical Neapolitan remorse. The result of this tragedy is that two women and seven children are deprived of means of support by this random combination of a shoe, a threat, and a transfer.

The second murder can be called "Miss, Misinterpretation, Misfire and Boom". In our coil winding department, there was an attractive dark-haired woman of 28 named Rosa. She had come to work at the factory a year before, somewhat to the displeasure of her parents, who felt she should be home, where all nice girls stay until they are married. However, as the marriage age in this town is rather young and as this girl felt her chances were not improving staying at home, she thought she better get herself a means of support and in the process potentially come into contact with an eligible male. Or perhaps the priorities were the reversed.

The eligible male with whom she came in contact worked in the maintenance department. He was a rather handsome 23-year-old fellow, and although his name was Marco, he looked more like a Lothario, and it was said he had a reputation that went with his looks. He took Rosa out once. Rosa's parents were very happy as was her brother, and even though Marco was a bit younger than Rosa, they thought he was a good steady chap and a satisfactory candidate for their son-in-law.

From what we were been able to gather about the situation, Marco was a perfect gentleman and did not say or do anything that could have been misinterpreted by Rosa as anything more than a casual show of interest on the part of Marco. And for Marco, it was no more than a casual interest because he did not ask her to go out with him a second time.

However, the parents of Rosa and particularly her brother, quite without foundation, had already been making plans for the future. When Marco did not show up again, they became first apologetic, then concerned, and finally enraged. "A nice girl should not be jilted in this way. Who does he think he is, building up a girl's hopes and then letting her down?"

While Rosa tried to deflate all of this nonsense, her brother Giacomo became even more infuriated and finally decided to confront the cur to see what his real intentions were. He stomped over to the house where Marco lived and burst in on him while he was playing cards. Without so much as an introduction, Giacomo said "When are you going to marry my sister?".

As could be expected Marco was a bit taken aback by this abrupt entry and accusatory question. His surprise turned to ridicule, and he replied with a tone of irony "You are out of your mind, I have no intention of ever marrying your sister!" This was just too much for Giacomo who had come prepared for more than an exchange of words. He pulled out a pistol and with a cry "If you are not going to marry my sister, you are not going to marry anyone else" and pulled the trigger. The gun misfired.

Marco was up out of his seat, and not caring to trust his life to the chance of a second misfire, bolted for the next room. Marco's brother, who was a policeman, had left his gun hanging on the wall. Marco grabbed it, rushed back to the room where Giacomo was still standing somewhat stupefied. As he entered, Giacomo looked up, and raised his pistol but Marco was quicker, and boom, Giacomo crumpled to the floor, killed instantly by a bullet through the heart. Rosa is now back to work after a leave of absence and Marco is in prison awaiting trial. It is likely that he will be exonerated on the grounds of self-defense.

As an attempt to partially overcome some of the problems in the south of Italy, the Italian government offers numerous incentives to encourage industry to move to the "Mezzogiorno" (the south). These incentives are intended to counter lower efficiency and lack of industrial base of the southern areas and infuse the more sedate emotional environment that is found in the north.

As can be found in undeveloped countries and in some sections of already developed countries, there are areas where large quantities of labor are available at low labor rates. Many international companies make the mistake of multiplying this labor rate with the number of labor hours required in the States or northern Europe to do a particular job and come up with an erroneous labor cost for their product. It is often overlooked by company managers that there is an economic reason for low labor rates on some areas rather than other areas. And the cost of experienced department heads will probably cost the company more in the south of Italy than in the north. Eventually the labor costs may become fairly close.

It is particularly disturbing to see the pressure on the part of the Italian labor unions to enact a minimum wage law on a national Italian rather than on a regional basis. The U.S. does this with its minimum wage which is not logical. If Italy passes a minimum wage covering the entire country, it will retard the development of an industrial base in the south of Italy. This movement is being pushed particularly by the Italian Communist Unions, who I'm sure see this as a way of creating further misery in the south of Italy, which in turn will make the southerners easier prey to the claim that the present form of government is unable to solve the basic problems of the south and consequently communism is the only hope.

Unfortunately, this movement is receiving some support from well-meaning socialists who approach the problem from the standpoint that it is unfair for a southern worker to earn less than a northern worker. Their message seems to be that needs are no less in one region than in another so why should he be discriminated against. While you can legislate minimum wages, unfortunately minimum efficiency cannot be legislated. Unless the present difference in labor rates is maintained, new industry will not move south, and unemployment will grow in just that area that needs employment most. But perhaps this superficial legislative approach which will aggravate the basic problem rather than solve it, is no more peculiar to Italy than it is to America. I am sorry to say there is some of this thinking taking place on the left side of the political spectrum in the United States.

1968: LABOR PROBLEMS IN THE NAPLES FACTORY AND BUSINESS IN ISRAEL

Regarding our travels of the past year, after having explored the western and northern shores of the Mediterranean, plus a few of the intermediate islands, this year we managed to reach the southeastern shore of the Mediterranean. A combination of business plus a few days of vacation allowed us to see a bit of Israel.

The time we were there was perhaps the most peaceful time in the past 18 months, being shortly after the Six-Day War and several months before the growing guerrilla clashes, some of which occurred in places we had visited a few days earlier. The contrast between the old Arabic bazaars with the bustling industry of modern Tel Aviv is striking. Old and New Jerusalem have special religious significance as Jerusalem is of great historical importance to three major religions. These differences give an unusual flavor as you are encouraged to duck when you hear a bang.

If this were not enough by itself, when you superimpose the above on a small area rich in contemporary archeological discoveries of Roman and Early Christian periods, predating the Roman occupation by many thousands of years, Israel is an area of great interest with a wide variety of historical and archeological differences.

The agricultural expansion of Israel is amazing. From an airplane it is interesting to see where the orderly circular agricultural communities that have brought water to the various parts of the land, stand out as oases of green in the midst of barren desert. Driving north from Tel Aviv, we saw luxuriant orange and lemon groves one side of the road and sand dunes on the other.

The attachment of the Israelis to the land is much stronger than we had ever imagined. This comes from the inhabitants of the current area of Israel and is added to by refugees from Europe who are willing to become farmers in the hot climate. The addition of newer immigrants from a wide variety of European countries, which managed to survive

World War II, has brought to Israel new energy with amazing changes taking place in both agriculture and industry. As we travelled about the country, this fierce sense of nationalism became one of the most striking features of modern Israel.

After having seen a Kibbutz from the air we were very curious to see one from the inside on the ground. We managed to visit one and stay overnight. The Kibbutz was a response to the early challenges facing Israelis. It was a substantial improvement for many of the early Jewish immigrants from the oppression and poverty they had experienced in Europe. While the challenge to the nation of Israel is as great as ever from the surrounding Arab nations, it is now a very different challenge from what existed before Israel become a country. Before that time, each Kibbutz was a self-contained community - an island in a hostile environment. The Israeli army has now taken a large part of the security burden. I would expect that the original Kibbutz form of organization will disappear before long.

Many people in Israel that we spoke with said they would not be able to live in a Kibbutz. It is a small communist community, where I would imagine a great amount of time is spent on decision making for the group. I'm sure each of the 800 people have their own ideas regarding what the proper mix should be between the various expenditures, and I would imagine interminable arguments would take place before arriving at a budget for the coming year for the community.

In the earlier days of the Kibbutz, we were told that all children lived all together away from their parents in separate quarters, and that the parents saw the children largely at mealtimes and in the few free hours in the evening. This is now changing and in most of the Kibbutz the children do live with their parents. There is a major problem regarding use of Kibbutz resources for higher education for the children that will become worse as Israel becomes more affluent. As could be expected, the decisions as to how many and who should be sent on for advanced education is decided on the basis of what is best for the Kibbutz community. Individual family desires are secondary.

For example, if there are three boys that all want to be doctors, and the Kibbutz only needs one, only one is sent to medical school. Having no money of their own, and without the ability to earn any, the parents themselves are not able to sacrifice and save in order to send their child to medical school. The inability to make these types of sacrifices must be hard on parents.

Had time permitted, we would have enjoyed seeing more of the actual operation. I would like to have seen an annual use and application of funds. Would you suppose there is a fair degree of egoism cleverly dressed in a robe of altruism as each tries to argue what he thinks is best for "the group"? When you have a small group of people living in an island, surrounded by a sea of hostility, it is easier for the group interest to be the path chosen. However, if there is peace in the Middle East and some degree of normalcy, it is my guess that in 50 years the Kibbutz concept will be replaced by capitalism.

Unfortunately, peace does not seem to be likely for some time, and there are many grim remainders of the proximity of danger and the need for the Israelis to work together for mutual safety. At one of the Kibbutz we visited, where the Jordan river drains out of the Sea of Galilee, there was a Syrian tank which had reached the perimeter of that Kibbutz in the war of 1948 before it had been knocked out. It stands as an ominous reminder of how close the enemy was in the attempt to kill as many Israelis as they could.

Our trip through Israel included a jeep ride from Eilat on the Gulf of Aqaba into the desolate and mountainous Sinai desert. Our ride took us over one of the main caravan routes which was used to bring spices, ivory and other products from India, China, and East Africa to Egypt, Crete, Greece, and Rome during the pre-Christian era. Seeing the mountains, hills and sand swept desolation of this desert, completely devoid of vegetation, we developed a lot of respect for the courageous people who traversed this desert. When the Portuguese explorers opened sea route ships rounding South Africa to reach India and China, the long camel caravans across Asia were replaced by Portuguese ships.

A short trip on a camel across the Sinai Peninsula from the Gulf of Aqaba to the Mediterranean takes at least two weeks and the availability of water is the main key to survival. Our guide showed us two water holes, which he said provide water almost all year around. One of them was at the bottom of deep draw and in a cool cave that was sheltered from the hot winds outside. Drops of moisture filtered down through the rock into a pool about three feet deep. Our guide told us that this spring is referred to in the Old Testament.

The other water hole is reached by making your way down a canyon similar to some of the side canyons one finds on the Yampa, Green, and Colorado rivers in Colorado. The walls of the canyon, formed by wind erosion, rise above you in the form of an elongated S, and in spite of the heat, are cool inside the canyon. As you follow the canyon down, you finally come to several excellent water holes which gather what rain does fall and keep it sheltered from evaporation. This water hole has also been known and used for thousands of years. On the sides of the sandstone walls, were ancient inscriptions which our guide explained to us.

Starting with Muslim inscriptions of the 8th century working backwards there was carving of a home-sick Roman soldier of the 10th legion, conquerors of Jerusalem. He carved into the wall "To see the Tiber once more" in Latin. There were even older Greek inscriptions, but it is not known whether these refer to the passage of the troops of Alexander the Great going east or on their return from India. There were a few inscriptions identified as Assyrian, as well as a number of ancient Hebrew inscriptions. The dating of these earlier inscriptions

1968: LABOR PROBLEMS IN THE NAPLES FACTORY AND BUSINESS IN ISRAEL

is difficult, but this was the area travelled by the patriarchs of the Old Testament.

As we climbed from the Gulf of Aqaba into the mountains of the Sinai, we passed through an abandoned United Nations camp, where a handful of about 40 Yugoslav soldiers acted as a paper-thin insulation between the armored forces of both Egypt and Israel. Although abandoned, it gave the appearance of being neatly kept. In fact, with empty beer cans, they had made a trim framework around the various paths and had even gone so far as to make the outline of the Yugoslav Star and the Egyptian Eagle with the word Nasser. We don't know whether the absence of a similar picture in beer cans of the Israeli star with the name of Dayan or Ben Gurion was due to being ordered out too soon, to their lack of impartiality of the UN troops, or to a lack of beer. A bit further on was an abandoned Egyptian camp with a few shoes lying about, and as we proceeded west into what had been Egyptian territory, we saw pieces of abandoned equipment.

Prior to returning to Eilat, we saw in the distance amid shimmering heat waves, an Arab caravan of eight camels, using the same form of locomotion, and with the same costume, as had been used on this particular route 6,000 years ago. While we were very impressed to see how the Israelis had made a former wasteland bloom after centuries of neglect, what was of particular interest to us was the basic question of who really possessed the legal and moral right to the land which the Turks, Syrians, Jordanians, Israeli, Palestinians, Saudi, and Yemeni, were disputing.

We had a chance to hear both sides of the story during this trip. On the one hand from educated and although intensely interested, reasonably dispassionate and objective Israelis, and on the other hand, again from an intensely interested, but also reasonably objective Jordanian, who we met in Jerusalem. Both of them had attended university in the United States.

The explanation of the Jordanian was that the Arabs had a greater legal and moral claim not only to Jerusalem but to all of Palestine. His arguments ran something like this: First of all, Saudi and Yemen tribes had been in Palestine for the past 3,000 years. They had been ruled by the Seljuk and Ottoman Turks. While the majority of the Jews had been there for a longer period, they had been driven out by the Romans 2,000 years ago. Prior to that time, various Arab tribes had occupied what is now called Palestine. He said it was his understanding the original Hebrews came Egypt and before Egypt had originated in the area of Ur.

From the religious standpoint, the fact that Mohamed flew to Jerusalem one night from Mecca, indicates special supernatural powers, which makes it the second most holy place to the Muslims. This happened about 600 A. D., long after the time of Christ and longer still after the time of Moses. When a matter is discussed from a religious standpoint, the time frame reference loses meaning.

The old part of Jerusalem, which our Jordanian acquaintance insisted must again be under Muslim rule, we considered as the most interesting of the places we visited thus far. As you walk down the narrow streets of the old city, you must give way frequently to donkeys loaded with various cargo or ridden by Arabs wearing typical Lawrence of Arabia head gear. However, unusual costumes were not limited to the Arabs in Jerusalem. Some of the Orthodox Jewish sects have their own particular form of dress, and its uniqueness from Western dress varies according to the degree of Orthodoxy.

A typical sabbath dress consists of black trousers slightly too short, covered by a black frock and a derby style hat which seems a couple of sizes too small. For the more Orthodox, a large Mexican sombrero type hat made of beaver skins is accompanied by a long robe under which are black "knockers". Long side burn curls are also much in evidence even among the younger Orthodox children. A trip to the

Wailing Wall, which is one side of the temple of Solomon, takes you to the most holy place of the Jews, and to the sacred Blue Mosque fifty yards away.

A walk through the covered bazaar of Jerusalem is a noisy, exciting, and odorous experience, and it is well to have a hand on your pocket as pick pockets thrive in these crowded areas. A common trick is for two members of a pick pocket gang to stage an argument to draw a crowd. As the principles curse each other and throw an occasional blow, their accomplices lurk among the outskirts of the crowd and relieve those most intent upon the entertainment of their wallets. We saw one such argument while in the bazaar, and it did seem more of a show than a real dispute.

From the bazaar we brought back an antique Yemenite curved dagger which looked like it had been worn by a harem guard during the period of the Arabian nights. The negotiations for this dagger took the better part of a morning and included several telephone calls in Arabic from the storekeeper to the supposed owner of this piece. We were quite proud to have obtained it for about half of what the seller had asked originally. I was curious to know whether the price he originally quoted was twice what he was willing to settle for or a factor of much more than that. However, we felt it was a fine buy. As we didn't have enough money in either Israeli pounds or American dollars, we had to pay him in European currency. He willingly accepted Italian Lire, but I'm sure King Leopold would have been shocked to hear he would not accept Belgian francs.

The most attractive monument in old Jerusalem is the Blue Mosque with the gold dome. This mosque was built in about 700 A. D. over the rock where Abraham was said to have started to sacrifice his son Isaac. It is a beautiful structure, and its large dome is a marvel from both an architectural as well as structural standpoint.

The Turkish walls completely encircles the old city, and Lydia and I walked on the parapets around most of the city. This would not have been possible six months earlier as the walls had been fortified by the Jordanians and soldiers with machine guns walked where we walked. Although most of the present wall was rebuilt by the Ottoman Turks and dates back to about 1600, there are still parts standing as well as foundations that date back to the time of Saladin as well as to the Roman era.

There is even one section that is built upon the ruins of the temple of Solomon. The Holy Sepulcher was another interesting landmark in old Jerusalem, and we were amazed to see how it has been divided among the various sects that claim it as their own. In the main part of the church, there are separate altars for the Roman, Armenian, Greek, Coptic, and Syrian Catholics. There was not enough room inside the church also for the Abyssinians, so they got the roof. They have a small altar up there as well as a number of small stucco single room cells, somewhat like squashed igloos where the Abyssinian priests live. Every Christmas they have a firebrand ceremony which is supposed to be the wildest of all the religious ceremonies in Jerusalem.

After seeing the Holy Sepulcher, we wanted to see Bethlehem, and our trip to Bethlehem was more interesting than the visit itself. At our hotel in Jerusalem, we were told that a taxi to Bethlehem and back plus a guide would cost about 15 dollars and take about half a day. On the other hand, the public Jordanian bus costs 15 cents. We took the bus.

This vehicle was probably one of the better ones that General Motors produced in – 1928 - because it was still running. The driver wore an Arab headdress and about one third of the occupants also wore the characteristic white cloth over their head, with a black or red braiding around the top. We expected to see some old rifles in their hands, but none were visible. However, in the folds of their white gowns, two or three rifles could have been hidden quite easily.

The landscape between Jerusalem and Bethlehem is hilly, full of stones and very unfertile looking. The stops of the bus seemed to be quite at random, and in the middle of nowhere. At these stops, a few Arabs would get off, walk across the rocky land, and disappear into a cave. At the entrance of many of these caves were cooking fires and children playing.

The snowy view of a cozy town as in many a Christmas song book was not what we saw as we approached Bethlehem. Although its position on top of a hill is attractive, the dwellings were plain, of sandstone color and not particularly picturesque. Only the very old church had some character. The entrance, which was once an extremely large, vaulted opening, has been successively reduced in size until now you have to bend over to enter, and there is just room for one person to pass through at a time. The last reduction of the entrance was built by the Crusaders to prevent people from riding into the church on their horses.

This church is the oldest structure in Bethlehem, and it is still standing because in about 600 A.D., a Persian army came through this area and razed everything but the church to the ground. The church was saved because of a mistake. A fresco on the front shows the Wise Men offering gifts to Christ. These Wise Men were dressed like Persians, and the Persian soldiers, mistaking the church for a Persian holy place, spared it.

As in Jerusalem, this holy place is again divided between four or five sects, each claiming that their altar is over the most holy place. This sectionalism was disturbing to us, but we know its elimination will be very difficult because of the many disputes over the centuries among the various old branches of the Christian church, Roman, Armenian, Coptic, Syrian, Greek Orthodox, Abyssinian, not to mention the relatively recent offshoot of the many Protestant sects, each proclaiming to be the true interpreter of Christ's teachings.

NINE

1969: Valeria arrives, Gary starts school, travels from Capri to Hong Kong

Our family in Milan is growing. Valeria Eleonora joined us on the 9th of September, weighing in at 5.5 pounds. Like her brother Gary, she was born with a lot of very dark hair which is gradually changing into a reddish blond. She also looks very similar to Gary when he was that age, but even at this point, a feminine character is apparent.

Older brother Gary is taking a very protective attitude towards his little sister and when walking with the buggy is quite careful that strangers do not look for too long at Valeria. That must be the Italian coming out in Gary although this behavior is more typical of the Sicilian rather than of the Venetian-Lombard background of his mother Lydia.

Gary and Valeria

His attitude towards females of his age is also Sicilian. We have sent him to a Montessori school in Milan. He enjoys learning and has developed friendships with the other boys. He is also protective of the girls. We went to pick him up at school yesterday. We were the next to last parents to pick our child. There was Gary, sitting on a bench with a cute girl of his age sitting beside him. One of his arms was draped protectively around the shoulder of this patient little girl and the two middle fingers of his other hand was in his mouth, as if it were a thumb and he was sucking the fingers. We are trying to get him to stop sucking his fingers, which he does instead of sucking his thumb. Our comment that only babies suck their fingers, or thumbs, hasn't registered with him.

Gary is now almost three and is exploding with discovery of his immediate environment. Pretty girls, cars, streetcars, buses, trucks, and numbers are his present passion. There is nothing like a streetcar with a big number on it to arouse his excitement. He knows most of the streetcar destinations of Milan by their number. He has also acquired (or inherited) my interest in castles and his favorite place to play in Milan is in the courtyard of the Sforza castle which is about a 10-minute streetcar ride (on number 26) from our house. The concern we had of him mixing up the Italian language and the English language has turned out to be no problem at all. At the age of two and a half we found him acting as a very capable translator for his two grandmothers.

Swimming has become an interest and we have been going once a week to a nearby swimming pool. For the first two sessions, he was just content to watch the other children and adults in the pool. He was particularly interested in those who dived. In spite of a certain initial reluctance to get in the water himself, he became an avid diver on our sofa at home. In the last visit to the pool, he reached a high-water mark and together we walked all the way across the entire shallow end of the kiddies' pool which was waist deep for him. After we reached the other side, he had the expression of one who had just conquered the Matterhorn!

Now that we have taken up the European habit of having an "Au Pair" girl to live with us and be a live-in governess, we had the opportunity of spending a few days at Capri. It is the first time that I had been to Capri. It was also the first time for Lydia. I had partially avoided Capri because I had heard it was very crowded, commercial, and overrated. If this is true in the height of the tourist season, it certainly isn't so the first week of November. It was in November when Ulysses discovered Capri on one of his travels from Athens along the Italian coast. It took a while before the word of this attractive island got back to the city of Ulysses and it wasn't until the 6th century B.C. that a group of Athenians decided to go there for a vacation. They liked the place so much they took up residence.

When they arrived, they found lots of wild boars, and that is why the island became to be known as Kapros, which means wild boar in Greek and became Capri when the Italians started going there. As the Greeks were pretty good hunters and took a fancy to roast pig, the species became extinct. Some of the current residents will tell you that large numbers of wild irritating boars can still be found on the island during tourist season.

Things were quite peaceful for the early settlers until the island was "discovered" by Augustus Caesar. When he arrived, legend has it that a withered oak started sprouting green leaves. Augustus took this as a good omen and being impressed with the beauty of the place, traded Ischia to the Neapolitans for Capri. This trade is vigorously denied by the Ischians as hearsay, although the transaction seems to be inscribed on a stone.

Augustus found Capri a fine retreat from the fast pace, bustle, and traffic of Rome and came here frequently. He was followed by Tiberius who ruled the Roman Empire for many years from his large villa perched on top of a rocky cliff on one side of the island of Capri. Tiberius constructed no less than 12 villas on different parts of the island along with numerous military towers. Many of the towers along with parts of his villas are still standing.

Augustus was good to the inhabitants and ordered the Greeks and Romans to exchange clothing as a show of friendship. Tiberius was not quite as gentle and played a much more ruthless version of the Augustus game of strip poker. In fact, he not only took the clothing and skin off the backs of the inhabitants but threw many pretty girls over the cliff during some of his wild parties.

Not much is heard about Capri after the disintegration of the Roman Empire until the 11th century when the Normans ravaged the island. It was a scene of battle in the 13th century when domination of southern Italy was being contested between the houses of Anjou and Aragon. The Saracens held the island for a short period in the 16th century and it was also fought over by Napoleon and Nelson. Now the descendants of all these invaders fight over the possession of hotel rooms during the tourist season.

Our hotel was at Anacapri, which is a plateau on the island about 1,000 feet above the sea and, as it was a nice balmy day, we took an open horse carriage rather than a cab from the small harbor at Marina Grande. The driver convinced us that a short detour to see the Marina Piccola (small beach) on the other side of the island was worthwhile and it was. The slow pace of the horse plus an absence of traffic allowed us to fully enjoy and admire the many lovely villas with their lush vegetation and still blooming flowers in November. As we reached Marina Piccola, we saw its famous swimming pool and the Faraglioni, the three large rocks in the water, one of which has a large arch through with boats can pass. Even though it was November it was warm enough to swim and several people were in the water.

The island of Capri is shaped like a saddle, with the town of Capri in the middle with Marina Grande and Marina Piccola on either side at the bottom where the stirrups would be attached if the Island was a horse. Anacapri is on top of a large plateau, somewhat like a pummel in front, and at the back of the ridge there is the high plateau where Tiberius had his main villa. The trip up to the plateau of Anacapri is very scenic and spooky. At one point, the road is not merely cut into the side of the cliff, but actually hangs out with 400 feet of air directly beneath it to the rocks below. Prior to the time the road was built (about 40 years ago), the only connection between Anacapri and Capri was by way of the Phoenician steps cut into the side of the cliff. We went down to Capri one day via the steps and they are still usable and in good condition.

When we arrived at our hotel, we were both flattered and surprised when the porter greeted us by name. We told him he was a good guesser, and he replied that in the hotel business you learn to pick out the guests very quickly. Then he added laughingly, as we were the only guests in the hotel on that November day, it wasn't very difficult for him to guess our names.

The porter turned out to be also the head (and only) waiter, as well as a tour consultant. His name was Fausto, and he gave us excellent service, suggested places to go and things to do, and he arranged for a boatman. He also kept us entertained with his skits and pantomime during dinner.

He was very amusing in describing the dining habits of different nationalities. The Germans come in to eat in a group of four or five couples, each ordering something different, and then divide the dishes between them. Then, rather than ask for the check and dividing it among themselves, they ask for separate checks, but not separate by couple, but separate for each individual.

The French say "merci" all the time, and when it comes time to pay the bill, they ask if service is included. He reluctantly says "yes", and they smile and say "merci" as they leave. (Even though service is included, it is customary to leave an additional small tip of about 5%). He said in his experience the French are reluctant tippers.

When the American comes in and starts looking at the menu, he doesn't read the names of the dishes, he reads the prices. When he starts to eat spaghetti, he puts his fork right in the middle until he has a big blob of spaghetti, almost half of the portion, wrapped around his fork, when he starts to lift this oversized mouthful, it drops off the fork back into the plate and all those at the same table get their shirts splattered with tomato sauce.

The Neapolitan is perhaps the worst diner because he thinks he owns the place, demands constant service and ice water in his room at all hours. The Roman is happy and content if you just bring him lots of good food. Next to the French, the Swedish are the worst tippers. The best clients are the Mexicans, the Spanish, the Japanese, and the Italians from Lombardy (Milan) in that order.

Through Fausto we obtained an old boatman to take us around the island. He suggested a rowboat as opposed to a motorboat so we could see the bottom more clearly. It was a marvelous ride with almost 10 miles of rowing in and out of the little inlets and lesser grottos. The water was calm and amazingly clear. You could see the rocks on the bottom in 70 feet of depth and, in one place, the bottom was visible at a depth of 100 feet. Had we brought masks and fins, we would have been in the water all day.

Apart from the Blue Grotto, which is now both a national monument and also a national museum, there are many other smaller grottos around the island which are very charming. At the back of the Blue Grotto, there is a tunnel, built by Emperor Tiberius that goes up through the rock to the top of the cliffs and was used as a quick getaway. As a national museum, an entrance fee must be collected from visitors, and outside of the Blue Grotto, there is a state boat bobbing on the waves. In the boat, there is a public servant sitting on a chair with a cash register on a small table, for making change and issuing tickets. We were told the Blue Grotto produced the second highest cash receipts of all of the museums of Italy, and half a million people per year hunch down in the bottom of the small boats to go inside. If you do not crunch down far enough, you risk hitting your head on the rocks at the entrance.

The villa of San Michele, given to the town of Anacapri by the famous Swedish physician Axel Munthe, is another attraction of Capri. It is built over the ruins of a palace of Tiberius and has a marvelous view of the Gulf of Naples, Sorrento and Vesuvius. In addition to the lovely view, it contains many relics of Roman times found around the island.

In contrast to the calm and beauty of Capri in November, the general environment of Italy has become very difficult in the last three months with almost everyone going on strike. The striking has not been limited to only some sectors of the industrial community, but it has also included the railroads, the power and light companies, hospital employees including the nurses and doctors, taxi drivers, bartenders, streetcar conductors, telephone operators, customs officials, post office employees, and letter carriers. As a rough comparison with prior years, so far in 1969, 400 million work hours have been lost, and the strikes are not yet over. This compares with the 150 million of work hours lost in 1962 which was the prior record of the last 10 years. As could be expected, striking students and their teachers add to the confusion.

The demagogic union leaders are pumping this growing state of discontent among major segments of the population with loud complaints about the growing cost of living and the need for more worker power. Their answer is to request, among other things, salary increases of 40%. With the annual growth of productivity around 6%, they will undoubtedly be shouting even louder in the next year or two as their requests can only increase the angle of inflation, particularly because Italy doesn't have much in the way of raw materials. What she sells, both for internal consumption as well as for export, is largely the cost of her labor.

While the main push for this high level of increase comes from an intense competition between the Communist and Christian Democrat union to get to the left of the other, the reception by the population of this pressure reflects some very basic problems in the Italian economy and its structure. The reply of the business community is that their labor cost today is about the same as that of the other Common Market countries. If this labor cost increases faster than the labor cost of the other Common Market countries, Italian goods will have a difficult time competing and the result could be a rise in unemployment. This reply, in spite of its logic, is not very satisfying to the Italian worker, who takes home substantially less than his Common Market counterpart in purchasing power.

The basic problem is the large and inefficient Italian bureaucracy which administers the social benefit funds collected from both the workers and the employers. If this administration were as efficient as that of Germany or Holland, the take-home pay of the Italian worker could be increased immediately by about 30%, without increasing the total labor cost structure. Unfortunately, it will take a long time to streamline and improve the massive and unwieldy patronage-ridden and overlapping offices which administer these social funds. Until the system is improved, I think we can continue to expect a higher intensity of labor agitation in Italy than in the other Common Market countries.

What is particularly disturbing about the labor agitation this year and in contrast with prior years in the 1960 decade, is the government attitude towards law enforcement. During the labor agitations this fall there has been a negligible attempt on the part of the police to prevent violations of the law, including vandalistic destruction of property and even assault and battery, if done within the framework of union activity and strikes. This type of partiality is disturbing to both private citizens as well as to members of the business community. However, since at the present time, Italy has a minority caretaker government, the avoidance of a direct confrontation is probably the lesser of two evils. As some of the alternatives to the present government would certainly be worse, probably the best policy under the circumstances is exactly what the government is doing, that is to let the agitation play itself out without adding fuel to the fire.

While we are experiencing a void of order, accompanying this void is a growth of an anarchic movement. In a recent demonstration in Milan, a policeman was hit on the head with an iron bar by one of a group of anarchist demonstrators. The policeman died and the entire nation was very upset by the incident. At the funeral, a group of communists and anarchists attempted to block the funeral procession and they were attacked by members of the funeral party, as well as by a group of neo-fascists. It was fortunate for the anarchists, that police were present to extract them from the fury of the crowd. I expect we will see more street battles between extremist groups this winter if the power void continues much longer.

Many of the older generation in Milan compare the present situation, the growing state of anarchy, and lack of effective central government law enforcement, with the situation that existed in Italy just after the first World War and prior to the rise of Mussolini. I can certainly appreciate and sympathize with the motives of the early Italian fascists whose scope was to restore law and order and make the trains run on time. The fiasco that followed the rise of fascism was certainly disastrous to the nation, but it did represent, for a period of time, one answer to the worse problem of growing anarchy.

As serious as these political problems are to one of Western mentality, my trip to the Far East in the late spring made Italy's problems seem mild in comparison. The deadly nature of political elections in Southeast Asia, the general corruption of the government administrative structures, coupled with areas of extremely dense population, varying religions, inadequate levels of employment and food supplies, all contribute to making Southeast Asia a very explosive area. However, at the same time, the economic growth potential is also very great. With a minimum of political stability, the area could have a very satisfactory development.

One thing that particularly impressed me on this trip was the energy and industry of the Chinese people in Hong Kong. Activity starts early in the morning, and in the late evenings as you walk past the one room shops, people are still working. It was also a surprise to hear that unskilled factory labor costs a company less than 20 US cents per hour. While you can appreciate that American labor with good machinery and in an efficient organization should be a lot more productive, you wonder if the difference is really in the order of magnitude of 10 times. And even if there is this enormous difference today, will it be the same in 10 years?

At this point, comes the sobering thought that perhaps the most dangerous thing for the Western world would be the rise of capitalism in mainland China. Would such a rise, and with it more industrial efficiency, threaten Western Europe and America with serious unemployment because we cannot compete with a modestly efficient company with a labor cost perhaps one fifth of ours? We are already seeing some difficulty of American manufactured goods competing with European goods where the labor differential including fringe benefits is about one half.

A partial answer to the Western world to this future challenge became evident to me on the flight from Rome to Manila. Along with the unusual combination of passengers, you would expect to see on a flight going from Rome to Tokyo with stops at Bombay, Bangkok and Manila – tall, bearded Sikhs, short Indians with Turbans, accompanied by wives in purple Saris, various sizes and shades of Indochinese and Indonesians, Japanese, Chinese and Filipino – there was also a number of American businessmen continuing with their subtle but peaceful invasion of the far corners of the world.

Our first stop was at Bombay at five in the morning. Even though I knew that Bombay was near the equator, I never expected the degree of pre-dawn heat that enveloped us as stepped out of the plane for its cleaning and refueling. It was like stepping into a hot, humid furnace. I was curious to know what it would be like at noon. Fortunately, the plane took off two hours later. The heat plus the rather small and listless looking airport attendants who were there to serve us tea, gave an unfortunate impression of Bombay. I made a mental note to seek an alternative stop over location on future visits. In contrast, the two-hour stop in Bangkok, although just as hot, was much more inviting. As opposed to the thin hungry looking male airport attendants of Bombay serving hot tea, at the Bangkok airport, transit passengers were met by attractive smiling Thailand hostesses who offered us chilled exotic fruit in pleasant surroundings.

In Manila, we had an equally pleasant reception and were met by attractive Filipino girls who gave each passenger a necklace of very fine smelling flowers. The smiling passport control official, who gathered up our passports, was our first introduction to the evils of the bureaucracy there. Apparently, there is a black market for foreign passports and two passengers that went ahead looking for their luggage before retrieving their passports spent the following day at their respective consulates getting duplicates. Fortunately, I had been warned about this game and stayed close to the passport table until they had finished stamping my passport.

To my surprise, I found that hotel prices are negotiable in the Philippines. When the hotel keeper quoted 15 dollars, I said that was too high and he immediately came down to 10 dollars. I sometimes wonder what daily price I could have reached had I continued to bargain. In both Hong Kong and Bangkok, I also noticed about a 30% reduction possible on purchased items if you negotiate. I am curious to know if 30% is a typical amount is added to the normal price to allow for some bargaining fun for both parties.

Incidentally, the price of 10 dollars for the ground floor room of my hotel was still no bargain. There was only a trickle of water in the shower, something I found out after I had stripped out of my soggy travel clothes and had a beard full of soapy foam. The plumber came quickly when I complained. However, his answer to the problem, after tinkering for a few minutes with the valves, was that there wasn't enough water pressure. Before I could resign myself to this state of affairs, he suggested I change my room to one on the 8th floor where he was certain there was more water pressure. Since I wanted a shower and was somewhat sleepy after the 18-hour flight, I didn't attempt to argue physics with the man, put on my clothes and went upstairs to the new room. There was plenty of water pressure in my new 8th floor room!

The number of servants kept by the well-to-do Filipino, as well as by employees of American companies in Manila, who might have a cleaning woman one day a week in the States if they were lucky, reminds one of the colonial days. A staff of four to five servants is not unusual and would include cook, housekeeper, nurse for the children, chauffer, and gardener. One person I know has nine servants. In addition to the above, he has two more nurses, one for each of his children, a cleaning woman who does all the laundry, and a houseboy that runs errands. If I remember correctly, a servant costs about 20 dollars a month including their food.

The life span of the agricultural Filipino is very long, but with the quickening pace of recent progress, longevity is being reduced somewhat. As an example, our driver told us his great grandfather worked until he was 115 and died at the age of 130. His grandfather only lived to 112 and had to stop working at 107. His father was now 90 and would have to stop working in a year or two. He concluded that people age a lot faster now than they used to. But looking at our driver who was 62, although he looked no more than about 45, I couldn't get too excited about his alarm at the creeping senility of the past 30 years. At first, I thought there may be something wrong with the way they were counting the years. The slow agricultural life with minimum strain and hurry, plus the diet of rice and fish, apparently was the answer.

This longevity may also be the case with Chinese farmers. On a trip to the Red Chinese border on the Kowloon peninsula of Hong Kong, I did see numerous older Chinese working the fields. I would have guessed that two of the men, carrying pails of water on yokes, each with a long, white, and slender Fu Manchu beard, must have been at least 80.

Of the cities I have seen, Hong Kong would be rated as the most beautiful from the standpoint of location, and one of the most fascinating. However, it also carries the feeling of one potentially doomed with an incurable disease, and only living at the whim of an irrational doctor. Apart from the uncertainty of being gobbled into Red China when the present lease expires in about 25 years, there is the ever-present danger that China will turn off their fresh water supply, in which case Hong Kong would run out of water in about a month. While it is to China's best interest to keep Hong Kong free, it is sobering to think that Hong Kong has a future only if a logical central Chinese government can maintain control of China.

With a population of less than 100,000 Europeans among four million Chinese, there is a strange mixture of a Western shell with a Chinese body inside. Outside of my hotel, a typical example of modern Western architecture, there were several rickshaw men in shorts and sandals waiting. While most of the Chinese you meet in shops speak English, I didn't have much luck with the rickshaw drivers. The two times I rode a rickshaw, I ended up in the wrong place farther away from my destination than from my starting place.

If you have only a few days in Hong Kong, the purchase of a tailor-made suit and a trip to the Aberdeen floating village should be part of the program; I managed to do both. How a suit can be made in two days starting only from the measurements and raw cloth, is quite beyond me. However, it wasn't beyond Lydia because she didn't care for the cut, and she found some defects in the workmanship. However, I think with a little more time and some instruction on Italian cut, the Hong Kong tailor that I found could make a suit to Lydia's liking.

The Aberdeen floating village contains 300,000 people who live their entire lives on the boats anchored in the bay. Approaching the village by boat, you are met by boys who dive for coins and other boats with children and their mothers that come by begging for money. It is discouraging to give them money as they curse you for not giving more. As you reach the village, there are several large Chinese floating restaurants. The storage area for their seafood is a large floor in their kitchen. There, suspended in many different nets in the water, is their inventory of live raw material. The storekeeper proudly pulled up the different nets and showed us a beautiful selection of lobsters, prawns, crabs, shrimps, small octopus, and many different kinds of fish enjoying their last swim. The food was excellent.

One of the best and cheapest tours of Hong Kong is the 15-cent round trip on the funicular to the peak behind the city. At the top station, there is a very pleasant hour walk that circles just below the peak and looks down upon the main city, harbor, and Kowloon. At night, it appears that you are flying over the city at an altitude of about 1,000 feet. This is a city worth several weeks to explore. I am hoping this dynamic city can remain free beyond the English mandate.

TEN

1970: Exploring Russia

The events of this year have been highlighted by a broken leg and a trip to Russia. Lydia broke her leg in February, and it was such a complete job that when it came time to take our trip to Russia in August, she still had her cast on. We had some concern that the Soviet border police would make her take the cast off to verify that she was not taking in microfilm strips of forbidden literature, or on the way out, the secret memoirs of Khrushchev. We brought along copies of her x-rays to prove that the leg really was in pieces, but no one ever asked to see them. We notified the US State Department of the laxity of Soviet security, and I wouldn't be surprised if there is a flood of tourists into Russia next year in casts.

With Valeria about six months old when Lydia broke her leg, it was quite a feat of acrobatics for Lydia to carry the baby while balancing on crutches. Valeria learned to grab hold like a monkey. She has now descended from the trees, is walking well, and is getting extremely cute. It is a surprise to see the distinct difference between the male and female personality at such a young age. She is very happy to play with her brother and he plays nicely with her. Even though she has about five distinguishable words to her vocabulary, she and Gary carry on long conversations, particularly when put to bed for their afternoon naps.

Gary has become a fine helper for his father. We took out a tree by the roots the other day and he helped me dig the hole. In the process, we must have examined 20 worms very closely. In fact, it took longer to examine the worms than to dig the hole. Gary is not only getting very observant but is also becoming very outspoken. We like to encourage this, but until he is able to develop a diplomatic way of expressing himself, this can be embarrassing to his parents.

At a restaurant the other day, he saw two effeminate men in flowery clothes at the next table. In a rather loud voice he asked, "Is that person a man or woman?" When Lydia said he should speak more quietly, he quickly replied, in a voice of no less volume, "Why should I speak more quietly?" The couple was so wrapped up in each other, we doubt they heard the comments and we managed to divert his attention to something else. After a short while, his eye caught another man at a nearby table. This man had a very red face with a small pug nose and not very much neck. As both Gary and I observed him, it became very apparent to me that this man resembled the pig in one of Gary's favorite books.

I could see Gary trying to make the connection with someone or something else he knew, as he studied the face of the man. I realized I had no more than 10 seconds in which to divert his attention, if we were to avoid another announcement in a loud, clear voice and perhaps this time also accompanied by a pointing finger. Fortunately, we managed to get his attention to something else before the silence of the restaurant was punctuated by his new discovery.

While Gary and Valeria are discovering their immediate environment, Lydia and I continued our exploration of foreign lands. This year we decided to go behind the Iron Curtain to visit Russia. We were anxious to get some feeling of that immense country, over 3 times the size of the United States, and get a better look at how their brand of socialism works. This trip to the Soviet Union was organized by the Harvard alumnae travel bureau and the itinerary included visits to Moscow, Leningrad, Kiev, and Sochi on the Black Sea. We had an interesting group of 25 people in the group who were good company. As far as understanding how communism works after spending three weeks in that country, our conclusion was - it doesn't work.

Our general impression of Russia was better than we had expected. The people appeared to be sufficiently nourished, and the cities were reasonably clean. Public transportation within the cities was very good and it was relaxing to see the wide and empty streets in which there was an astonishing lack of traffic and smog. Much of the pre-revolution artistic heritage is preserved and made available to the public. The Hermitage Museum in Leningrad is one of the very best museums we have ever seen, and the treasures of the Czars are breath-taking. The Bolshoi Opera House is superb, and tourists are able to obtain tickets at reasonable prices.

Seeing people waiting stoically in many lines around the city, we obtained the impression of a well-disciplined, courteous, and extremely patient population. We did get a chance to meet and talk seriously with a few Russians without being observed and we found those people, while guarded at first, more open at expressing themselves than we had expected. The Russian women made quite an impression on us. They were the most powerful looking women we had ever seen. I'm sure the Notre Dame offensive team would have a real difficulty in moving the ball against a defensive line selected at random from the strong large Russian women we saw in Moscow.

One aspect of Russia's power, as personified in their women, becomes more obvious as you ride the Moscow subway. If you didn't exit quickly at your stop, you ran the serious risk of being pushed back into the car by two or three determined women moving ahead shoulder to shoulder intent on entering your subway car. Holding one's ground, much less moving ahead against this flying wedge of Russian women power, requires more agility and strength than I have. As our group consisted of average size humans, it was surprising that only once one of group was imprisoned on the subway car and had to exit at the next stop. However, with the trains running every 80 seconds and the stops close together, he exited at the next stop and was back to us in less than six minutes.

It was our impression that if a person were to spend about a week in Moscow with a well-organized group, visiting the Kremlin and other sites, he would probably come back with a surprisingly good impression of the country and of the communist system that produced it. On the other hand, if one stays for two to three weeks in Russia, the sluggishness and lack of spirit of the Russian people becomes more and more obvious and heavy. While the people don't look unhappy, they don't look very happy or energetic either. You don't see either the purposeful hurry of the Anglo Saxons, nor the relaxed happy manner of the Italians. The people seem to go about their business without enthusiasm and a lack of expression. Perhaps apathetic is the best word to describe the demeanor of the people we saw on the streets of Moscow.

The apathy of its inhabitants left us with the impression that the Great Russian bear was half asleep. And we believe it had been this way even before the Mongol invasions of 11th century. We understand that these passive attitudes of "what's the use" has been unchanged since the 300 years of rule by the Romanoff family. When you add 50 years of communist dictatorship it is understandable that 95% of the population shuffles ahead without an optimistic spirit.

Russia has enormous potential, with its large land mass and valuable land and materials yet has a sad history. With a population of 240 million people and occupying a territory much larger than Europe and United States together, with more natural resources than any other country, this mammoth country entered the 20th century as one of the most backward countries of Europe. In the decade of 1890, an extensive famine in the Volga River area, widespread persecution of Jews, and the passive reaction of the ruling class, resulted in a deadly famine in Central Russia. While the landowners continued to sell their grain to western countries, their citizens had no bread. This situation produced a lack of trust in their rulers which paved the way for revolution.

At that time, 90% of the population were serfs bound to the land and their status had not been much greater than that of the American Negroes before the American Civil War. The owner of the large farms where they were living had the power of life or death of its peasants. The wealth, land, and power were in the hands of a very few aristocratic hands. The secret police of the Czar ruthlessly stamped out any liberalization movements. It is small wonder that the attitudes of many was to overthrow their chains and their government.

A short three-word sentence of a man we meet casually in Leningrad summarized what reflects the disillusionment of many at the results of the revolution to erase famine and provide freedom. Lydia and I took a walk on the banks of the Neva River in Saint Petersburg near the Czar's magnificent winter palace. We happened to stand next to a man of about 70 years and he started up a conversation with us in English. He had joined the merchant marine in Leningrad at the age of 14 and had then joined the British Navy in the First World War. After the war, he went to Philadelphia where he spent 10 years. He returned to Russia about 1930 to see what the new freedom was like. He replied, "There wasn't any, and food was scarce and very expensive."

While the standard of living for the great majority of the population has improved since the frequent famines, the status of the people has not changed. As opposed to being subjects of the Czar, they are now subjects of the Communist party. The membership of the Communist party is less than 5% of the total population, and those that rule are an infinitesimal number.

There is only one state tourist agency in Russia which is responsible for making all hotel, travel, and tour arrangements for both foreigners and Russians, tourists, and businessmen. Any changes of plans in all areas of Russia had to be funneled back through to Moscow to be rescheduled. It is an enormous task and at that time it was terrible disorganized mess. Imagine how difficult and chaotic it would be if all travel arrangements for both tourists and businesspeople visiting the United States were centralized at one of the New York airports.

Our flight from Vienna to Moscow provided a first indication of the limited amount of exchange there has been between the free world and Russia. Our airplane from Vienna landed at a minor Moscow airport rather than at the main Sheremetyevo International Airport. It gave us our first contact with the slow and clumsy giant called Intourist. Our Austrian Airlines plane, which seats about 100 people, had only 16 passengers - and this was at the height of the tourist season. Of these, there was not one Russian. Due to mechanical difficulties, we were asked to leave the plane and have drinks courtesy of Austrian Airlines and we became acquainted with some of the passengers. There was a diplomat from Afghanistan, two Armenians on their way to Iran, two New Zealanders, one Austrian, five American tourists, Lydia, and me. There was also a courier from the U.S. State Department who was not communicative and a Peruvian doctor.

As we took off from Vienna and flew over Czechoslovakia, Poland and into Russia, I had a spooky feeling. After the plane came to a halt, we sat inside for 20 minutes, seemingly in quarantine. It was midnight and raining. When the door of the plane finally opened, the first Russian we saw was in military uniform and he came into the airplane. He had cold, suspicious eyes and he looked at each one of us with a half-smile as he took our passports. His smile was not a smile of welcome but the smile of a hungry fox that fortune had blessed, seeming to say, "You are most welcome to see my den, you curious and silly chickens. Won't you come in please?" I would have rather given that man my shirt than my passport but there was no choice.

Once inside the airport there was great confusion. The entrance hall was full of people milling around, there was no one in charge at the counter who knew what to do. As we looked for custom declaration forms, we found them on the counter in most every language except English and the major European languages. There was Burmese, Chinese, Thai, Arabic, Finnish, Hungarian, Urdu, Swahili, and Bulgarian, to mention a few. We finally came upon eight entry documents in French. There were two Armenian fellows who could speak Turkish, Persian, Armenian and about 10 words of English. We helped them fill out their French forms as best we could. While we were fairly certain what the questions were in French, it was quite a job to fit these questions into the ten-word English vocabulary at their disposal. When they thought they understood, they wrote down the answer on their form and returned it to us to verify.

There was an "Intourist" office and two representatives of that inefficient company at the airport. I felt sorry for the two overwhelmed employees that were at the information desk. They seemed to have no idea of what they should and could do. One of the problems of this single, and only, tourist agency in Russia was to book in a hotel of their choice. I asked of the Intourist representative at the counter if he could tell me the name of the hotel where we had been placed. I felt embarrassed asking the question since it seemed ridiculous that the clerk should know the answer. Suppose all travelers landing at Kennedy airport had to ask at an information desk, at what hotel they had been booked by the US Government tourist agency.

This first "Intourist" representative appeared somewhat puzzled by my question "the name of your hotel?". "Wait," he said, "we will arrange it." But he did absolutely nothing. After about 20 minutes, with no answer I put the same question to a second representative. He took a more active interest in our problem and began looking through a pile of papers on his desk to see if our reservations were there. They were not in his pile. So, he got on his phone, and I assume called the head office and talked to someone named Mischa. We had heard him speaking with "Mischa" several times earlier while we were waiting. I assumed Mischa was a key employee of this Russian Government owned and managed travel agency at their central office in Moscow. Mischa finally responded that they had found our file. Now we knew the name of the hotel was Rossia, which was close to the Kremlin. The next problem was to get there.

The Intourist rep said he would arrange for transportation. But he did nothing. As it was now 1:30 a.m. and we were getting tired and impatient. Finally, at 2:00 a.m. we found that another American couple from our plane, had been assigned a taxi and they were reserved at the Rossia Hotel also. We asked if we could share their taxi, they agreed, and we were off into the night.

Up to this point, security had been pretty loose. We had gotten our passports back after 20 minutes of landing. No one had checked our baggage, currency, or our custom declarations. We now walked out of the airport without anyone checking our documents and could probably have walked off into the countryside and no one would have known the difference. However, once into the cab, and traveling to the hotel, security began tightening up. We found that the task of the taxi driver doesn't end when he drops you off at your hotel. He comes inside and must write down the number of the room to which you are assigned. I'm not quite sure for whose benefit he does this or who checks to see whether he wrote down the right number. Actually, if the police wanted to know our room number was, it would be sufficient for them to call Mischa, the know-it-all on night duty at the Intourist office at that minor airport.

Once in the hotel, we took the elevator to the third floor. Just outside the elevator door, there was a woman at a desk who manned the third-floor desk near the elevator exit. She could not find our reservation and spent 10 minutes pawing through great stacks of paper. Finally, she picked up the telephone. The first word she said was "Mischa". Mischa knows all and told her which room to which we were assigned. I'd like to meet this Mischa fellow and I'd hate to imagine what happens when Mischa gets sick or takes a day off. Then we went up the elevator to our floor. We presented ourselves to the floor mistress, a hefty specimen who had probably thrown the javelin in her youthful days. She looked us over suspiciously and gave us our room key. Judging from her smile, I thought she must be the wife of the man who took our passports at the airport.

When we entered our room, we were delighted with the large picture window, reaching from our ankles to the ceiling, looking out on a street scene just off Red Square. Our pleasure with this fine view turned quickly to chagrin when we realized that there were no curtains on the window. Despite both of our theatrical tendencies, there are times when we prefer not being on stage. We discovered that there was no place in the room where you could undress without also being able to see and be seen to the people in the street and vice versa. Our chamber maid assured us that tomorrow there would be a curtain, but tomorrow never came while we were there. Maybe what she really meant was next year or that the curtains are in next five-year plan. The next morning, from our bed, we had a fine view of people walking to work. And I assumed they had a fine view of us. We could also almost converse with a team of construction people working on an old church just in front of us. It was only necessary for me to prop myself up on my elbows to get a completely unobstructed view of the street.

Our first day in Moscow we became familiar with the problem of elevators in Russian hotels. The problem stated simply is that you may have to wait a long time for an elevator. In our section of the hotel, there was a bank of three elevators on the right and three on the left. Only about half of the elevators seemed to be working and a great mob of people were waiting at the elevators. In each of these elevators, there was an elevator operator. Since the elevators were very easy to operate by pushing a button for the floor you wanted, it seemed that the purpose of the elevator operator was to keep the elevators from being overloaded. And the load limit, controlled by weight, was reached when the elevator was only 2/3rds full. When the red overload light went on, the operator was very ungentle in telling the last person who got on, to get out. If the person didn't move fast enough, he or she was pushed out ungracefully.

For the balance of our first morning, we went to visit the breathtakingly beautiful Red Square. Much of its appeal is the lack of traffic. In most places in the West such an important square in the very middle of the city would have a large parking lot nearby. But in Red Square no cars or vehicles are permitted. The square must be almost 200 yards wide and 600 yards long and the reddish medieval walls of the Kremlin fortress serve as a backdrop for the two religious monuments of Red Square. One of these is Lenin's mausoleum in the very middle of the square, and the other is the multi-colored onion domes of the church of Saint Basil.

There was a long line of people waiting patiently in line to get a glimpse of Lenin's mummified body. Before the entrance to his tomb there is a long line that snaked back upon itself several times before it trailed out of Red Square and disappeared in the distance. It must have been at least a mile long. Several days later, we waited only 45 minutes in the relatively short "foreigners' line" to see the preserved body of Lenin on his coffin. As you enter the pyramid-type mausoleum, a sense of mystery envelops you as you walk down in the semi darkness two by two.

Although the actual distance from the entrance of the mausoleum to the tomb is not very far, you have the feeling of going down into the depths of a pyramid, and as you turn corners, you pass by motionless soldiers at attention. When you finally come into the large tomb room, your eyes have become used to the semi darkness and, as such, you are dazzled by the illuminated altar-like platform raised in the middle of the room on which Lenin's body lies enclosed in glass. The lighting is done very well and leaves the rest of the room dark, while highlighting Lenin's corpse. His hands are folded, and he gives the impression of just having fallen off to sleep. The official party line, as told to us by our guide, is that there has been no facial make up added or any retouching of the body. This aura of sainthood is part of the religious legend which surrounds Lenin.

Lenin seems to have replaced the Russian Orthodox Church as the religion of the country. The observations of several doctors in our group cast some doubt on the party line and leads one to strongly believe that the hands and face must be of wax. From what we were told, cadavers kept completely immersed in formaldehyde at medical school begin to show signs of skin decay after about one year. As Lenin died about 45 years ago, barring supernatural explanation, some break in the skin should be visible now regardless of how well the tomb room is ventilated, temperature and humidity controlled.

As you leave, you pass by the names of numerous heroes of the revolution and international communists on the wall of Kremlin behind Lenin's tomb. There are also busts of several of the more prominent communists. The bust of Stalin is back again but it doesn't have any more prominence than the other collection of busts.

Looking across Red Square from the walls of the Kremlin is the department store Gum, and we decided to go in to have a look around. Before going in, we thought to try a drink from one of the soft drink automatic vending machines but changed our minds as we got closer. We saw that disposable paper cups were not dropping into a waste basket after each drink, but rather there was one community glass was being used by everyone. Even though there was a spray arrangement for washing the inside, though not the rim of the glass, we decided we weren't thirsty, and settled for an ice cream sold by two women carrying trays. The ice cream was quite good, but the price was surprisingly high at 20 kopeks, or about 20 cents each. Despite this, they were selling very rapidly and were all gone 10 minutes after we had bought ours.

The layout of the large retail store GUM is more like that of a Turkish bazaar than of a Western department store. Inside the building there are broad aisles, about the width of two cars. On either side of the center aisle there are stalls and rooms containing merchandise. The same type of merchandise seemed to repeat itself every 9 or 10 stalls. As far as clothes were concerned, the variety was very limited, and the quality was poor. There were some appliances and TV sets, refrigerators, and 1920 style sewing machines. In the toy section there were large plastic trains, trucks, missiles, and cars and a few different kinds of dolls. Although the variety was again limited, the quality was not bad.

One article particularly in evidence all over the store was a red leather box about the size for two packs of cards decorated with Egyptian designs. It was priced at 9 rubles, about 9 dollars at the present official exchange rate. This was apparently Nasser's contribution to the Russian standard of living in exchange for all that Russia was doing for Egypt. With so many of these boxes in evidence, we assumed that the Russian consumer wasn't very interested in giving about one and one-half days' pay for such an article.

The price of wool at Gum was puzzling and had a wide variation which seemed to be based entirely on color. A hank of greyish white wool was 3 rubles 50 kopeks, blue wool was 4.50 and green was 5.50. I didn't see any difference in either the quantity or quality. We made a purchase at Gum of a pack of playing cards for 2 ½ rubles. We found out later that we could buy the identical article in the same color at the hard currency shop in our hotel for 1 ruble. This perhaps gives a better idea of what the exchange rate really ought to be and the amount the Russian citizen is taxed.

With Russia as the second largest industrial power in the world, we were interested to see to what extent the individual benefits from this large industrial output. From what we understood, there is virtually full employment, and everyone can have a job although it may be somewhat difficult to change jobs. It is pretty hard to get fired unless you are obviously much worse than the rest, or if you engage in "subversive political activity." Everyone has sufficient food and very modest housing. Medical and dental care is available to all, and illiteracy has virtually disappeared.

In comparison to Czarist times, the majority of the former peasant population is much better off, and they are well aware of it. In addition, they can see that things are getting better every year. What they don't know, thanks to a complete censorship of Western books, magazines, and newspapers, is that the standard of living of Western Europe and North America is also much, much higher than it was prior to World War I.

To get a better idea of the purchasing power of the Russian salary, I went into several food and clothing stores in Moscow, Leningrad, and Kiev and priced the articles. As a frame of reference, bear in mind that the average monthly salary in Russia is 120 rubles. There isn't much difference in pay between unskilled labor and professional people. While a factory worker will earn about 120 rubles a month, bilingual guides and doctors earn about 150 rubles per month, as do the bus drivers for tourist buses. A judge earns 250 rubles per month and a street sweeper's salary is about 90 rubles per month.

From my pricing excursions, it seems that 120 rubles in Russia has less purchasing power than 120 dollars in the United States. Here are some examples of what goods cost in Moscow, which I'll express in dollars for ease of comparison:

Eggs	$1.20 per dozen
Milk	$0.60 cents a quart
Butter	$1.50 per pound
Sugar	$0.40 cents per pound
Cheese	$0.80 cents to $1.20 per pound
Rice	$0.40 per pound
Bread	$0.15 cents per pound
Chickens	$1.20 to 1.60 per pound
Beef	$1.50 per pound

As far as beef is concerned, the only kind I saw in the stores was 80% lard and 20% red meat. Except for small apples, fruit was nonexistent and there was not much variety in fresh vegetables other than an abundance of cucumbers, tomatoes, and cabbage.

As far as clothes were concerned, a pair of shoes for which you would pay 12 dollars at Sears Roebuck costs 32 rubles. There were shoes available for 10 rubles, but they looked more like house or shower slippers. A cotton shirt costs 19 rubles for one you could purchase for 5 dollars at Sears Roebuck. The cheapest canvas fabric shirt was 7 rubles. The cheapest men's suits were 50 rubles, and the low-priced winter coats were 70 rubles. Plastic raincoats were 25 rubles. Incidentally, in a music store which was supposed to be the best in Leningrad, there were no good quality brass or string instruments for sale.

The housing situation is very sad. While the average Russian only pays about 6 rubles per month for housing, he doesn't get very much in the way of space. Even if he wants to spend a larger part of his salary for housing, it is impossible to improve his housing situation unless he has some kind of political pull. Each person is allowed 9 square meters, or about the size of a 9 x 12 rug, or the space occupied by two large double beds. This assigned space excludes the entrance hall, kitchen, and bathroom, but in most cases these conveniences are shared by two families. A person can purchase his own apartment and, in this way, at least insures having a private kitchen and bathroom. Even so, they cannot have more than the 9 square meters per person. The cost of such an apartment is about 2 ½ year's salary and it can be purchased with a 40% down payment, and the balance paid in 20 years. Our guide had such an apartment.

Public transportation is cheap. The subway costs 5 cents, the surface bus 4 cents and the streetcar 3 cents. There are also inexpensive camping places Russians can go for vacation and tickets for sports and musical events are about a dollar each. As far as cars are concerned, these are presently beyond the reach of 99% of the population. The cheapest car coming out of the new Fiat factory in Togliatograd will cost a factory worker 4 years' salary. One measure of the extent of motorization in Russia is the number of gas stations in the cities. In Leningrad, a city of just under four million people, there are four gas stations. These are indicated on the city maps. In Moscow, a city of seven million people, there are now eight gas stations.

For a country that has much greater natural resources than the United States, and which has a high-level of industrialization, the population hasn't seen a reflection of much wealth. In fact, I think we could conclude that even if you factor in the Russian average salary of 120 rubles per month, the equivalent cost in the U.S. of a small one-room apartment and free medical and dental care, the standard of living for most who are not insider communist members, which is 98% of the Russian population, is quite far below what is considered the level of poverty in the United States.

One reason of this low standard of living is due to the allocation of a large part of the national income to the military and to heavy industry.

Another reason is the extreme inefficiency and wasted manpower of the Soviet system. There is also an extremely slow work pace that has resulted from the lack of personal incentives. From what we could see in our brief stay in Russia, the people work at about one-half to one-third of the speed we do in the West. This is particularly noticeable in both the construction and the services areas.

In stores, there is no effort to serve the customers or to complete a sale. In the department stores we visited, you would often see two salesgirls at one end of a counter talking, and a patient line of customers waiting at the other end of the counter. When one salesperson finally did come to serve someone, it seemed to be as a great favor to the waiting customer. Even in the shops limited to foreigners who pay in dollars, where it is the interest of the Russian government to sell as much as possible, this desire certainly isn't reflected in the attitudes of the sales personnel.

When one of our groups wanted to buy a Balalaika, he had to beg the clerk to look in the stock room to see if there might be another one, as I had just bought the last one on display. The salesclerk happened to find seven more in the stock room and this fellow got one. When another customer came in and wanted a Balalaika, the salesgirl said "nyet". When we explained that we knew there were at least six instruments still in the stock room, the salesgirl finally took the trouble to get another one and the purchase was made.

In addition to the general listless attitude of sales personnel, the byzantine bureaucracy in the Russian retailing area must also share the blame for inefficiency. The salesclerk does not handle any money. After she has helped you pick out what you want, she adds up the various items on her abacus, and then writes out a sales slip in triplicate, even if it is for only a 25-cent purchase. She keeps one slip, and you take the other two to the cash cage where you wait in line. The girl at the cash cage then rechecks the addition on her abacus, accepts your money, keeps one slip, and returns the other two to you marked "paid".

It all happens quite slowly as there is usually a long line at the cash cage. Several times our wait at the cash line was over 20 minutes. When you get back to the girl that helped you initially, she is usually busy with other customers so you must wait in line again to pick up your purchases. Therefore, to buy something you usually have to wait in three lines, one after another.

Adding to the time required to purchase something is the whimsical and arbitrary closing of the cash cages. Every now and then, one of the girls at the cash cage would decide to close and start counting her money. This would naturally cause the lines to double up at the remaining cages. The criteria for a girl closing her cage, was never very clear and I never noticed a manager of the store present to regulate these whims in proportion to the volume of business.

We ran into another example of a lack of desire to make a sale at the Black Sea resort of Sochi. We wanted to take out a small rowboat which can be rented on the beach. At one end of the beach there was the cash cage where you pay your money and a slip in triplicated is filled out. Then, you walk to the other end of the beach to the boat dock with two of the original three slips. There were three young men in swimming suits in charge of the boats. I handed my slip of paper to the boat operator who was sunning himself in a deck chair, and he told me to come back in ten minutes. When I came back ten minutes later, he said to come back in half an hour. Seeing about ten boats in the boat building, I asked why I must wait another half an hour. The man indicated that I must wait until one of the four boats already out in the water returned.

My protesting was of no avail. While it is possible that all ten of the boats in the shed may have been broken, I'm sure the only reason for the delay was that he didn't want to take the trouble to get up out of his comfortable deck chair even though it would take a mere two minutes to pull a boat out of the building. When I told him I couldn't wait for another boat to come in and wanted my money back, he said fine, just go back to the woman at the other end of the beach where I had paid. She gave me my money back without any argument and without any concern that the state enterprise was losing a sale. Neither of them really cared whether the income from the rental of the boats paid their salary and maybe a little more to take care of the repair of the boats and a portion of the sale to pay for overhead and profit.

The Russian taxi drivers also have an indifferent attitude towards obtaining business. We have never come up against such a selective group of taxi drivers in all our travels. If they don't like the looks of you, they won't stop. If they stop but don't like where you are going, they won't take you. And this attitude isn't directed just at the foreigners who can be identified easily by their clothes and shoes. The taxi drivers also take this attitude with the Russians, and it is not limited only to the Moscow drivers as we found the same attitudes also in Leningrad and Kiev.

To get a better idea of the taxi system, I stood in a line of people waiting at a taxi stop in Kiev for about an hour. When a taxi arrived, it seemed that the driver would not ask the first person in line where he wanted to go but told him where he was going with his cab. If the person happened to be going in the same direction, fine. However, if the first person wasn't going where the cab was going, the driver would announce his area and people from the line would run up to get in. The person at the head of the line had to wait for the 4th taxi in a time span of about 20 minutes, until he found one going to his section of town.

While all of this was going on, I noticed two other cabs parked a short distance away with their on-duty lights off. Apparently, they had already made their quota and there was no reason to continue serving the public even if there was a line of 30 people waiting for cabs. I'm sure the apparent shortage of cabs is due to the fact that there is no connection between the number of fares a cabby can handle in a day and his salary. If they were put on incentive, I imagine their output would increase by at least 100%.

The slow work pace of the Russian construction worker must be seen to be appreciated. There were numerous construction projects underway in Moscow when we were there and at each one, we saw the construction workers either moving as if they were drugged or just plain loafing. In more cases only one person was working, that person was working at half speed. The other three persons were just sitting. In addition to being surprised by the Russian work pace, Russian quality is not very good. This is particularly noticeable in the finishing work on construction projects. In some sections of Moscow, nets are hung over the sidewalk at the second-floor level to protect pedestrians from crumbling masonry of new buildings.

Mechanical things don't inspire much confidence either. In a central Moscow subway station near our hotel there were 20 coin changing machines and not one was working. Instead, a long line was waiting at a cash cage to obtain change for the automatic toll gates. At our hotel in Kiev, the shoeshine machines didn't work, and we heard they hadn't worked for months. Elevators break down frequently and the taxis don't look too dependable.

One of our Russian acquaintances, while defending vigorously the Communist system, did admit to us in private that the effect of not having a free market did contribute to the low quality of Russian consumer goods in comparison to Western products. However, he added that the principal reason for the admittedly low quality of Russian manufactured good is due to the emphasis at the factories on quantity to satisfy the large and growing internal demand rather than on the quality of the products. While this is certainly a factor, I'm convinced the main problem is again one of incentive. The individual doesn't have much incentive, be it carrot or stick for producing either quantity or quality of merchandise.

While 50 years of Communism has not produced a good standard of living, what is even more striking to the tourist is the lack of freedom of the people and their fear of the police. On the way back from a performance of a ballet one evening, we found ourselves walking beside a lovely girl of about 18. She looked like a student, and we spoke with her in English. She was studying English and enjoyed talking as we walked along. We asked her if she would like to join us for a drink. She said fine, but as we approached our hotel and she realized that the outside bar was closed, and she said she would not come to the bar inside the hotel, and she politely declined. When we asked her why not, it would only be for 30 minutes, she replied with an expression which showed both disappointment and fear and said, "I cannot, because of our police."

One of our Russian acquaintances, whom we saw several times, didn't want to come to dinner with us at the hotel a second time because it might look odd. When we asked if we might send him books and magazines from the West his reply at first was that they could receive all with no troubles. But later, when he realized we were serious about sending something, he indicated that we should be very careful about what we send. Curiously enough, he defended the tight censorship in Russia on the grounds that the people believe what they read and if they get several conflicting views, they will become confused. What he didn't say, but what was implicit in his reply, was that there was the danger that if Russians were aware of both the freedom and standard of living of the West, their status quo would be in danger.

The awareness that he who questions the status quo gets sent to prison or to an insane asylum, is so much a part of the Russian personality that virtually all but a handful of intellectuals go about their daily business with blinders on. Those that do protest can get away with it only if they are innocuous and not considered to be challenging the political system. We heard of a protest movement by a group of intellectuals from an American newsman in Moscow who had been at the protest demonstration. The intellectuals were requesting that the Russian Government observe its constitution. The 30 troublemakers paraded in front of Pushkin's statue and the extent of their protest was tipping their caps to Pushkin as they passed. Apparently, this has an historical significance. Security forces both uniformed and in plain clothes and members of the foreign press outnumbered the protestors four to one. As soon as the protestors had doffed their hats, one of the agents announced that the road must be cleared for traffic and the demonstration was over.

Although we could walk about freely in the cities we visited, we did have a feeling of the omnipresence of the secret police. While the thought of anyone bothering to listen to what we had to say in our rooms seemed ridiculous, we weren't entirely convinced that our room was not bugged. For one thing, the radio in the wall in our room could just be turned down so you couldn't hear the volume, but it could not be turned off. One day Lydia complained that there was no mirror in the room. When we returned that afternoon a panel of the desk was raised, and it contained a mirror. Another couple had a similar experience. They complained that the towels had not been changed. Ten minutes later, there came a knock on the door, "Here are your clean towels." On the other hand, if there is someone or a group of persons listening in at random to personal conversations in hotel rooms, they must get a terrible earful of drivel. On some of our museum tours an extra person seemed to be tagging along. When the same one appeared at two different museums, on two different days, our suspicions of being tailed may not have been unfounded.

I was curious to see whether I could identify any of the secret police loitering in public places. A most obvious place to look was in Red Square. One afternoon I went to Lenin's tomb in Red Square where a large crowd gathers to watch the changing of the guard. I began looking around to see if I could identify people that were either trying to blend in with the crowd or who seemed to be watching other people.

After about 10 minutes I had picked out five likely looking suspects. Now came the changing of the honor guard. As the crowd began to disperse, four of my suspects didn't leave, and consequently they became more suspect. With the crowd much sparser an additional five candidates became obvious. At this point, the man whom I labeled as the squad leader of the Red Square section of the KVB gave himself away. He made a motion with his hand and two of the suspects I had identified approached him. He spoke to both, and they moved off in different directions. One of them spoke to another of my KGB identified agents and the other spoke to a man who I hadn't yet identified but who I added to my list. Then, the chief walked away from Lenin's tomb. I watched him. When he got to the edge of the square, he stopped and leaned against a tree and looked back at the square. He then moved to his left and walked slowly under a row of trees. After about 100 yards, he stopped to talk to another person; this fellow I would never have identified as an agent. He was standing by a tree looking back at the square and had with him on the ground a suitcase and package and looked like he was waiting for a bus or cab. It then occurred to me that no buses or cabs go by the place where he was standing. It was just part of his disguise. After this stop, the chief completed his cycle and came back to where he started, put his hands behind his back and looked at Lenin's tomb like the other tourists.

When the next changing of the guard came the following hour, and the same ten people whom I had identified as agents were still there, it confirmed my suspicions that they hadn't come to watch the changing of the guard but were there to watch the people watching the changing of the guard. Another suspect I had under observation was standing at the edge of the square away from most of the crowd. He had a camera around his neck. He also had Russian clothes. After having him under observation for two hours and noting that during that time he neither took any pictures nor did he move from his position, I felt there was an 80% possibility that he was also a member of the secret police, trying to look like a tourist.

When two or three people in the crowds would start to talk to each other, one of my suspects would approach casually and stand with his back to the group. Although he was looking in the other direction, you could tell his ear was tuned in. A tall blond agent gave himself away with his obvious furtive eyes. While his face was immobile, his eyes were going from left to right, watching. He seemed to be particularly interested to observe people who had packages. While the changing of the guard at Lenin's tomb takes place every hour the changing of the KGB takes place at 7:00 pm. The chief of the second shift arrived about 6:55, and after a short conversation with the chief of the first shift, which probably included a word to keep an eye on that American disguised in the Italian suit, the first chief left.

As our hotel was only a five-minute walk from the square, I enjoyed playing this game several times. One evening I tailed another KGB agent. He stopped about every 50 yards to look around. Once he stopped and waited in a line at a taxicab stand. Apparently, the conversation he overheard was not too interesting, because, after ten minutes, he left the line and proceeded to our hotel. On his way, he followed two people for about a block, then into the lobby where he looked like he was waiting for someone. Then he waited between the elevators for about ten minutes. Finally, he got into an elevator, and I lost him, or maybe I should say at this point he finally shook me. I don't think he was aware of being tailed.

One day I took Lydia to Red Square to play this game. At first, as I pointed out three agents, she was amused. But when she realized that six agents I had identified for her were between us and the entrance to the Lenin tomb and that some were in a semi-circle back of us she began to get uneasy. When one started to move towards us, she took my arm and said, "Let's get out of here, we are surrounded!" We left and went back to the entrance to our hotel.

While security at Red Square seems to be well organized, the Intourist agency is not. Despite the claim that Russia is a planned society, Intourist seemed to be making plans for our group only one day ahead, and most of those plans didn't work out as planned. At each mix-up, our guides, two very nice young women, were put in the position of either blaming the Intourist Company – where the blame belongs – or they had to think up fantastic stories to save face of their Intourist organization.

One evening we were supposed to go to the ballet. When our group got there, it was discovered that the Intourist head office had arranged for transportation from our hotel to the opera house and had made seat reservations at the theatre for the next day. Returning to Moscow from the Black Sea resort of Sochi there were no buses to meet us at the airport. Since we had to wait an hour and a half for the bus, it was obvious that someone at headquarters had forgotten to give orders for the bus to come to pick us up. When we got to our hotel at 2:30 in the afternoon, there were no reservations for us for lunch. The attractive and hardworking Intourist guide was almost in tears of embarrassment. At this point she announced, "Someone will be punished for this." After an hour, she did manage to get us in to a special dining room for a late lunch.

The next morning, we were supposed to go for a tour of the city and were told to be ready in the lobby by 10 am. No buses. When the buses finally arrived, we discovered that they had been sent to a different hotel. We were also told that Intourist had made reservations for us for lunch the day before, but at a different hotel from the one where we were staying, but the notice of that change was not conveyed to us, and no one had informed our guides of this change. And the next morning the buses for our tour had been sent to the hotel where they had reserved lunch for us the day before.

Buck passing in the Soviet Union and the desire to avoid responsibility must be enormous. One of our friends in the group who spoke fluent

Russian wanted to eat something other than our dull hotel food and tried to book at a restaurant several days ahead. The manager of that day said he couldn't book us places for the next day because he wasn't on duty on the next day. Calling the next day and speaking to the manager on duty, he said he couldn't take reservations for that evening because he didn't know what reservations had already been made by the other manager for that night.

After three weeks in Russia, you begin to become dulled to the fact that the system doesn't work very well. If you try to fight it, you will just get frustrated and can do very little to improve the service. You begin to accept disorganization as the normal as the citizens Russians have done. Although the trip was more an educational experience than a vacation, we are anxious to return to Russia, sometime in the future, maybe the distant future, to see what changes there will be when the present political group will have been replaced with a new group. Apparently, the changes in the last ten years have been substantial, particularly in the growth of consumer goods. Perhaps the next ten will bring with it a bit more freedom.

One thing that will accelerate profound changes will be the increase of car ownership. The car will make people more mobile and take them away from surveillance. It will stimulate their desire to enjoy the fruits of a consumer society and will cause considerable strain to the present social fabric. I predict that there will be growing corruption in Russia and more and more public resources will be diverted into private pockets.

The leaders will then be faced with the alternatives of heavier and more repressive punishments for economic crimes, or the more dangerous solution of modification of the economic system. If the second alternative is followed, China will have even more justification for criticizing Russia for betrayal of the real philosophy of Communism and this could accentuate the struggle between the two. Apart from the external problems, there are enormous internal problems connected with modification of the economic system.

In order to increase the availability of consumer goods, the people will have to increase their work pace, and this will require additional incentives. Apparently, the hope of receiving a Stakhonovich medal hasn't worked very well. Managers must be given more autonomy allowing them to use their intelligence to determine the best use of resources and base production of goods on anticipation of market desires and needs. For that to work one would have to have a free market, which will encourage questioning, creativity, and a pragmatic action rather than a party line approach to problems. At present, the system discourages creativity and questioning. How to encourage these attitudes in the economic area, but at the same time discourage them in the political area is a big problem.

Perhaps the most striking experience of the whole trip was stepping off the Aeroflot jet in Amsterdam. It was like moving into an entirely different world, with an environment of friendly service, the ability to buy all kinds of newspapers, even Communist ones, and stores with a great variety of merchandise of good quality served by smiling clerks who were helpful and efficient. It was a breath of fresh air meeting the West again. We felt like shouting Hallelujah!

ELEVEN

1971: Gary's first day of school, Sicilian Fish Soup, and doing business in communist countries

Gary will be five on Christmas day and Valeria is two. I told Gary that now that he was five years old, he is old enough to receive a weekly allowance which he can spend anyway he wants to, excluding candy. I explained that with his growing knowledge of math it is a good idea to understand where his money is going. I gave him a piggy bank, a budget book and showed him how to keep track of income, subtract spending, and to arrive at his net worth at the end of each week. I told him if he writes down his income and spending each week and balances that with a count of his actual cash in his piggy bank, he will develop a good control over his income and spending and know where his money is going.

Gary likes math and he understood the concept of reconciliation. He was enthusiastic about keeping track of his money and enjoyed the discipline of the weekly tally. He thought this was a great idea and he looks forward every week to bringing me his budget book and piggy bank to show me that his accounts are balanced and ready for the weekly addition to his income.

Valeria was nearly three at that time and anxious to keep up with her older brother. She asked when she could start with a budget book, an allowance, and a piggy bank. She was also good at math and liked the idea of managing her money as well Gary. Valeria's vocabulary is expanding rapidly. She has just discovered the flavor of "big lemons" (grapefruit) and is becoming interested in stories and songs. She is now at an age where she can play with her older brother. She follows Gary around and tries to do what he does. This is convenient for Gary who often needs an actress for a play or a following for a parade. Valeria and our big German shepherd, Sultan, gives Gary the needed mass for his productions.

After having seen the opera Aida this summer, recreating the opera was the great game for many weeks for both of them. Gary takes the part of Radames, and Valeria is, naturally, Aida. He has even taught her a few lines and when prompted she comes out with them. Sultan, the German shepherd dog, played the part of the lion. Although I don't remember a lion in the original version of Aida, the kids' version of the opera produced good theater.

Gary has developed a great interest in grand opera, and I'm sure with her early experience as Aida, Valeria will follow suit. We took Gary to see his first opera last spring, a matinee performance of the Barber of Seville at La Scala. He was fascinated by it. He sat on my lap for the entire performance and was very absorbed by it. The only minor incident was when he said in a loud voice during a soft part of the overture, "When are they going to take away that tent so we can see the singers?" This summer we took him to a performance of Aida at the Arena of Verona. We had planned to stay only through the second act which includes the triumphal march, but Gary didn't want to leave at the end of the second act. We tried again to leave at the end of the third act as it was already midnight by then. But again, he wanted to wait until the very end. By the end of the 4th act, Lydia and I were beginning to droop, but Gary was still all attention and wide awake.

1971: GARY'S FIRST DAY OF SCHOOL, SICILIAN FISH SOUP, AND DOING BUSINESS IN COMMUNIST COUNTRIES

After having had a first year in the Italian nursery school, we started Gary in Kindergarten at the American school this fall. The jump into the unknown was a bit frightening the first day, but things are going fine now, and he enjoys it. Part of his enthusiasm for school is due to the fact that he is the first one to be picked up by the bus in the morning. Not only does he have the whole bus to himself (for the first 5 minutes) but also, he gets the seat right behind the driver, who is his good friend and with whom Gary speaks in Italian. Many of the young students at the American School of Milan only speak English.

Lydia and I took Gary to school the first day. We arrived early to acquaint him with the school before classes start. First, we walked out to the playground to examine the swings, parallel bar,s and sand box and he was reasonably impressed. Then we walked into his classroom and examined the various materials. He liked the blocks, the books, the puzzles, and the piano. By the end of the inspection, he seemed pleased and reasonably full of confidence to meet the new experience. There were also several children there with their parents and they seemed to be calm and reasonably pleased anticipating the first day of school. Then came a crisis. A little girl didn't want to be left by her mother and was crying desperately. Gary's expression while still positive became a bit puzzled,

"Does that little girl know something about this school that I don't know? Does she have reason to cry?"

But he held firm and gave only slight evidence of an erosion of his brave front.

Then came a little boy dragged into the room by his older brother. The cry of the little girl was now doubled by the wail of the new boy and a very unsettling duet was produced. Gary's expression darkened by several degrees, and he said "Does that little boy know something about what this teacher does to the children?"

As we left the room, we could see that Gary was becoming less and less convinced that this school was the proper place for him and given the slightest excuse would have gladly left. As we shut the door, and still heard no cry from him, we felt he had overcome the first hurdle. But once outside I realized I had forgotten to leave with him the bag with bib and towel. Without thinking of the consequences, I went back into his room to bring these to him. As I opened the door, I saw him sitting on a chair with moist eyes, his mouth wrinkled, using all of his self-control to keep the tears from coming.

My reentry was the straw floating by and as he saw me, he screamed "Daddy". The dam of tears broke, and he came running over to escape the dark unknown school and wrapped his arms round my legs. We managed to extricate ourselves, left and he made it through the first day. Now he is well in the swing of things and looks forward to school and the bus ride every morning. However, the other day he told us it wasn't really necessary that he goes to school.

"We learned London Bridge today, but I already knew it." We asked what else they do at school. The teacher says, "line up children." "Then what?" I asked. "Then we all go and do peepee"

Both children help us to take care of our garden at Brunate, the small village 3,000 feet above Lake Como. We purchased an old two-apartment house with Lydia's father, and we spend weekends and most of the summer there. It is only an hour-drive from our apartment in Milan, and also an hour drive from the factory where I work so the commuting is not bad. The climate in Brunate is excellent. We are at an altitude above both the fog of Milan in the winter and the Milan heat and humidity during the summer. The air is clear, and the sky is vast and blue.

1971: GARY'S FIRST DAY OF SCHOOL, SICILIAN FISH SOUP, AND DOING BUSINESS IN COMMUNIST COUNTRIES

David, Valeria, Gary and Sultan on porch of summer home above Como

Both children have wicker baskets which they carry on their backs to help us take weeds and leaves to our compost pile at the bottom of our property. Valeria helps me pick tomatoes and is very enthusiastic about picking wild raspberries, which grow on our land. We had a good harvest from our garden this year. The new peach tree increased its production 20-fold, from one peach last year to twenty peaches this year. The apricot tree surpassed all expectations and gave us 80 juicy apricots. We also had 6 handfuls of raspberries, 20 cherries, and 8 strawberries. The fig, persimmon, and pear trees have yet to provide us with their fruit. With this prolific beginning, we expect having a bumper crop next year. The flower side of the garden, under Lydia's able and intensive care, produced a great variety of color. She is slowly making her way down the 30-degree slope of our land, taming the jungle in the lower part of the garden.

To expand our horizons, we decided to see something of the south of Italy during our vacation. Our trip this year was to the Aeolian

Islands, a group of seven islands of volcanic origin, situated about 30 miles north of Sicily, just above the strait of Messina. My mother came from Chicago to take care of our children while we took our vacation. These islands are the site of much ancient Greek and Roman mythology, due undoubtedly to the extensive volcanic activity and the unusual geologic formations. The main island of this group, Lipari, had monopoly in the Mediterranean of several natural resources much sought after in the Pre-Christian Era: pumice, alum, and volcanic glass. The volcanic glass was used for tools and weapons until iron became widespread, and pumice is still being mined, serving as a base for talcum and face powder.

First traces of human habitation on these islands date back to around 4,000 B. C., and the Aeolians were active trading partners with the Phoenicians, Egyptians, and Greeks. Volcanic glass of Lipari has been found at Alexandria and at Knossos, and in recent excavations at Lipari both Egyptian and Phoenician pottery have been uncovered. These islands have a long tradition of hospitality towards visitors. Around 1,100 B. C. refugees from Troy found their way to Lipari and were welcomed by and mixed into the local population. Hannibal, who came from North Africa was warmly received in Italy around 250 B. C. He used Lipari as his headquarters before making his famous attack on Rome by way of Spain, southern France and across the Alps with his elephants, to defeat the Roman army in central Italy.

Along with many friendly visitors these islands have had, from time to time, unfriendly visitors. Once in 1,250 B. C., and again in 850 B. C., the town was completely burned to the ground by invaders and there are no historical references as to who the invaders and destroyers of the island were. The islands have had long periods of peace and prosperity ersed with periods of sieges and invasions. Between 2,000
 e time of the Carthaginian invasions of Italy, the center of
 vn was transferred back and forth many times between
 venient but indefensible lower harbor region and the

1971: GARY'S FIRST DAY OF SCHOOL, SICILIAN FISH SOUP, AND DOING BUSINESS IN COMMUNIST COUNTRIES

virtually impregnable higher acropolis on a cliff overlooking the town and sea.

While lacking historical reference to many of the invaders, there is ample literary reference to two famous gods who lived on the island. One of these was Aeolus, God of the wind, who was the one who taught men how to use sails for propulsion of their boats. The other was Vulcan, God of the forge. There is also much written about another famous character who has spent some time on these islands. Ulysses stopped at Lipari during his travels and was given a very unusual and useful present by the King of the Islands. The present was a bottle in which the four winds were kept. If used properly, a sailor could uncork the bottle and call out the wind he wanted to hurry him along this next port of call. Apparently, Ulysses wasn't listening very attentively when King Aeolus was giving him instructions on how to use the bottle. In his carelessness, thanks perhaps to another bottle to which he may have been giving more attention, Ulysses let all four winds out of the bottle at the same time, In the dreadful fight that followed, a tremendous storm resulted. Ulysses and his crew barely escaped with their lives.

Visitors to the nearby island of Volcano must also be prepared for certain risks. The god Vulcan lived at the top of the main crater of the island where he had his forge and, when angry, caused violent volcanic eruptions. During the time of Augustus Caesar, Vulcan must have been particularly angry as eruptions were more frequent and violent than they had ever been, and many of the small villages on the shore were wiped out many times. Augustus Caesar decided to send a senatorial mission to the islands to placate the angry god. After the Roman senatorial mission left, Vulcan did not get angry again for 700 years, and then caused an eruption of only minor intensity. He hasn't been angry since that time. Unfortunately, it is not recorded what sacrifices and rituals were followed by the Roman delegation, but whatever they did, it worked.

Just a few months ago Filicudi, another of the Aeolian Islands, was brought to public attention. This is where the Italian police transferred from Palermo fifteen presumed Mafiosi for temporary detention, in the interest of public safety. The episodes that followed the transfer of these fifteen men make fine material for a comic opera.

To guard the 15 Mafiosi and to monitor the single telephone, about 50 Carabinieri were sent to Filicudi. When the residents of the Island began protesting against the presence of the Mafia members who had been transferred, claiming it was hurting their tourist trade, another 150 Carabinieri were sent as reinforcements along with several armored cars. To make the protest more dramatic, the occupants of the island all left with their belongings, not quite filling one of the hydrofoil boats plying between the islands, vowing not to return until the Mafia had gone. These unwelcome guests were finally transferred to another island, much to the disappointment of the children of Filicudi. Many more tourists came to Filicudi to get a good look at the leaders of the underworld.

While righteously contrary to the presence of the outlaws, the Aeolian islanders shouldn't speak too loudly because their ancestors, the famous pirates of Lipari, preyed on merchant ships from Roman times up until as recently as the 17th century. The Lipari pirates got their start in the piracy business after a heroic battle in which they defeated a much larger group of pirates. About 650 B.C. a fleet of Etruscan pirates were sighted off the coast and five ships from Lipari went out to meet this superior force and engaged them in battle before they had a chance to land. Interested as much in honor as in prey, the captain of the Etruscan band didn't think it fair to attack the Lipari ships with all 30 of his ships, and only sent five of his ships against the Liparese, who were superior sailors. The Liparese defeated and captured these five Etruscan ships.

A second group of five Etruscan ships were then sent against the Liparese, and again the Etruscan pirate ships were defeated. A third

1971: GARY'S FIRST DAY OF SCHOOL, SICILIAN FISH SOUP, AND DOING BUSINESS IN COMMUNIST COUNTRIES

time another group of five ships were sent against the tiring but courageous defenders, and for a third time the Etruscan pirates were beaten, and their ships captured again. Up to this point the Liparese hadn't lost a single ship. Even though the Etruscans had only 15 ships left, the pirate captain still let his sense of chivalry take precedence over his desire for revenge or bounty, and instead of going after the tired Liparese with his remaining fleet, he sent still another group of five ships against them. Again, the Etruscan pirate ships were captured. At this point, the Etruscan pirates gave up and sailed away while the exhausted, but victorious Liparese returned to a hero's welcome with their 20 captured pirate ships.

Not only did this battle give these islanders a full awareness of their superior mariner skills, but also some new capital in the form of these 20 ships with which they could initiate a new venture, more lucrative than fishing. From that time on, they began extracting tribute, referred to it as a protection fee for keeping the area free of pirates, from the ships passing the Strait of Messina and plying the Calabrian coast. There is some dispute among ancient historians regarding the exact status of the Liparian pirates. Some refer to their action as that of cleaning the lower Tyrrhenian Sea of pirates, while others claim that in ridding their sea of the Etruscan pirates, the Liparese pirates merely replaced them.

While Ulysses and Hannibal were famous visitors who slept at Lipari during ancient times, Ingrid Bergman joins the Mafia in bringing attention to the Aeolian Islands in the 20th century. She made a film with Roberto Rossellini named Stromboli, in 1947. Lydia and I took a trip to Stromboli, the only island of the group that still has an active volcano and climbed up to the top of the crater to have a look.

Three times a week there is a ship that travels the 30 miles from Lipari to Stromboli, and as you approach the island, it looks like a near perfect cone rising 3,000 feet out of the water. The island has two small towns, one with the name of Ginostra along with the town of

Stromboli. Neither town has a dock. The ships anchor offshore, and row boats come out to ferry the passengers and freight ashore. During much of the winter and, occasionally in the summer, the island remains isolated, as the row boats are unable to do the loading and unloading in rough seas.

As we disembarked, we were met by Salvatore, our guide for the trip to the top of the volcano, with his dog, Max. We started the climb at 6:30 p.m. and were at the top by 9:00. For about half of the climb the trail cuts back and forth through terraced land that until recently was intensively cultivated with figs, olives, and grapes. It is a bit sad to hear the story of the recent depopulation of the island. In 1920 Stromboli had 6,000 people. Now there are less than 600 people. The rest have left the rather difficult fishing and farming life on the side of the live volcano to find their fortune elsewhere. Recently, however, there has been an influx of former residents who are returning to Stromboli for their retirement.

For anyone wanting to work the land, this is a nice place. There is plenty of fertile acreage available at a low cost, however, to reach the farmable land one has to hike up 1,000 feet up from the sea. Between 1,000 feet and 2,000 feet above the sea the land is very fertile. Between 2,000 and 3,000 feet above the sea the path goes through an area of rock and warm sand. A mere 6 inches below the top of the warm sand it is so hot fingers can burn if put into the sand.

We passed the active crater on our right at an altitude of about 2,200 feet and continued up to the peak, which is over 3,000 feet. It was dark when we arrived and looking down at the crater, we saw two red holes. From each of these holes, a shower of red-hot ashes and stones were thrown up about 100 feet every five minutes. Prior to the eruption you could hear the buildup of pressure which it sounded like a combination of the clank of an iron foundry and a puffing steam locomotive.

1971: GARY'S FIRST DAY OF SCHOOL, SICILIAN FISH SOUP, AND DOING BUSINESS IN COMMUNIST COUNTRIES

Occasionally, there would be a shower of flaming red rocks and cinders thrown high up into the air. Lydia and I were sitting 800 feet above the opening, we had to look up to see the top of the trajectory of the red-hot rocks, sometimes reaching height of 1,000 feet above us. These high shots of volcanic material were accompanied by a rushing hissing sound. We stayed on our seat for about two hours. During this time, we became enveloped in a fog which held acrid fumes and made breathing uncomfortable. The wind pushed the fog aside from time to time giving us a new view of the eruptions.

We were amazed when the guide informed us that his dog was 20 years old, the equivalent of a man of about 140 years. The guide told us he wouldn't feel comfortable going up without his dog, as the dog seems to be able to sense unusual activity and danger from the crater well in advance of a human being. He told us of a trip he took with a group of Germans several weeks earlier. That particular night a black smoke was emerging from the potholes between eruptions and, in addition, the noise coming out of the crater was more clanking than usual. As his dog was showing signs of uneasiness, he told the Germans that it was getting dangerous, and they had better descend because an explosion was building up. They refused and indicated they wanted to stay until dawn. Ten minutes later the dog began to get very agitated. He even started whimpering.

At this point our guide said he told the Germans that they must go down now because it was getting more dangerous. The Germans replied they didn't want a frightened and superstitious Italian with his silly dog spoiling their vacation. The guide finally managed to convince them to descend. As they got up to leave and start down, the noise emerging from the crater was growing, accompanied by increasing whining of his dog. One hour after they reached the town, there was an enormous explosion and eruption which threw rocks the size of tables four kilometers from the crater. A few of these piano sized rocks struck a few of the houses in the town of Stromboli. The observation point where they had been sitting earlier had become unrecognizable and was now covered by new rocks and hot ashes. Our guide told us this group of German tourists packed their bags and were waiting on the dock to get off the island as quickly as they could.

Our guide told us of another near disaster. He had a small group of French students who, while watching the eruptions, saw a particularly large flaming rock the size of a chair flying in their direction. He pushed one of the girls out of the path of that flying rock. The force of the impact, 30 feet away, threw them both to the ground. The bed sized rock we were sitting on was that rock.

The trip down was more difficult than the trip up. We went a different way, primarily because it was safer with a ridge stood between us and the crater. The first half of the descent was on a black sand and the angle seemed like we were sliding down a 70-degree slope, although it was probably about a 45-degree slope. We took long sliding steps and covered lots of ground with each step. Then we came upon a zigzag path on top of uneven rocks and finally dropped into a jungle of cane stalks and brambles about 12 feet high. The dog knew the way and we followed him in almost pitch darkness. After much winding through this thicket, we finally came out just above the town. The next morning, after a swim from the black sand beach, we were rowed back to the big steamer anchored 100 yards offshore and said goodbye to our exciting visit in Stromboli.

Lipari, the main island of the group, is supported by fishing. There is a large fleet of small fishing boats that move out of the harbor at dusk and return in the early morning with sword fish, bonita, orate, tuna, and other varieties. We were told that a few of the fishermen in the last few years have discovered that fishing for and with tourists in their boat during the summer season, produces a higher income than just fishing to sell the fish to the town fish market.

1971: GARY'S FIRST DAY OF SCHOOL, SICILIAN FISH SOUP, AND DOING BUSINESS IN COMMUNIST COUNTRIES

There was a fishing boat that came to our hotel every morning around 9:30 in the morning to pick up passengers for a daytrip to one of the other seven islands in this group. It looked like a long tugboat with the cockpit in the back and could take about 30 passengers, who were sprawled in various positions on the deck and on top of the cockpit taking the sun. The usual program would be to cross the open water between the islands, normally a two hour-trip, and find a cove or small bay where all the passengers could swim and skin dive in the clear water of the nearby island. The water was very clear, and we could see the bottom of the ocean which was 100 feet below us. At about 1:00 in the afternoon we would go to a village on the island where we would have a fine fish luncheon at one of the rustic restaurants.

On one of these trips, we found ourselves a part of a Sicilian melodrama and an incident that could have easily became a tragedy. The problem arose over a bowl of fish soup and a different interpretation between the owner of the restaurant and the guests as to what should be included in the contents of a bowl of fish soup.

The setting for the drama was an open-air restaurant on the island of Panarea, perched on a small cliff above the sea. On this hot July day, we were very comfortable in our bathing suits, in the semi shade of the straw matting roof, and with a slight breeze blowing through the dining room. Adding to the attractiveness of the restaurant were the French and Italian waitresses, lovely girls around 20 years old in brief bikinis.

Offsetting the festive setting was the proprietor's wife who was also the cook, a rather stringy looking woman of about 50, who seemed upset to see 30 people of dubious pedigree coming into her restaurant. Although it was a public place, she apparently preferred to select her clientele, and asked several of the guests in which hotels they were staying. The implication was that certain luxury hotels put them in the "in" group while those staying in the more modest hotels and pensions put them in the "out" or socially unacceptable group.

We sat at the table with our two fishermen guides and waited for the meal. On the menu was "zuppa di pesce" (fish soup) which in Sicily is a meal by itself, with large pieces of fish floating in a rich tomato and seafood sauce. Many of our group ordered it. When it came, it was a small bowl of broth with no resemblance to the hearty Sicilian dish we had expected. One of the guests remonstrated that this wasn't what he ordered, but the proprietor insisted that that was "zuppa di pesce." Our boatman feeling responsible for the welfare of his clients went into the kitchen and told the cook that this was not "zuppa di pesce". Also, she should have put larger pieces of fish into the soup.

This suggestion was not welcomed by the mistress of the restaurant. She said this was a French style "zuppa di pesce" and besides, she had spent two days cooking it. When the boatman tried to also correct her Italian as well as her cooking by telling her this was a "passato" (or strained soup) and she told him to get out of her kitchen. After a few more words with the client, the proprietor, a rather large muscular fellow, proposed a Sicilian way of coping with a customer complaint. "If you don't like my wife's "zuppa di pesce" would you step outside, and we can settle the matter here and now."

Another guest who had also received his bowl of "zuppa di pesce" without large pieces of fish in it and reflecting the growing anger of some of the other guests, sweeping like a wind across a dry brush fire, announced in a loud undiplomatic voice, that besides the misrepresented dish, he didn't want to be served by "several half-naked sluts."

While the first boatman was leaving to go outside, the second boatman got to his feet to accompany the guest to his meeting, and potential fight, with the proprietor outside. As if one strong wind were not enough to fan these flames, the proprietor, like the careless Ulysses, let out other strong winds by casting doubt on the ancestry of the second boat man. This was all that was necessary to remove the last bit of restraint from the growing Sicilian tempers. It appeared we were

1971: GARY'S FIRST DAY OF SCHOOL, SICILIAN FISH SOUP, AND DOING BUSINESS IN COMMUNIST COUNTRIES

going to be present at a knife fight and a scene out of the Sicilian opera, Cavalleria Rusticana. Our boatman raised a chair by its one leg and came forward screaming epitaphs at the proprietor, who was now flanked by two of his waiters. We expected to see knives drawn but one of the guests managed to restrain the offended boatmen.

Over the soaring oaths of the two protagonists, the proprietor held back by two waiters, and the boatman restrained by a few guests, was superimposed the voice of the wife who could be heard in parrot like fashion repeating over and over again "If you don't like my soup - get out. If you don't like my soup - get out," and gesticulating with her big wooden spoon. If Verdi could have been there to catch this moment, he could have produced another quartet as famous as the one in the last act of Rigoletto.

Tempers finally became calmed, and we returned to our meal. Insult was added to injury when the bill came as it was somewhat higher than should have been expected. This then infuriated the member of our party who had been able to restrain the boatman previously. He was also Sicilian, and his temper flew off and several of us including the boatman (who was now calm) had to restrain him. Finally, we all got back on the boat and set sail for the island of Lipari, leaving behind the lovely but turbulent island of Panarea.

Speaking with the boatman on the way back about life on Lipari, he described some of the storms they had in the months of December and January, and the dangers associated with making a livelihood from the sea in that season. He described that his boat would climb up a wave at a 30-degree angle and then go racing down the other side as a surfboard to bury its bow in the bottom of the trough. He called this great fun.

During this stormy weather all members of the crew would have ropes tied to their waists as the waves were sweeping over the boat. He added that winter was the best time to fish, and they would be pulling in many swordfish and tuna while trying to keep their balance amidst bobbing about in the tall waves. Assuming that the calm of the summer waters and the more lucrative summer tourist cargo made for a more pleasant life, I asked him if he didn't prefer the summer season. "No," he replied, "sometimes the tourists vomit in my boat."

Drinking water is a problem on the islands and most of the houses have flat roofs and collect rainwater in large cisterns. Ciccio, our boatman, has an eel swimming around in the cistern of his house to keep it clean. Going further into the particulars of his water purification system, it came out that Ciccio's eel is at least 34 years old. It had been purchased by his father 34 years ago and had been there ever since eating insects and any other thing that might find its way into the cistern. In spite of the quality work of the eel, the cistern must be emptied and cleaned out every three years. Ciccio described the fear he had as a little boy when he had to climb into the cistern to clean it. "Eels do snap", he said, and he had to work fast as his father was busy trying to catch the eel or at least to keep it occupied at the other end of the cistern.

Ciccio was a very versatile fellow. In addition to being a brave fisherman, an even braver tourist pilot, and keeper of a rather old eel, he also plays guitar in the evenings, singing at several of the hotels on Lipari. He told me he also composes songs, one of which he proudly told us had been published. We spent many of our evenings with Ciccio as our guide. One moonlight evening we went out in his boat to try our hand at fishing for Totani, better known as a Sicilian variety of octopus or more accurately, if you count their arms, it should be called a decapus.

Lydia caught 20 decapuses, more than the professional fisherman and I together that evening. However, I claim that it wasn't a valid contest as Lydia, with a scream, turned over the line to one of us every time she got the decapus to the surface. She thought they were horrid creatures and didn't want to touch them. She also had the fear that one of the three-foot arms of the decapus would swing around and grab her by the back of the neck and pull her into the depths of the ocean. At night in the moonlight, they were very spooky. As one of them broke the glassy surface of a calm sea, their arms would be coiling and reaching out to you, which made for a frightening appearance.

They moved by pumping water through their body. As they were pulled out of the water when we had hooked one of them, they would still have a cylinder full of water. This water would squirt in our direction, providing an unwelcome shower. Somehow Lydia managed to avoid the shower, while the fisherman and I got squirted many times as we approached the writhing beast to take it off of the hook. The next day the cook at our hotel fixed us a three-course meal starting with decapus soup, followed by fried decapus arms and a decapus ring salad. It was delicious.

We finished our vacation with a leisurely drive up the Western coast from Reggio Calabria to Naples, where we got back on the Autostrada that passes Rome on our way to Milan. There are still miles of deserted beaches along the lower Italian coast facing Sardinia. We hope these beaches will still be deserted for future vacations to the south of Italy.

In the business area I am now the Director of Finance and Administration of General Telephone of Italy, a manufacturer of telephone equipment with our headquarters in Milan. Our Company has grown rapidly and now has over 5,000 employees in three Italian factories and annual sales of $ 65 million. Along with the rest of Italian industry, our company has been doing an increasing amount of exporting to Eastern European countries. The telephone systems of Eastern European countries are still very backwards.

An interesting and difficult to define element growing out of the increasing trade between Italy and the Eastern bloc, is the effect of this trade on the Italian labor movement, and the impact of the growing Italian economy and its increase of employment compared to the Communist countries of Eastern Europe. The cry of the Italian Unions, half of which are Communist sponsored is. "We want more purchasing power, and freedom and autonomy for the worker." A request rejected by the management of Eastern European communist countries. The response of the elite communist's boss was "keep quiet and your head down and do as you are told."

A recent incident at the Italian rubber company, Pirelli, illustrates the consequences of the exposure of the Eastern European Communist factory employees to the increased trade and contact with the free largely semi-capitalist countries of the Common Market. At the Pirelli plant in Milan, which specializes in manufacturing rubber tires, one of their workers, a skilled Italian factory worker who was also a sincere member of the Italian Communist party, requested a transfer to the new Pirelli plant being built in Romania.

Pirelli was selling a complete tire factory to Romania and the purchase contract included a group of skilled Italian technicians sent to Romania to assist in the construction and installation of machinery as well as a period of training in its use for the unskilled Romanian factory workers. Pirelli management was only too happy to transfer this skilled worker from Milan to the Romanian factory as he was a troublemaker who led strikes in Milan against his factory there. When this Italian communist labor organizer was transferred to work in the Romanian factory, he was amazed to see how the low his pay in Romania was in comparison to what his Romanian salary could purchase. He also was unhappy that working conditions were much worse in Communist Romania than in the modern Italian plant in Milan.

As a skilled labor union organizer, he decided something must be done about this unsatisfactory situation. He took it upon himself to organize the labor in the Romanian factory. Naturally, this attempt was met with a very cold reception by the Romanian power structure. A few not so friendly warnings to stop his counter revolutionary activity were not sufficient to deter this determined Italian Communist. Finally, to protect the labor peace and perhaps to avoid a Polish type of spark, the Romanian Government expelled this Italian communist.

For a sincere Communist, to be a "persona non grata," in a Communist country added insult to injury, and this fellow sent off a fiery letter of protest to the Romanian Communist party. A copy of this letter, along with a comment, "Please don't send any more of those kinds of people to us again, or our commercial relations will be strained", found its way back to the Pirelli management in Milan. Pirelli management felt this was just cause for Pirelli to dismiss him.

At this point the worker complained to the Italian Communist party. An interesting aside is that the Italian Communist party which had been sent a copy of the letter at the time the original was sent off to Romania, kept quiet about the matter and preferred to avoid publicity of this incident. However, two weeks later, with a firing on their hands, there wasn't much choice for the Italian Communist party but to jump into the battle. They took up the cause of the fired worker and also sent a letter of protest to the Romanian Communist party. They asked for a detailed explanation of how and why a letter addressed to them found its way to the management of Pirelli.

To make matters worse, the other two Italian Unions wanted to protest the firing and requested to see a copy of the letter so they would be cognizant of the entire situation. The Italian Communist party refused to make the letter public. The letter must have been a beauty. The position of the Italian Communist party is that a worker does have the right to organize and call a strike. But striking in a communist state is not allowed in countries of the Russian block.

Just before the Pirelli incident, a delegation of Italian Communist Union members paid a visit to the Fiat factory at Togliatti Grad. Their findings apparently were not too rosy either. They found worse examples of exploitation of the workers in Communist East Europe than found in the Capitalistic West. When suggestions were made by the Italian consultants who were helping to set up the car factory in Russia regarding improvement of pay and working conditions of the Russian workers at the new car factory at Togliatti Grad, the Italians were told by the Russians to "mind their own business."

In Sweden, a Russian trading company, exporting equipment to Sweden, and maintaining the Russian equipment, is being brought before the Stockholm court because the Swedish company fired the Union organizers in its shop. The Russian company refused to hire employees who are Union sympathizers. It refused to recognize the right of the Swedish Union to represent the employees, and it did not even pay the earned termination pay for those employees fired, as established in Swedish labor law. This case received much publicity in Italy.

In the Italian arena some breaks in the stranglehold of the left-wing unions upon the passive majority are showing up. In the Ancona region, a group of workers from one factory, exasperated by the long strikes they were called upon to carry out, marched through the streets with placards saying, "Down with the dictatorial power of the unions." The unions bought a suit for libel against the demonstrators. The suit was quickly withdrawn, both because of pressure from their own central union headquarters, and also because the initial group of workers accused of libel, were made heroes by hundreds of other workers who joined in to support them. At another company in the same region, the workers went on strike. As a condition to return to work, the workers requested that the company fire the union representatives whom they felt were acting against the best interests of the workers and only in their own personal interest.

1971: GARY'S FIRST DAY OF SCHOOL, SICILIAN FISH SOUP, AND DOING BUSINESS IN COMMUNIST COUNTRIES

It would be very beneficial for the Italian economy and its labor movement if the unions would give attention to some of these problems and start to move towards a more moderate and responsible labor stance. On the other hand, if the unions lose their influence on the workers and become weak, industry is left with no counterpart, or a much-splintered counterpart with whom to negotiate.

In the semiprofessional area, I have become a Director of the American Chamber of Commerce in Italy and have recently been named as the treasurer of that organization. The man I replaced held that job for 54 years. While I am pleased to volunteer my unpaid services for a good cause, I hope the job is not that thankless that I will have to match his envious 54-year record. I would like to turn the job over to someone else before I reach the age of 96.

I have also been active this year in the formation of a middle management business school in Italy, known as ISTUD. It is patterned after the Harvard Business School, Stanford, and MIT and receives support from professors at these schools. The response of the students has been enthusiastic, and the school fills a need in the Italian industrial environment. While Italy has moved very rapidly into the post-war period with the growth of a professional managerial cadre, the family-owned business with relatives in management positions is still the norm. Most of the current Italian industry is still being run as a family affair by a small group of enlightened and sometimes not so enlightened "padrone." There is still a substantial degree of nepotism draining away the vigor created by the earlier captains of Italian industry, who have famous last names like Agnelli, Marconi, Olivetti, and Pirelli. The lack of professionalism in the management of many of these companies is certainly one of the factors contributing to the labor problems of the past five years. Perhaps the new the school, ISTUD, can have some impact on building up a professional management cadre.

TWELVE

1972: Visit to Orsara Di Puglia and Pickpockets in Naples

One of my new responsibilities as the production manager of the GTE switching division in Milan was to set up a new factory in the south of Italy in a small town outside of Naples. At this time the Sylvania branch of GTE had invented the 4-sided disposal flash cube and sales were very good in the US. The company was importing the flash clubs from Sylvania factories in the United States but thought there would be substantial benefits from manufacturing this product in one of the Common Market countries. The Italian government wanted to stimulate employment in the depressed south of Italy and were offering subsidies and long income tax holidays.

We put together a proposal for bringing the production of the Sylvania Flash cube to an area in the south of Italy where there was unemployment, and it was accepted by the Italian government. For setting up a 1,000-person factory near Naples, Italy to make mechanical parts for our telephone systems and the flash cubes, we would obtain a tax holiday for 10 years. The project was approved, and I was put in charge of this new venture.

1972: VISIT TO ORSARA DI PUGLIA AND PICKPOCKETS IN NAPLES

The small town we picked for the new factory was called Marchinese, ten miles from the center of Naples. It has a population of about 20,000, most of whom are engaged in agriculture on their small family plots of land. I was put in charge of the project, and we started construction of a new factory. We also transferred some portion of our telephone assembly work being done in Milan to the new factory, which required a higher level of skill.

Paul Schiavone was the Vice President of Finance of GTE International in New York to whom I reported. He was interested in this project because Paul's mother and father had both been born in the town of Orsara in the south of Italy about 50 miles from Naples and had immigrated to American in the early 1900s. Paul was interested to visit the town where his parents came from and also to visit any of his relatives who may be still living there. He went with me on one of my monthly visits to the Naples factory.

On the weekend we drove to the town of Orsara which is in the province of Puglia on the Adriatic side of Italy. It is a very scenic drive from Naples and about an hour north of the city of Bari. It is from Bari where many ships from Italy took crusaders to Jerusalem to liberate it from the Moslems in the 1200s. The town of Orsara was founded by the Greeks over 2300 years ago and is famous for growing "hard" wheat used in making the best spaghetti. This agricultural area is also famous for growing tomatoes and eggplant used in their famous spaghetti sauce. Grapes for red wine are also grown in this area to complete the meal.

The land owned and farmed for hundreds of years by the Schiavone family is a long narrow strip on the ridge of a hill about a 30-minute walk outside of town. In this area of Italy, the ownership of land is in long parallel strips. Most of the property owners have donkeys to carry their tools to their farm site and donkeys to bring the produce back to town. The Schiavone family house in the middle of the village is a two-story stone house on narrow road in the town. On the main floor of the house is a large living-dining -kitchen room and there are two bedrooms on the second floor. There was a small room behind a curtain of the living room on the first floor. I was surprised when I heard a "knock, knock, knock" coming from behind the curtain.

Paul's cousin went behind the curtain, and we heard a sound as if someone turned on a faucet and was filling up a bucket with water. Then his cousin, carrying the bucket, walked through the living room, opened the door to the road, and threw the contents of the bucket onto the dusty cobblestone road. When she came back in the house, Paul asked his cousin why she filled a bucket with water and then threw it out onto the road. She replied that it was not water that she threw out in the road, but donkey urine. They kept their donkey inside the house behind the curtain.

If they left the donkey outside there was a chance that someone might steal the donkey. During tough times people in the town were known to eat donkey meet. To keep their donkey from getting stolen he is kept in the house and is considered a member of the family. She proudly stated that he is a housebroken donkey. When he has to pee, he will stamp his foot, which is a signal to bring him his bucket. Then he fills it up, and the contents are emptied onto the dirt road outside.

Paul's aunt prepared a delicious lunch using their own wheat to make their spaghetti, including a tomatoes and eggplant sauce with home grown herbs to make the spaghetti sauce. His aunt also brought out her homemade cheese, bread, and wine. The meal was delicious.

As we were building our factory in Marchinese, there was a very entrepreneurial fellow living in that small town. He offered to find employment for people in his town. He went around to the coffee bars in town and told them that there was a new U.S. company coming to build a factory and that he may have some connections. He told them,

1972: VISIT TO ORSARA DI PUGLIA AND PICKPOCKETS IN NAPLES

"If you give me $5, I will see what I can do to put you in line to get a job at the new factory. If after six months, I have been unsuccessful I will return your money." As many of the coffee drinkers were unemployed, a number of them agreed that was a fair deal and gave him $5.

This fellow did absolutely nothing to influence the hiring of his many clients, but he was honest. After six months our company had hired about 300 employees. Some of those hired had paid this "agent" five dollars and were pleased to have been hired. They thought it was money well spent and thanked him. Of those at the bars who were not hired after six months, he sought them out and, as an honest man, said, "I am sorry I was unable to get you a job. Here is your five dollars back." This is a typical example of a Neapolitan man living by his wits.

The old city of Naples has some beautiful architecture and is a colorful and large city. It is awake and alive until past midnight. At 11:00 pm some mothers send their young boys to pick up groceries from the neighborhood street venders. It is after dark that skilled pickpockets initiate their evil business. One evening we had a few engineers from our main factory in the U.S. where the Sylvania flash cube had been invented and was being produced for the U.S. market. The two Sylvania engineers from Salem, Massachusetts, had been sent for a few weeks to help the manufacturing startup of our new flash cube production.

In the evening I took the two engineers out for dinner at an attractive restaurant in Naples. After dinner the city continues to be alive, and many people are singing in the streets. Three 15-year-old boys came by and asked, "Are you American?" I replied that we were.

One boy said, "We have a beautiful fountain to show you" and he took the arm of one of the engineers and tried to steer him to the left. I replied that we did not have time and told my guests to keep walking.

"Okay," said one of the boys, "if you are here tomorrow, the fountain is nice." And the boys left. Our Sylvania engineer from the U.S. put his hand in his pocket and realized that his wallet was gone. The boys had disappeared with it, and we were down one wallet full of dollars.

We went to the Naples police station to report the pickpocket incident. The police were very understanding of our loss. They took the information, filed the report, and gave us a copy. Then they said, "We are happy to provide you with a document which you may be able to use for whatever insurance you have for theft by an unknown pickpocket. However, by this time, the skillful young pickpocket has probably destroyed the contents of the wallet after removing the cash and we have no proof to charge them with pickpocket crime."

The police chief added, "this is one of the negatives of 300 years of Spanish and French rule in Naples. When Garibaldi united Italy in 1865 and defeated the Spanish in the south and the French in the north, we Italians inherited both the good and the bad habits of those two countries."

The moral of this story is to always keep your hands in your pockets when you visit Naples.

THIRTEEN

1973: Au Pair troubles and more adventures in Sardinia

Valeria has joined Gary this year at the American School of Milan. Valeria, aged four, is in the nursery class and is thrilled to ride the school bus. She tells us she does math at school. Using 10 fingers her addition is very accurate up to 5 plus 5. Gary is in the first grade and enjoys it very much. The language teacher is reading them episodes from the Odyssey in Italian and Gary tells us the stories enthusiastically with only an occasional inaccuracy. Last night we heard about the big war between the Greeks and the French and the wooden horse.

Lydia is also very much involved in the school as a member of the PTA and room mother for the first grade. This responsibility includes arranging field trips. Next week the first graders will visit the Motta chocolate factory. Keeping 160 fingers from getting too sticky will be one of her major tasks. Together we have organized the spring and fall picnics for grades K through 8. We had Olympic Games and races for the children and an egg throw for the parents.

Gary tells Val the Trojan horse story

I have been elected as a board member of the school and am serving as its volunteer finance director. In addition, I have been promoted to Controller of the European Telecom Division of GTE, which will involve significant travel to our operations in West Berlin, Antwerp, Madrid, and Naples. Given our busy schedules, we thought it might be worthwhile to consider having a live-in Au Pair girl.

The European Au Pair tradition provides young women who want to become fluent in another European language the opportunity to live as a member of the family and function as a junior Mary Poppins. The Au Pair is given a private room, eats her meals with the family, is a babysitter, and receives a modest stipend. It is a good system that has both pluses and minuses. Our first Au Pair student was Pamela from Atlanta, Georgia. Pamela was excellent and became a lifelong friend. She spent a year with us and, enjoyed taking short trips in northern Italy and learnt Italian. Under Lydia's tutelage she picked up the many fine points of Italian cuisine.

1973: AU PAIR TROUBLES AND MORE ADVENTURES IN SARDINIA

Our second Au Pair turned out to be disastrous. She was from a wealthy family from a suburb of New York. We left her in the apartment one evening with our two children and went to see an opera in the center of Milan. While we were at the opera, she turned on the gas in the kitchen and tried to commit suicide. Luckily it was a short opera, and Lydia and I returned earlier than expected. As we opened the door to our apartment, we found her lying on the kitchen floor with the gas on and the oven door open. She was groggy. We turned off the gas, opened the kitchen window and called the fire department. Within five minutes we heard the siren of the fire truck, and two of the firemen ran up the 15 floors to our apartment. They explained they didn't want to be stuck in the elevator if something happened to the electricity. We appreciated and admired their energy and this good decision.

The firemen revived her and took her into the fire truck along with our two young children. The firemen said it was lucky that neither of us smoked. They added that a small spark could have ignited the escaping gas in the kitchen that could have blown out a wall of the kitchen. Fortunately, the report from the hospital was both children and our Au Pair was okay.

Early the next morning, I made the most difficult call of my life to the mother of the Au Pair girl.

"Your daughter tried to commit suicide last night. I think it would be better that you fly here and take her back home." Her first comment was "I hope we can keep this out of the newspapers". When I met her mother at the airport it was clear why the poor girl was disturbed. Her mother told me that she and her husband and the eldest daughter were extremely intelligent. Her major concern seemed to be to make certain it was not printed in their local papers and it clear that she was worried that their family status in the community might be reduced by a rung or two.

Our 3rd Au Pair was May Britt, a very lovely and most attractive Danish girl from Copenhagen. She was so pretty that she kept getting invited by Italian men to parties. She became pregnant four months after she arrived in Italy. She returned to Copenhagen to have the baby, before completing our year contract.

On the agricultural side, Lydia has conquered the jungle in the lower area of our garden at Brunate, our weekend home near Lake Como. New grass and flowers give a fine appearance in contrast to the great underbrush that had been there before. The mail strike has wreaked havoc with our corn production this year. The seeds of Hybrid Golden Bantem, imported especially from Burpee, spent the better part of the spring in the bowels of the Central Post Office of Milan. The postal clerks returning from the strike delivered the seeds to me by late June. Despite the setback on the corn side, progress is being made on the fruit sector. Raspberries and apricots were good and abundant, and our pear section is finally producing results. We had one pear this year. As we have three pear trees, that is not a very good average. Nevertheless, it is the first pear for this tree. I could tell it would have been rather good tasting too, had I left it on the tree until it became fully ripe. It was harvested a bit in advance out of fear that it would fall off and rot on the ground before we had a chance to taste it.

I had threatened to pull out all three pear trees and replace them with a more eager variety if they didn't produce this year. But modest as the yield was this summer, I can see that they are trying, so I'll give them still another year. The young fig tree on the other hand is doing nine times as well as our entire pear section. We have one fig tree, and she has given us three figs this year, her first since being planted four years ago. Cherries and strawberries were more abundant this year, but they ripened while we were on vacation, and we missed them.

Our vacation this year took us to Sardinia. We went with the Mediterranean Club again, this time to a small island off the northeast

1973: AU PAIR TROUBLES AND MORE ADVENTURES IN SARDINIA

coast of Sardinia. It took us three different boat rides to get there. First, we had the overnight ferry boat from Genoa to the main island of Sardinia. Then a three-hour car ride from the northwest to the northeast coast of Sardinia. In Palau we took a ferry boat to the island of Maddalena. At that island, we parked our car and then took a boat to the island of Santo Stefano. Just behind Santo Stefano is the island of Caprera, where Garibaldi the hero that unified Italy in the 19th century, spent the end of his days. Garibaldi's fame as a great national hero isn't shared by all Italians including Lydia. She would have preferred that the north and the south of Italy had remained as two separate countries. As we were right at the edge of the Bocche di Bonifacio, the channel that separates Sardinia from Corsica, known for its winds the sailing was very peppy.

The major sports at this club to which my attention was devoted are sailing and scuba diving. This club has a very well-organized program and averages five students per instructor. We went out at 8:30 A. M. and with many large and small islands in the vicinity we were usually able to find a cove or inlet protected from the waves.

I spent two days in the shallow water re-adaptation program before I took my first deep dive. It went smoothly and after having spent 25 minutes roaming around with the instructor and four other novices at a depth of 25 meters (about 80 feet), I felt like a veteran. When the first student went on his reserve air, we all started up for the surface. We stopped about five meters below our boat and there grabbed hold of the lines that hung over the side. We stayed there for about three minutes, the time necessary for decompression and re-absorption of nitrogen bubbles into our blood stream.

The next morning, we had a beautiful clear, warm day with no wind and the surface of the sea was as flat as an ice-skating rink. As I had completed the 25-meter baptism I was now eligible for the underwater exploration trips. Five divers plus an instructor are the normal squad and a 30-minute dive at depths of 30 to 40 meters was the daily program. I was amused at the obvious nervousness of the three new fellows on our boat who had graduated the day before from the 5-meter school and who were about to take their first 25-meter-deep water baptism. Even though I had taken the baptism just yesterday, I felt like an old veteran. I watched with a growing sense of overconfident superiority as they tested their air bottles and mouthpieces three and four times, chatting nervously and asking many questions of their instructor.

My group was called first when we arrived at our diving location, and I found myself among some amazing French pros. The first one in the water did a flip instead of the normal feet forward jump. In spite of being just one day away from the baptism, I tried the forward flip also. I didn't land quite right and had the air partially knocked out of me. It was a poor start and getting back my breath I took in a little water and used up quite a bit of air in my bottle before we went down.

Once all five of us were in the water, we dived straight down descending slowly in a lazy spiral with arms spread in front in the position of a parachuter before his chute opens. It was the same sensation Alice must have felt as she fell through the mirror into Wonderland. The depth meter registered our plunge, 15 meters, 20, 25, and 30. As we neared the bottom of the sea we pulled out of our dive and landed with a slow bending of our knees finishing up in a kneeling position on the sea floor with arms folded. As each diver touched bottom at almost equal two second intervals, it was as if this was a planned routine of a swimming ballet group although this was the first time, we five had dived together.

The monitor looked straight at each of us and made the sign "all okay." Each diver gave back the okay signal with military vigor. The instructor rose up slightly on his toes and pushed off. We followed and began our exploration. I glided along with a marvelous feeling of weightlessness.

1973: AU PAIR TROUBLES AND MORE ADVENTURES IN SARDINIA

With only a minor arching of the back and negligible effort I could change my altitude and glide upwards away from the ocean floor like a fighter plane in slow motion climbing into the sky.

A little water got into my mask, so I stopped to clear it. After clearing it I saw an interesting shell and went to pick it up. This stop and detour had only taken a minute but in that time our squad had moved 50 meters ahead, I had forgotten to observe cardinal rule number one, which is to always stay close to your partners underwater. If anything goes wrong at a depth of 35 meters, the results can be disastrous, but if you are in a group most situations can be taken care of with minimum difficulty. If you are alone, you don't have much spare resources.

I began kicking at a faster rhythm to catch up to our group and it took about 30 seconds to reach them. It was a long 30 seconds. I glided past the last member of our group and took a position in the squadrilla, just to the right and above the monitor. In formation we proceeded for another 100 meters before reaching some underwater cliffs just ahead.

Another squadron of six swimmers, swimming parallel to the cliff, passed in front of us. The face of the cliff was rough and uneven and little fish came out of cracks to look at us. What looked like two strings of seaweed growing out of a cleft in the rock turned out to be the two antennas of a lobster. He climbed out and swam off. Farther ahead was an opening in the cliff and we entered. It was a tunnel about 10 meters long and we swam through it. On the other side of the tunnel, we found a very cold-water current near the bottom. Even with the wet suit you were aware of changes of temperature in the water, and I sought the more comfortable warmer temperature. At this point I found myself directly above the monitor and two of the other divers. Then it happened.

I was suddenly aware that it was hard to pull air out of my bottle. It was time to pull my reserve handle. This was the first time in my diving experience that I had exhausted my normal air supply and had to go on reserve. During our adaptation course one of the signals we learnt was how to request help if you had difficulty going on reserve. Therefore, I preferred to be near the monitor before putting on the reserve, just in case. I panicked worrying that the reserve handle might get stuck or that after pulling the handle there would be no reserve air. My composure left me, and I became an apprehensive air breathing creature out of his normal environment rather than a confident fishman. The monitor was six meters below me.

As I changed my altitude to swim down to the monitor, the little air that was left became even harder to pull out of the bottle. While at my former depth I could still get a partial breath with difficulty, at three meters lower the increased pressure reduced the air in my bottle and I could get no breath. I let myself rise to the point where I could get a full breath of air. This maneuver put me eight meters above the monitor. I felt as if I was a balloon on a string above the heads of a group of people who were walking. I wanted to attract their attention so they would pull me down to earth. But they kept going ahead and didn't see me.

Even though I know a person can stay for at least two minutes without breathing and with no ill effects, it is easy to forget this physiological fact when you are not sure where your next breath is coming from. I could feel panic growing. I was undecided as to whether I should make the great effort to reach the monitor before pulling my reserve, or whether to go ahead on my own. If I pulled my reserve and was unable to release the additional air and was some distance from the group, I would be in serious trouble. However, if I used this last breath to reach him and was unable to release my reserve, I could use his spare mouthpiece and tank.

With the sweat now pouring out of my brow and fogging up my mask, I made my decision, and pulled hard on my reserve shaft. Fortunately,

I did not pull on my shoulder strap buckle, a common mistake of novices. That first deep breath of air from my reserve was one of the most comforting sensations I can remember in the past five years. I swam to the instructor and with as much nonchalance as I could muster and with my lungs gloriously full of air, I gave the signal for being on reserve, a clenched fist of the right hand held next to the forehead. The instructor gave the reply signal, looked around to make sure all of the other divers of our group were there and motioned that we should start heading up to the surface. We changed our altitude to about 10 degrees off the horizontal and slowly moved up.

Looking down at the cliffs below us which were getting smaller as we rose, it seemed as if we were a group of space explorers out of Buck Rogers with motors on our backs flying up and out of a city. Looking up, the underside of our boat and propeller looked like a spaceship parking in orbit waiting for us. We came up under the boat, grabbed hold of the decompression lines and did our three minutes of breathing before coming into the boat. As I went up the ladder, the exhilaration of having spent 30 minutes gliding under the water pushed the few seconds of horror of being without air into a misty background.

There were an interesting group of people among those that went exploring with the scuba diving equipment as well as some odd ones. One of these was a nervous French woman in her fifties. I had first met them at the restaurant and was struck by the strange longish hair style of her 60-year-old husband. Next time I met them was on the scuba boat. The husband was completely bald. I admired their athletic prowess, especially in connection with their age, but her nervousness got her into frustrating situations. One day, she started off with our group but went back immediately to the surface to adjust her mask. We waited for her at the bottom. She didn't return. Our instructor went up to look for her and then came down and we proceeded. We found out after that she had dived again but had attached herself to another group thinking it was us. The only trouble was that the other group was just completing their dive. Five minutes after she joined them, they started coming back to the surface. She complained bitterly all the way back on the boat about having had such a short swim. I don't think she realized that she had gotten with a different group.

One memorable underwater scene was the day it was quite wavy. Underwater you don't feel waves but near the surface it was another matter. The boat moved vigorously and with this movement the ropes over the side for the decompression stop moved up and down like the ropes in a belfry. The swimmers holding on to these ropes looked like monks being pulled up by the bell ropes, legs flying off to the side.

The last dive of the vacation was a very exciting one. We parked the boat about 400 meters from shore. The depth there averaged about 40 meters with the exception of the two underwater cliffs that reached up to just one meter below the surface. Over the past 2500 years many ships had hit these rocks and sunk, Last year divers had gone down here and had found pieces of pottery that were from 100 B.C.

The movement of the water currents changes the bottom sands, and objects exposed the year before can become covered and new objects become visible. As we reached the bottom, I could see hundreds of pieces of pottery and began picking them up. Our monitor motioned to come farther ahead, and he stopped at a place near the cliff base, and he started digging with his pick. I followed suit as did the other divers in our group. I uncovered a large piece of pottery that was curved and the size of two palms, I looked to our monitor to show him my find. He had his head down and was digging. He didn't show the same attentiveness and concern for his charges as had our other monitors on prior dives. He was intent on one thing which was to come up with an amphora, and his complete attention was on his work.

I can visualize the cartoon now, our monitor with his eyes on his digging with a group of novice scuba divers around him in various stages

1973: AU PAIR TROUBLES AND MORE ADVENTURES IN SARDINIA

of danger, one without air, another with one leg entwined by an octopus, a third wedged between two rocks. Remembering my frightening experience with the reserve air, I decided that the best place to dig was next to the teacher.

Digging with my hands I came upon something hard. I pushed away the sand and uncovered a handle. I pulled at it and found it was the upper part of an amphora with one handle intact and part of the other handle. It was covered with shells and seaweed. The other fellows in our group found the tops of two amphoras with neck and both handles intact, and one of the girls found a complete plate, which probably belonged to the captain of this Roman Galley. The deck of our boat was covered with many such treasures as we headed back to camp.

At the end of our vacation, we took a few days for some sightseeing in the northern half of Sardinia. Lydia and I had been there 10 years earlier and we found things quite different in many places. There is much construction taking place and the tourist population is increasing. However, you can still find deserted beaches. One day we and a family of three were the only ones on a four mile stretch of beach. At another place that had a series of half-moon beaches, each framed by rock outcroppings, we saw no other people as far as we could see which was about a mile in each direction.

The roads were somewhat better than 10 years earlier and we didn't find much traffic. We did find a number of tight police roadblocks. The police, carrying rifles and sub machine guns were looking for kidnappers and bandits for which Sardinia has been, and is still, famous. We were stopped by five roadblocks in three days.

We visited again the town of Calangianus where ten years ago we had found a craftsman who did beautiful work with cork. He was still there, but in place of his one room shop that contained him, his apprentice, and his many knives, we found a three-story apartment building.

On the ground floor was his factory employing 20 people and some heavy machinery. His cork products were still attractive, but we were disappointed to see the charm of the craftsman converted into mass production. He used to make pictures out of various shades and shapes of cork pasted on canvas, but he has no more time for this.

Another change that has taken place in Sardinia is the sharp decrease of the seal population. There is a large grotto, reaching many miles into the rock at a place called Cala Gonone. Ten years ago, there were hundreds of seals living in this underground lake connected to the sea by a tunnel. Until five years ago there were still about 80 seals that called this cavern their home. Three years ago, the population dropped to twenty and this year there were only about six.

In spite of the changes taking place, the Nuraghi of Sardinia remains immutable. These are the Bronze Age fortresses that dot the countryside. The circular towers made of stones, beehive shape, reach in some cases to four stories of height. The larger ones have staircases inside the walls. The normal structure has three large rooms in the center, one on top of the other. The place of the chief is in front of a large key shaped opening where he is silhouetted against the light so no one can see his expression. In the courtyard of the Nuraghi was a well and outside of the main walls were many small one-room stone structures. We had a fine spooky time going through the dark passageways.

The contrast in Sardinia between the old and new is very marked. While the old is charming, the new is sometimes a poor copy of what you find on the mainland. Castelsardo, a town perched on a rocky promontory high over the sea is a good example of such contrasts. The town is medieval in construction but undoubtedly was a village even before the Roman times due to its well protected location by the sea. A typical Sardinian scene in these old towns is the gathering of the old men. They wear black floppy hats and sit in a long single file along a wall, puffing pipes, like so many black crows on a telephone wire.

Down below along the beach one finds modern hotels. We stayed at one of these "modern" hotels. The wind had blown half the sign off. The door to our room was not fitted properly and wouldn't close. There was a light in the bathroom ceiling but no light switch. The hot water didn't work, and the cold water leaked. The toilet seat wasn't attached very firmly, and you had to be literally on your toes to keep from falling off. Even the bed let us down. The first time I relaxed on it, one of the slats gave way and the top half dropped to the floor. The illumination was meager and a small naked 20-watt bulb in the ceiling was fighting a losing battle against the darkness. The hotel was only two years old, but the new plaster walls were cracked and some of the paint was peeling. The Venetian blinds went askew as you pulled them up. We had the impression that the hotel had been built by a group of comedians rather than by a group of craftsmen. While Sardinian heritage includes shepherds, fishermen and bandits, they can't compete with the Swiss as innkeepers. However, a few inconveniences don't detract from the impressive beauty of Sardinia with its rugged coast lines, mountainous and unpopulated interior.

After leaving Sardinia, the family spent the rest of the summer at Brunate. We have started to take the children on hikes in the hills above Lake Como. There are many nice paths going through the woods and following the ridge line. The ridge line runs from 3,000 to 5,000 feet above the lake and there are wide pastures on one side. Cow bells around the necks of both goats and cows can be heard frequently. On these mountains above the lake there are many rustic refuges. One nearby refuge has a farm that becomes a restaurant on Saturdays and Sundays for the hikers and is reached only by foot. The cow bell music comes from his flocks as does the meat, cheese, milk, and salami served.

On one trip we were three families with a total of nine children. The hikers stretched out for quite a distance, and in one stretch of woods, I found myself alone with Gary. We had some interesting conversation about the nature of the world and things we saw, including butterflies, bees, grasshoppers, lizards, and flowers. Gary asked me how this all came about including the world we were walking on. I told him that no one really knows, but that there were several theories about it: One of them being the passing suns theory and the other being the gravitational pull of small particles in empty space making larger and larger balls of matter. After a few minutes' reflection on my explanations, he said: "I have another theory, God made the world." He quickly followed this by asking if God's sneezing is thunder. I think he thought of this because he had in mind God putting together a dusty earth and dust certainly makes one sneeze.

Valeria is a bit small for these long walks, but the pull of love brings her out. Gary's friend Jimmy came to join us one weekend and Jimmy has two older brothers aged 9 and 11. When Valeria heard that Jimmy's brothers were coming on the hike, she had to come too. We had heard Valeria speak frequently of Jimmy's brothers and we had even heard that our 4-year-old waited outside the school door for the older pupils to pass to have an opportunity to say hello to them. Having these boys as our guests for a hike was something special and Valeria managed for most of the time to be either on the shoulders of these two grand boys or walking hand in hand with them.

Playing house is the major game now. When Filippo, a boy of five, comes over, Valeria, Gary, and Filippo make a fine trio for the game of house. Gary and Filippo go off to war with swords, helmets, and garbage can covers as their shields. Valeria is the wife. It is not very clear just whose wife she is as both of them call "wife, I'm coming back, get the food ready." She is very busy at their home base making the meals with her dish set and then prepares the bed for all three of them.

Both Lydia and I enjoy partaking of the fantasy of the children in their many games and we pretend to nap on the terrace so we can overhear their conversations. Their fantasy takes on many forms, and we sometimes wonder what the limits are. One day, we sent Gary and Filippo

1973: AU PAIR TROUBLES AND MORE ADVENTURES IN SARDINIA

to run an errand. They took about twice as long as it should have taken. When questioned as to why they took so long, Filippo said: "We stopped at the cemetery as Gary wanted to show me where his dead uncle was buried." Interesting explanation as we have no dead uncle buried in Brunate. I took Gary fishing this summer in Lake Como and he had the thrill of catching his first fish. It wasn't a very big fish, about half the length of my finger, but it was a fish and he caught it.

On the business side, I'm starting my second year in the job of Controller of the European Telecom Division of GTE. I still spend a good part of the time travelling between our factories in Antwerp, Berlin, Madrid, Milan, and Naples. Between fog and airline strikes the time travelling can become long. For the past six months the air controllers in Germany have been striking intermittently and when they do, you can spend hours circling the skies above Frankfurt and Duesseldorf.

On a recent trip to our factory in West Berlin, I decided to travel by way of Vienna and East Berlin to avoid this curse of the Western democracies as they revert to strikes. The first thing I noticed that was strange about flying into East Berlin from Vienna was the silhouette of the aircrafts that are parked at the airport. The droopy wings of the Ilyushin jets are quite different from the profile of the Boeing, Caravelle, and Douglas jets which are the familiar vehicles of West Europe airports.

The second thing that was quite different from western European airports is the screening process at passport control. I found myself in the midst of a group of dark swarthy fellows. I happened to see the passport of one of them and discovered they were from the Royal Hashemite Kingdom of Jordan. It took ten minutes of checking for the first of these fellows to get through. When my turn came, the passport officer made a lengthy study of my passport and close scrutiny of my face. After I removed my new glasses, a glimmer of recognition came over the officer's face and he finally satisfied himself that the passport was really mine and that it was authentic. After a payment of a $2 transit fee to cross into West Berlin, the East German police stamped my passport and affixed a tax stamp. After that I was allowed to cross out of glum Communist East Berlin and crossed into West Berlin where people were smiling.

The bus driver had an obstacle course to follow as he threaded the bus around and between the concrete barriers that kept people from the Communist countries of East Germany from the freedom in West Berlin. The turns were so tight the driver hardly made it without having to back up.

A frontier policeman came to check our papers on leaving the People's Democratic Republic of Germany, but he didn't give the appearance of being a very democratic person. He had a small attaché type case hung around his neck and a set expression which conveyed the message: "I let no one pass unless I say so." The front cover of the attaché case opened forward, and, in this position, it became a hanging desk. A stamp pad and rubber stamp were in one corner of this portable desk and his head jerked forward each time he stamped the passports after assuring himself that the transit visas were authentic. Two people were removed from the bus by the policeman and were pushed into a police car that sped off. After the frontier pole was lifted and we passed onto the other side, I thought I heard a sigh of relief coming from the person just in back of me, but it was probably only my imagination.

Once into West Berlin I thought the slow bureaucracy and tight control was finished but not so. Sitting next to me was a small dark man with a rather sad expression. He carried a carpet bag and I discovered that he was from Damascus. When I asked him what brought him to Germany, business or pleasure, he answered somewhat equivocally, "a little of both." This raised my curiosity and I wanted to pry deeper. I tried to find out more about him and his business but met with little

1973: AU PAIR TROUBLES AND MORE ADVENTURES IN SARDINIA

success. A wry smile partially illuminated his sad expression as he pretended not to understand my questions.

When the West German police came on the bus, I realized that it was probably anxiety rather than sadness which enveloped the man. The West German police looked at his Syrian passport and barked out a short clipped one-word command: "Aussteigen!" The man got up and walked out of the bus. However, the Syrian wasn't the only one to receive a less than cordial welcome into West Germany. There were three other Arab looking fellows in the back of the bus who were also welcomed into West Germany with the same sharp "Aussteigen!" greeting. They also filed off the bus and removed their baggage from the trunk. They took their luggage to a special house where a most thorough check of Middle Easterners was being made. My Syrian seatmate missed this bus, but his place was taken by another Arab who had been on the bus which left the airport an hour earlier. In spite of the slight delay for the rest of us in the bus, I was relieved to see the stringent security against potential air pirates. Apparently at that time people living in West Berlin could visit relatives living in East Berlin but not vice versa.

FOURTEEN

1974: Robin arrives and a trip to Nigeria

A Robin was sighted in early September. Strangely enough she was accompanied by a flock of storks. The storks dropped her off at the Piedmont Hospital in Atlanta, Georgia, and came to rest in the crib named Robin Scott at the nursery of the hospital. We had not expected the Robin to arrive until early October, but it was no less exciting welcoming her a month in advance. She had probably been forewarned about the pending cold wave this fall that was to keep so many sparrows and sparlings and storks on the northern side of the Alps. Robin represents the fifth member of our family. She has cast off her feathered cloak and has turned into a lovely baby girl.

Both Gary and Valeria are very pleased with their baby sister whose complete name is Robin Giuliana Scott. Gary is particularly interested and keeps Lydia on her toes. Whenever Robin cries, he goes to Lydia with great indignation, "Aren't you going to feed your baby?" Valeria enjoys feeding her baby sister. She understands better than Gary that it is good for a baby to cry. She explains that it makes their lungs strong, and it is important not to spoil the baby.

It was an accident that the baby was born in the U.S. Unlike Lydia's other pregnancies this one gave no particular trouble until the end of the 6th month. Two days before we were scheduled to return to Italy from a home leave vacation in Atlanta, Georgia, trouble started. Lydia was put on bedrest and waited out the pregnancy in my mother's house in Atlanta, Georgia. It was touch and go for a while as Robin gave indications of an even earlier arrival. Lydia managed to hold on for two more months, during which time she had the opportunity to become familiar with American hospital practices. In comparing the U. S. and Italian hospital systems, from this brief and limited exposure, Lydia found that while the U.S. hospital has excellent modern equipment, a private Italian hospital is more personal, less bureaucratic, and equally, if not more efficient, than a private U. S. hospital and certainly less expensive.

In spite of all the troubles avoiding a premature birth, we are both very pleased with the results and enjoy having a Robin in our nest. She looks like she came from exactly the same mold as Gary and Valeria and her features and expression are identical to them at that age. She has accepted the change of environment from Atlanta to Milan without much fuss. She lets her parents sleep at night and is a very good little girl.

Baby Robin, Valeria and Gary

Both Gary and Valeria benefited from their lengthened sojourn in the States. They both had a chance to understand something of the U.S. environment and they liked it. Gary started second grade and Valeria attended kindergarten in an Atlanta public school within biking distance from my mother's house. They found no difficulty adjusting to the school and Gary was the top student in his class. Valeria picked up quite a southern accent in the short time she was in kindergarten. I also had the chance to take Gary on a trip to Disneyland and I'm not sure which of us enjoyed it most.

Some of the other events of the year included substantial progress by Gary on skis. Although he doesn't ski faster than his parents, he never stops. We now take him with us on the expert slopes in the Dolomites. While we stop to catch our breath every so often, he just keeps on going and usually gets to the bottom before we do. He also made great strides in swimming. While still in Atlanta we took both Gary and Valeria to a 2-week swim course at the YMCA and Gary was swimming at the end of it. He now does as well under the water as on the top. Valeria made progress, but it will be next year before she is really swimming. The important thing is that they both gained confidence in the water.

Back in Milan, Valeria is starting ballet lessons in the same ballet school where Lydia began her dancing lessons. She enjoys showing us the various movements she has learned. Wearing the ballet costume is a big part of her enjoyment. Lydia has been active at the American School of Milan. She was the room mother for the second graders and organized several field trips for the children. Together we ran the spring school picnic with races and games.

This year I had the opportunity to do some hospital testing and I chose an Italian State Hospital for my research. I broke my leg skiing at the Cortina ski area in the Dolomite Mountains just south of Austria. The excellent hospital, service, and environment, compensated for the shame of having of broken my leg. The break could not have happened at a better place. The Codavilla hospital in Cortina is connected with the Bologna medical school and specializes in bone work. It has the reputation of being one of the best Italian State Hospitals, particularly for those who break their ankle bones.

The first aid part of the cure was rapid and efficient. I was picked up from the slope in a snow tractor within 10 minutes after my fall. I was put in a cable car and rode to the bottom of the mountain. As the rescue patrol had called ahead, the ambulance was waiting at the bottom of the chair lift. Once inside the hospital, an x-ray was taken, and I found myself in traction within minutes of entering the hospital. The traction apparatus and attachment were a bit spooky, and it gave me a start to see and hear it being attached, but surprisingly enough, there was no pain. The sight of the doctor with a Black and Decker type hand drill and a foot long piece of steel tube that is supposed to go through your heel bone, as you are put into traction, created a bit of anxiety to say the least, particularly when he said a local anesthetic was not necessary.

From the time the doctor touched the heel until the time the steel bar was pushed through to the other side of the bone was a matter of 30 seconds. The only thing I felt was a slight prick, no worse than an injection, as the steel screw penetrated the skin. This was followed by the smell of burnt powdered bone as the high-speed drill whined through my heal. Before you really have a chance to savor the smell of cooked powdered bone, the steel bar is through to the other side. Two corks were placed at both ends of the steel bar and a horseshoe shaped cable is attached over a pulley, and weights are added. The bones are now in place to start growing together.

After four days of traction, I was given the opportunity to have the famous "Dalara" screw put in my leg. This is a new way of keeping a broken bone together while it heals and was patented by the Italian surgeon Doctor Dalara. I was the 1,640th patient to have received the Dalara screw. This technique is supposed to reduce the time spent in a cast by from six to four weeks. The screw goes through the back of the ankle bone, and both ends of the screw stick out through the skin. When the bone has healed the screw is screwed back out, and in most cases the patient walks away with a well-healed leg. I was one of the "most cases". There is no need for even a local anesthetic as there is no pain as the screw is unscrewed from the bone. It was as if one were unscrewing a metal screw from a piece of wood. My beautiful stainless steel Dalara screw, 4-inches in length, is now on display over our mantelpiece.

Apart from the excellent doctors, who are experts on fixing broken ankles and legs, the Codavilla hospital has very attractive smiling nurses and fine gourmet Italian meals. Just outside my hospital room there is a lovely large balcony with space for five hospital beds. During the middle of the day the nurses wheel the beds of patients recovering from broken legs out onto the balcony. It is glorious to spend a few hours in the early afternoon absorbing the warm sun and brilliant blue sky of the beautiful Cortina Mountain scenery from the comfort of the hospital bed on a broad porch.

Being tied into traction, one appreciates the happiness and pleasure of freedom and mobility. You can hardly move when you are in traction. What is really difficult is sleeping. I never realized how much one moves and changes position when sleeping. But with traction, every time you roll over you wake up. Even a slight movement of the hips wakes one up. Washing hands, cleaning teeth as well as other needs require an attendant to bring and take away containers and receptacles of various sorts. There was a whole new level of happiness that I became aware of after the traction was removed. It was wonderful to be able to get up to clean my teeth and wash my hands. It is amazing the sense of freedom that comes from being independent, first walking with crutches, then walking with a walking cast, then finally having the cast off as summer and warm weather arrived. I have concluded, as a result of this experience, that it is good for people to be deprived every so often of something that they take for granted. It sharpens your appreciation of the absolute pleasure of mobility.

Apart from enjoying the care at the Cortina hospital, the year 1974 produced other interesting events and episodes. One episode was an attempt to track down a large sum of Arab petrodollars for a loan of working capital for our Italian company. Following rumors about elusive pots of gold, I felt somewhat like Ponce De Leon. But instead of an Indian chief describing the Fountain of Youth and pointing in its direction, the messenger bringing news of the fabulous petrodollar deals around the corner, came in the unlikely guise of a short Neapolitan lawyer.

The idea of a rich Arab Sheik using a short Neapolitan lawyer as his intermediary seemed strange. But as our need for working capital was large, unusual paths seemed justified. This particular trail ended in the office of the President of a large Belgian bank. The last 50 yards of this trail added to the mystique of the search. We were greeted at 10:00 a.m. in the morning by a man wearing a suit of black tails and white gloves. He was the usher. We followed him, at a respectable distance, as he led us down an elegant corridor with intricately woven 17th century tapestries on one wall and fine sculptured faces in stone niches along the other wall.

With this formality and dignity, I had visions of being led into a large conference room with a fresco by Tiepolo on the ceiling and a group of stout turbaned sheiks, sitting on pillows in a semicircle, with their pots of gold at their sides, smoking water pipes while awaiting our visit. It was an anticlimax being led into the office of the President of the Bank, who had only one assistant at his side, a thin pale Belgian with a rather sad expression. This Belgian bank did have funds from Kuwait and Abu Dhabi deposited with them and was seeking a secure and remunerative investment vehicle for their excess cash. However, the conditions were far less attractive than those described initially by the Neapolitan lawyer, and we took the deal off the table.

While one trip followed a trail to obtain Arab oil money deposited in a Belgian Bank, another trail was to the middle of the African continent where the source — Nigerian crude oil of very high quality and low sulfur content, better known as "Sweet Nigerian Oil" which was discovered in great volume in the southwest corner of Nigeria on the Atlantic Ocean. It is the very best quality crude oil in the world.

GTE has a large telecommunication contract with the Nigerian post office which is responsible for developing a portion of the undeveloped Nigerian telephone system. Nigeria is a very large country and is the size of France and Italy together. It is just five degrees north of the equator in tropical and humid West Africa. The Nigerian Census of 1973 indicates a population of about 80 million, compared to the population of France and Italy together of about 100 million. Nigeria's population is growing rapidly and is expected to exceed that of France and Italy in less than three years.

Current estimates are that the population of Nigeria will keep increasing at a rapid pace because of its large Muslim population in the entire northern half of the country. The Moslem religion, as practiced in the Middle East and in parts of Africa imposes a limit of four wives to a prosperous man. There is a Benjamin Franklin-like qualification in the Moslem religion regarding the limitation of number of wives a man can have, which is "if you can keep them". The qualification is that if the man wants to have four wives, he must be able to support them. I assume this also means keeping them out of each other's hair, presumably not an easy task. In Nigeria, the four-wife limit does not seem to apply and if a man is prosperous his household size is limited only by his wealth (and patience) rather than by Moslem religious law.

The production of petroleum from wells already identified in Nigeria, puts the country among the world leaders in production of oil and, currently, they are presently producing 2.5 million barrels of crude oil per day. This gives the Nigerian government close to six billion dollars per year of oil royalties and an annual trade surplus of about three billion dollars. Their currency is one of the strongest currencies of the world, having been revalued recently against the dollar, with prospects of a further revaluation. Nigeria is now the largest supplier of oil to the United States, having recently surpassed Kuwait, Iran, and Saudi Arabia.

Ninety percent of the population of Nigeria currently engages in subsistence farming, not much different from what had been going on over the past five hundred years. With a sudden jump into the industrialized 20th century, the future looks prosperous and challenging. A poster vividly illustrating this contrast between the old and the future Nigeria, was just released by the national Nigerian Telephone Company. A picture of our newly constructed GTE (General Telephone) earth satellite station in the jungle in the center of the country shows the sharp contrast between the past and the future. The illustration is of a native Nigerian drum, alongside of the large microwave transmission antenna on top of the Satellite Station recently installed by GTE.

David in Nigeria with his driver

The Nigerian government has an aggressive five-year plan for the development of many large infrastructure projects. These projects include an expanded telephone system, superhighways, enlargement of airports, increased electrical power systems, seaports, schools, and hospitals. The lack of skilled manpower is limiting their ability to spend the money coming from the export of their petroleum which today represents about 85% of Nigerian exports.

Regarding the current telephone network, today there are 50,000 telephones in the Nigerian telephone system, which computes to about one phone for every 1,500 people. This compares with one telephone for every four people in France and Italy and one phone for every two people in the United States. The Nigerian five-year plan includes the addition of one million phones by 1980. This is a 20 times growth of telephones which requires a large cash investment and significant resources to train skilled personnel to run the new systems. GTE hopes hope to participate in this growth and help Nigeria improve their telecom network.

With this first two weeks spent in Nigeria I can understand better the difficulty one encounters in working in a developing country. The difficulties start even before your plane lands in the capital as it is necessary to obtain a visa which takes three photos and several days of waiting. Conversely, a visa for nearby Ivory Coast takes six pictures and can be obtained in one hour. While I feel flattered knowing my pictures are on file with many government agencies, I am puzzled as to the need for six copies of my photograph.

The Lagos airport procedures are slow and confusing. The airport staff is under dimensioned and has difficulty handling the current volume of traffic. Passport, health, and customs clearance, takes over an hour. The problem, however, is not due to large crowds being discharged from several jumbo jets at the same time as at Kennedy Airport in New York City. The planes that land and take off at the Lagos airport are fairly small because of the short length of the runways. The number of passengers in each plane is currently about 100 passengers and only a few international flights land at Lagos every day.

The problem is that the processing of a passenger through passport and import controls, takes five times longer than at an American or European gateway airport. It seemed that the officials at the airport are looking for reasons why you should not be admitted into their country. The airport staff reads through every word of your documents, and then slowly and deliberately, to make certain no word was missed the first time, they read your documents a second time.

GTE has an American manager living in Lagos who handles a large number of problems of Nigerian red tape. He has been in Lagos for three years and is very skilled at cutting through the bureaucracy and getting one through the airport bureaucracy. His duties include living arrangements and transportation issues of the many engineers, installers, and managers making visits to our operations in Nigeria. He met me as our plane landed and expedited my entry through the airport into the country. We then drove the 15 kilometers from the airport to the center of Lagos. The highway from the airport to the center of Lagos is one of the main highways into the country and, unfortunately, it is still under dimensioned.

The car population has grown faster than the increase of road construction. If you are lucky, it normally takes 90 minutes for the 15-kilometer trip from the airport to the center of Lagos. This can become three hours depending on the number of breakdowns on the highway. Once inside the city the traffic becomes even more clogged and chaotic. One can be stuck for 30 minutes without moving, even with policemen directing traffic. The Lagos traffic jams make traffic jams of Rome and Naples look like free-flowing futuristic cities. Fortunately, the Nigerian people that I have met are not nervous people and there is an amazing lack of noisy and impatient honking of cars stuck in Lagos in heavy traffic. This traffic makes keeping timely appointments very difficult.

Shortage of hotel rooms is big problem of Lagos at this time. It is now necessary to make reservations many months in advance for a hotel room in Lagos. Once a reservation is booked and paid for there is no assurance you have a room for the night. GTE has rented on a long term lease a two-bedroom apartment near the center of Lagos for our telephone technicians who may require many months of installation time.

Our local manager had made a weeklong reservation for me one month before I arrived. He paid for the room in advance and had picked up the key in the morning of my late afternoon arrival. That afternoon when I arrived in Lagos, I noticed many signs along the road from the airport to the center of the city, welcoming Mr. Gnassingbe Eyadema, the Prime Minister of Togo, who was arriving the same day as me for a state visit bringing with him Togolese government officials. When we arrived at our hotel, the hotel manager advised us that our reservations had been cancelled to make room for the Premier of Togo and his extensive staff of Togolese diplomats. Apparently, the Togolese Ambassador in Lagos had forgotten to make hotel reservations for this important state visit.

The Lagos English paper had a picture of the Prime Minister of Togo, Gnassingbe Eyadema, in a warm embrace with General Yakabu Gowon, the Nigerian Prime Minister. Mr Gowon had been the Prime Minister of Nigeria since 1966 and came to power in a coup following a civil war that resulted in three million deaths. He attended school in England and was famous for converting the Nigerian currency from the English systems of shillings and pounds to the decimal system. He was replaced in coup in 1975 while I was there. Until that time, he ran the country fairly well and had fairly good relations with neighboring African countries.

I saw from the local Lagos English language newspaper the description of the arrival of the delegation from Togo.

General Gowon was quoted as saying "Welcome Prime Minister Gnassingbe Eyadema to Nigeria."

Dictator Eyadema responded "It is a great honor to come to your rich and modern country"

General Gowon "These kind eulogies embarrass me. Where are you staying, Prime Minister?"

Dictator Eyadema "Did you not make the arrangements for us, Great General Gowon?"

General Gowon "Of Course your Excellency, your comfort is in our duty. How many worthy

Ministers from your Togo have you brought with you on this trip?"

Dictator Eyadema "57 ministers, which includes all the leaders of the opposition party."

General Gowon "Wise foresight, great leader of men."

General Gowon then sent Major Ogonwulu to the Palace Hotel with orders to obtain 57 rooms. That was the hotel where I was supposed to have a room for my 7-day visit. Fortunately, the manager of our Nigerian project found another room for me in a private house. While I regretted not having an air-conditioned hotel room that evening, I admired the foresight of Premier Eyadema to bring his opposition party with him so he could protect against a coup in his absence from his country. Most coups in Africa have occurred when the prime minister is away.

To solve the problem of limited rooms for skilled foreign workers, many companies doing business in Lagos rent extra hotel rooms to protect against large diplomatic visits between neighboring countries. General Telephone had already rented on a yearly basis a three-bedroom house in Lagos for their telecom engineers. That house was already full, so our country manager obtained a short-term bed rental from National Cash Register for our employees. I stayed there on several subsequent visits. Unfortunately, that house had a noisy air conditioner in each room. If you turned the air conditioner off, the room became too hot and muggy for sleeping. During the night one alternated between being kept awake by the noisy air conditioner and being kept awake by the moist equatorial heat and one had to choose between being hot and sweaty, or dozing off and being kept awake by the noisy air conditioner.

Some of the American and English companies worked well together in Lagos and when one had an extra room and no individuals arriving, they would make the space available to another friendly company. In our group of friendly companies, that shared the difficulties of working in Nigeria were Barclay's Bank, Lloyds of London, National Cash Register, IBM, Xerox, and Chase Manhattan. Luckily, it was not necessary to ask our major competitor IT &T if they might have a bed for the night in Nigeria. That company had been blackballed by the other American companies and was not at that time considered to be a worthy competitor.

There was a dentist office next door to our office in Lagos. Fortunately, I did not require any dental work while in Nigeria. I looked at their equipment and saw that the drill was operated not by an electric motor but by a foot pump to turn the tooth cutting tool. I assumed the dentist must have had an assistant that operated the foot pedal that turned the tooth drill. I would expect it was not the dentist that used his foot to provide rotary power to the tooth drill at the same time he was guiding the drill in the patient's mouth.

On the other side of the dentist office there was a pharmacy. In the window was a crow impaled on a stick, along with the beak of a small colorful bird. There was a mummy of a monkey and there were spiders of various sizes attached to a medicine board with pins stuck through their bodies. There were also various kinds of seaweed that were ground up into a powder which was supposed to be very effective if one had a headache as well as several sizes of dead scorpions. There was a sign that suggested you tell the medicine man what your ailments were, and he would grind up the appropriate potions that would provide a cure. During my several trips to Nigeria, I was fortunately in good health, so it was not necessary to purchase any medicines from this Nigerian medicine store. I don't think the GTE comprehensive health plan had included ground up bat wings or stuffed rats to be boiled in coconut oil to relieve headaches.

For later trips I stayed at the company house which had three bedrooms and a steward that would cook our meals. He also took care of our laundry. One would give him a few bills of local currency to buy food. There would also be a sum of money to cover a "dash" (a tip) as appreciation for his work. While his accounting for where all the food money went, was somewhat vague, his cooking was good, and he treated those of us from GTE like gods and referred to us as "Master". I was a bit startled the first time I entered the apartment and met the steward. As he bowed, he said,

"Good evening, Master."

Before I had the chance to answer he continued,

"Shall I wash your shirts this evening, Sir?"

The next morning, I was greeted with, "Sir, your breakfast is served."

At first, I thought this attitude may have been unique to the steward at the first apartment, but all stewards I came across were equally respectful. This Grand Hotel type of service and respect was last seen in Europe shortly before the start of the first World War.

Not being able to count on firm reservations is not limited to hotels, but also to internal airline flights. One of the people I met in Lagos had a recent confirmed reservation on a flight to Soketo, an inland city in central Nigeria. He got to the airport at 7:15 am for an 8:00 am flight.

As he presented his ticket he was startled by this reply:

"I'm sorry Master, the plane has already left."

"What do you mean it already left? The schedule and my ticket say 8:00 a.m., and it is only 7:15" said my friend, as he wound his watch and brought it up to his ear to listen to it tick.

"But master, the plane was full by 7:00 so it left."

"But how can that be, I have a confirmed reservation?"

"I'm sorry Master, but it became completely full, so it left."

"Okay, I guess there is not much I can do now. When does the next plane leave for Soketo?"

"In two days, master."

I understand that if you try to fight the frustration you may go mad or die of a heart attack. Lagos was not called the white man's graveyard by the British occupiers without a good reason.

A walk in the center of Lagos, a city of almost two million people, presents a very interesting view for someone on a first visit. The most striking thing is the women with their uncanny sense of balance and carrying capacity. They carry amazing loads on their heads and in addition many women have concurrently a baby strapped to their backs. The baby rides lower than a papoose and just over the hips. This method of carrying the baby probably explains the profile of Nigerian women with their carriage thrust backwards to provide a platform for the baby. The most common head load is a tray about twice the diameter of an umbrella on which all sorts of goods are carried. I imagine in the rainy season it also serves as an umbrella.

I watched with fascination as one woman walked down the main street of Lagos, carrying a tray full of oranges on her head. The oranges were stacked three layers deep. In addition to the tray being heavy, the slightest change on its angle would probably start the oranges running off, and once started the rest would probably follow. But with beautiful posture, a slight swaying of her hips, and her arms moving freely at her side, she walked down the street gracefully as if she had nothing on her head but a rather large hat.

The women are also the main retailers, and their retail store consists of a place on the sidewalk or side of the road. Their inventory is as much as they can place on their tray. I thought Italy had a large number of small retail outlets, little mom and pop stores for fruit, dairy products, meat, cheese, clothes, and hardware. But the size and number of retail outlets in Nigeria makes Italy look like a land of supermarkets by comparison. These little sidewalk stores stay open long hours, as late as ten pm at night. Each has a little lantern or candle in the middle of the tray, which is just enough light to attract attention, illuminate the wares, and make change. It is hard to imagine with such a small selection and inventory, that turnover is enough to be economic and worth their while, but it must be. The men also do a lot of selling in the streets but more of an ambulatory hawking nature while the women remain fixed in one place and wait for the customers to come to them. You have the feeling in Lagos that this is a country of retailers.

Small wonder that in the decree aimed at having Nigerian citizens own and run the economy, the retailing profession both big and small is restricted to companies (and women) that are 100% owned by Nigerians. Wholesaling, distribution, and some small manufacturing requires a 40% Nigerian stock ownership, while companies of modern high technology are not required to have any Nigerian ownership. As they need and want high technology companies to help build their infrastructure, minimum obstacles are put in the way of such companies. Ours is such a company. There is the gnawing doubt that if you do begin investing and become profitable, what is going to stop the Nigerian government from saying one day, now you have to be 40% owned by only Nigerian stockholders. No one can give that assurance.

I did receive some assurance from a former Nigerian Ambassador to the United States that the Nigerian Government was well aware that they would lose their credibility in the Western world if they tried to force a change in the percentage of Nigerian ownership participation. That is a rational argument and if rational people remain in power in its government Nigeria will probably follow a logical path. General Gowon, the present Premier, seems to be a sensible and reasonable person and so far, has not resorted to Big Daddy Amin (of Uganda) type of antics. If he can stay in power with his military government for five years, the country may have a good tradition of law and order.

When the government was turned over the civilian rule in the past, things became quickly chaotic. The target date of 1976 for turning the country back to civilian rule has been retracted by General Gowon. So, the military government will probably try to stay in power until almost 1980. The main problem he will have to fight is complaisance and corruption among the bureaucrats, who will begin to feel that they own their ministries and that the public is there to serve them and not the reverse. In so far as Gowon mentioned the elimination of corruption as one of the conditions to be met before the government is turned over the civilian rule, the military may have to stay in power an awfully long time.

In addition to nationalization there is another problem for all foreign owned operations, and that is called indigenization. There is considerable pressure on companies to train Nigerians so that at some later date they can be capable of running the economy. This makes good sense. At our company in Nigeria, we have a few skilled Americans working on maintenance contracts for the oil companies and they are training Nigerians to take their places.

Other Nigerians training in our company include our male clerk, Mr. Friday Ogonwulu, who can type as fast and as accurately as any Italian, and also the head of our motor pool, Mr. Sunday Tackteboo, who is very competent and conscientious driver. But if you ever need a car on Friday or something typed on Sunday it can get confusing. The first names Friday and Sunday seem to be quite common in Nigeria. I asked our office manager if he ever ran into an occasional Tuesday or Thursday. He said frequently, along with many named Fridays and Sundays and no one with the first names of Monday or Saturday. We also have a Nigerian working as our controller in the Lagos office. Adiza is the first controller I have worked with at GTE who is one of 45 children and whose father had 10 wives, all at the same time. None of our other controllers in GTE have even 20 brothers and sisters. Adiza is proud to have the distinction of being the only one of our GTE International controllers to have ever made a pilgrimage to Mecca.

The main concern for foreign companies in Nigeria is that the government will force the pace of indigenization and the replacement by local management faster than it can be effectively installed. And that seems to be happening. But in spite of this, the foreign English-speaking expatriate community in Lagos seems to be growing and presently numbers about 10,000 people.

Being equatorial, Nigeria has more than its share of insects, flies, mosquitoes, lizards, and scorpions. While in Russia I went looking for bugs in my hotel room, in Nigeria the bugs come looking for me. I was reading one evening in my hotel room (after the Togolese Premier left), and a large cockroach came crawling up the side of my lamp table. Even though the cockroach was merely curious I was startled to see such a huge beast a few inches from my elbow. He was one of those large hard-shelled variety that produce a crunchy sound if you step on them. In the prior week while staying at one of the company apartments, my appearance in the bathroom frightened two roaches out of their hiding places, and they went scurrying across the floor. One I was able to crunch and the other one got away. He scurried under the door, out into the living room and then under the door of the bedroom of the other employee of GTE in Nigeria. I did not want to wake my friend by giving further chase and assumed it was not the only large cockroach in his room.

Many of the people I spoke to in Lagos find the life there is quite tolerable, once you get used to the bugs, the heat, humidity, and the incredibly high prices of goods. Servants are cheap and having a chauffeur, cook, maid, and full-time nanny are not uncommon. While there is crime and occasional voodoo and witchcraft practiced, it is probably safer to walk the streets of Lagos at night than many U.S. cities, provided you are not afraid of evil spirits.

Regarding prices, a three-bedroom apartment rents for $ 5,000 per year in Lagos and you must pay five years rent in advance. Food is also very high. A box of corn flakes for example costs $1.20 and apples 50 cents each. Imported fresh meat is $5.00 per pound, compared to local meat at $2 per pound. After visiting the meat section of a local market, I would prefer to eat imported meat at $5.00 per pound. There was an open running sewer a few yards from the tables of meat and the flies seemed to be making frequent trips from the sewer to the meat and then back to the sewer. Most restaurants indicate on their menu that their meats are imported.

Not only are imported foods very expensive but their supply is very sporadic due partly to the overload at the port. The port of Lagos is very under dimensioned for the present traffic and the situation will get worse before it gets better. The tonnage of imports is growing rapidly not only to support the growing oil industry but also for the growth of other sectors of the economy. You find ships waiting ten to twenty days outside the harbor for a berth. I counted 34 ships waiting on the high seas when I was there. This adds considerably to the transport cost of the imported goods and many steamship lines try to avoid carrying merchandise to Lagos because of these delays.

Another addition to the cost of imported goods is the substantial pilferage that goes on, which must be reflected in the prices. Pilferage is perhaps an understatement. While I was there the newspaper announced that a whole cargo of cement, amounting to about 400,000 one hundred-pound bags, which was laying on the docks, disappeared one night. The proportion of this is incredible. If four men - two on a truck and two on the ground - could load a 100-pound bag every ten seconds, you would need 150 four-men teams, or 600 men and 150 trucks to do the job in one night. It must have taken a week, or else some official hanky-panky was involved.

When Nigeria begins to develop many of their own industries the cost of goods should be reduced substantially. The economy is moving in this direction, and I saw a large modern looking Volkswagen assembly plant under construction just outside of Lagos. Other industry is beginning to move in. If they can maintain political stability for ten years, Nigeria could become a fast-growing prosperous country and a leader in central Africa.

So, I'll be adding Lagos to my normal circuit of Berlin, Antwerp, Madrid, and Milan. Other developing countries in between may be added at a later date. One of the positives of Lagos is the magnificent beach and surf on the Atlantic Ocean. There are wonderful waves at the beach in the ocean just outside of Lagos. However, be warned, beautiful as the surf is, it is very dangerous on some days. There is often a rip tide that pulls one sideways and out into the ocean if one is not careful. The weekend before I arrived, an airline pilot of an American airline company went swimming in the surf. He was caught in a rip tide and was unable to swim out of it, He was pulled out to sea, and he drowned.

Perhaps the growing commercial ties and the potential prosperity Nigerian Oil will bring, will help pave the way for a peaceful and prosperous future in this large undeveloped country with much raw material.

FIFTEEN

1975: Nigeria and the Two-Step Viper

The highlights of our past year included a trip to Nigeria for Lydia and me, a delightful vacation on the Sardinian coast, athletic medals for the children and new responsibilities for Lydia as President of the Parent Teachers Association at the American School. Lydia was elected President last year and has done a beautiful job in encouraging capable parents to take part in school affairs. Before school started this fall, she had all of the fifteen committees organized and staffed, and many more parents are becoming involved this year than in the past. There is excellent cooperation between the parents and teachers and I'm sure a good part of this attitude is due to Lydia's enthusiastic work.

As far as relaxation is concerned, we spent our vacation in Sardinia. We were 15 miles south of the port of Olbia which is at the same latitude as Capri. The water was clear and clean, and from a rowboat, you could see the bottom of the ocean 60 feet down. We rented a small three-bedroom house five minutes' walk from the beach and a small boat with an outboard motor. We took short trips to nearby islands where we found beaches just for our family. The weather was fine with a warm sun, dry climate, and cool evenings.

While the dry climate is good for the tourists, it is not so good for the farmers. Fresh water has always been a problem in Sardinia and this year it was a major problem. While we had washing water in the house, we had to fetch drinking and cooking water in 5-gallon plastic containers from a fountain seven miles away. Every third day we would make a water run. Some people went by mule, but a sturdy car would also make it.

We made friends with a nearby farmer who made yogurt from goat's milk and cow's milk on alternative days. Their yogurt culture had been in their family for generations. They also provided us with fresh eggs and chickens. The Sardinians are extremely hospitable and a trip to buy a dozen eggs and a quart of goat yogurt ends up in a 45-minute visit complete with coffee and Sardinian pastries. It was almost impossible to make a purchase without a long visit.

As the Sardinian coast is being developed for tourists, the interior is still primitive and undeveloped, and it has been that way ever since Roman times. The Romans colonized the coast but did not make much headway in the interior. The only thing that penetrated into the interior was the Latin language, and once established, it stayed. There were not many outside influences to change it and today the dialect of central Sardinia is still much closer to Latin than to modern Italian.

Sardinia supplied Rome with timber, salt, and granite, and the Trajan column in Rome comes from a granite quarry ten miles from our vacation house. An inscription on a rock near the quarry was discovered recently and is identified as a law made by the emperor Trajan. This law had to do with the transport of large blocks of granite from Sardinia to Rome by raft. Large wooden rafts were built, and the enormous granite pieces were lashed onto these rafts. The law stated that any galley that passed this floating raft must tow it for 15 miles towards Rome, upon pain of death. Since Sardinia is about 200 miles from Rome there must have been at least 15 different galleys compelled to bend a heavy oar to bring this material to Rome. It would be interesting to know whether Roman police boats patrolled nearby to make sure that no passing galley shirked its civic obligations. Also, one wonders how many galley captains were crucified for not towing a raft of granite.

We found a good way to fish by using our masks and snorkel and floating on top of the water with the rod held in front. This way you could see the fish gather around the bait. The more courageous ones would strike and nibble at the side. It was particularly enjoyable to float over a depth of from five to ten feet and locate the bigger fish hiding under rock ledges and then try to maneuver the bait and line so that it slowly floated past their noses. Sometimes, when done skillfully, we had an immediate strike as the fish saw a wonderful lunch passing by and would come out to grab it. Other times the fish were more suspicious and would swim by many times studying the menu before partaking.

Athletic progress this year was not limited to swimming and a number of medals were acquired by the children in other sports. Valeria took ski lessons at Selva in the Dolomites, and in her class of 18 she took a second place in their giant slalom ski race and told us she did not miss a gate. Gary won a second place at the school giant slalom ski meet. Shortly after, he followed in the family tradition and had a cast on his leg for three weeks. It was not a break but a sprain of his ankle, which he received trying to be a ski jumper. He was proud to have a cast and it did not slow him up at all. He was back in top shape for the school Olympic meet in the spring and won first place by a healthy margin in the 50-meter dash for second grade boys and a second place in the 400-meter run. Every parent is amazed at the rapid growth and progress of their children, and we are no exceptions.

This past year I thought it was high time to expose the children to the Bible. The stage was set to make it a pleasant experience. It was Sunday evening, they had just had their bath, the sofa was drawn up in front of an open fireplace and the wood was crackling, giving out an inviting warmth and captivating flickers. I thought it would be best to start at the beginning and Genesis was our first lesson. I got no further than the part where God had created the heavens and the earth when Valeria interrupted with a small question, "Does God really exist?" After answering that one as best as I could, I was interrupted by Gary. Between the 22nd and 24th verse of Genesis, there is a rather wide jump after the creation of fish to the creation of cattle. "That's not true," interrupted Gary, "the dinosaurs came first." By the time I had finished my explanation to that affirmation it was time for bed and the first Bible lesson was over.

Our parental pride at the precociousness of the children turned to a bit of concern a few weeks later when Gary had his 8th birthday party. I arrived home early to participate in the games of his second-grade class. They were playing "Simon says" when I arrived, and Gary was the leader. Remaining in the game were four girls and one boy. Gary was whispering some instructions into the ear of the little boy and their expressions were enough to tell that something sinister was afoot. Gary stepped back and gave the next command. The boy missed the command and stepped out. Now with the four girls (where he wanted them) Gary gave the command.

"Simon says, pull up your skirts and pull down your pants". Before there could be any thought about the command and without resorting to "Simon says", I interrupted the game with: "I veto that command."

I was aware of the early maturation of the children these days but was not aware it was this early. I do not remember every playing that kind of game when I was in the second grade. This was then followed by Valeria telling us she would like to have a bikini bathing suit with a brassiere. Robin, our one-year-old, has not been able to find the words to startle her parents yet. Up to now she is just reminding us how much fun a baby is. She is a very gregarious explorer and likes to toddle into the same room where the other two children are playing, they make a nice trio.

The trio was broken up in July when Robin stayed with the family of Lydia's brother and my mother took Gary and Valeria to visit relatives in Denmark. Prior to leaving, my mother asked each child to write down the rules they thought would be important for good traveling companions to follow. While the children were following their rules traveling north, Lydia came south with me to Africa. She had heard my stories of trips to Nigeria and wanted to see the country for herself. In the process we had a real modern-day African experience.

As our airplane approached Lagos there was a replay of my first trip to Nigeria. The pilot announced that there was an important visitor in the plane ahead of us and we were not allowed to land until the visitor had been officially greeted. The visitor was the king of Lesotho and General Gowon met him at the airport in a manner befitting a king. Our plane circled the Lagos airport for one and a half hours as the king was being greeted.

When we got to our hotel where reservations had been made two and a half months earlier, we found there were no rooms available. This time it was the unexpected visit of the king of Lesotho and again neither he nor his host had remembered to book hotel rooms. Our room was one of those commandeered for his royal presence, so we were happy to know our room was fit for a king. Fortunately, the king of Lesotho did not bring 57 ministers with him as had the Premier of Togo on my last visit, so every nook and corner were not occupied by a bed. After much searching the manager of the hotel did find one room free on the top floor. He explained that it was not really in condition to let out. It was the rainy season, and the roof was leaking. At least that was what we were told. The pool of water was only in the bathroom and the problem may not have been restricted only to the roof, as the rainwater did seem a bit darker than I would have expected. Fortunately, the visit of the king of Lesotho was of only one day duration, the foreign policy matters must have been simple, and I doubt there is much complicated trade between Nigeria and Lesotho. The next day we got a room that was dry.

As opposed to the heat and humidity of prior visits, the weather this time was very pleasant. It was towards the end of the rainy season and the rains had stopped the day before. It was sunny with fast moving low clouds in the skies and the temperature was about 70 degrees. The air was fresh, and the foliage was green and lush. Lydia was particularly impressed by the different kinds of plants and flowers and Nigeria certainly has a wide variety of equatorial and typically African foliage.

Also very typically African is the marketplace. We went through the market in Lagos and were particularly impressed by the pharmacy section. Along with bottled medicines, the pharmacist sold various kinds of bones, deer antlers, rhinoceros' horns, monkey hands, lizard heads, cows' hoofs, frog legs, and even a few skulls which I thought were rather large to be of monkeys, but I may have been mistaken. We asked a fellow from the office who accompanied us how one went about selecting medicines at this market.

"Do you normally get a prescription from a medicine man?"

"No," he replied, "you just select a few of the items which you like, take them home, grind them into a powder, add a little water, and give it to the person that is sick."

"How do you know the proper proportion of each item," I asked.

"Oh, you just feel it."

One startling article in the pharmacy section was a dried rat impaled upon a 2-foot stick. I knew that prisoners of the Turks during the Renaissance and even after were impaled but was not aware that rats were crucified in this manner.

"What are these rats used for," I asked.

"Medicine men buy them and carry them in front of them when they walk into a house of a sick person. They feel it helps to drive away the evil spirits, much the same as your missionaries carry a cross in front of them when they walk someplace."

I was somewhat taken aback at his comparison of what I felt was a black magic ritual to Christian practice, but I had to admit myself that even though the two objects carried are very different, the basic principle is not. We then inquired about the price, and we were informed that the cost of a good, impaled rat was about eight dollars. Our guide complained that everything is going up with "Udoji", another name for inflation, and six months ago they only cost five dollars. We decided that at eight dollars it was a bit overpriced and after all it was not really the type of souvenir from Africa that our aunt would appreciate.

The "Udoji" to which he referred has been quite a traumatic shock in Nigeria. Udoji is the name of a minister who was asked at the beginning of 1974 to prepare a report on what the pay scales should be for civil service employees. The report was issued at the end of 1974 and proposed to increase the lower paid civil service workers by 100% and the higher ones by 30%. The government did even more than Mr. Udoji proposed and also increased the highest paid bureaucrats by 100%. This decree took place in December 1974 with retroactive effect to April 1st, 1974 and sent a sharp impulse of new money into the economy. But with no more goods produced and the port clogged preventing new imports, this new money in circulation sent prices up. Shelves of stores were swept bare and sales of appliances and motorcycles more than doubled. People nicknamed their motorcycles Udoji, and a Lagos theme song became 'In my Udoji Hacienda."

Then came the reaction of the workers outside of the Civil Service. They wanted their Udoji also. They presented their demands in virtually all sectors of the economy at the same time. The private sector was not prepared for this onslaught nor did most of the private companies have the financial reserves, as did the federal treasury swollen with oil royalties, to cope with increases of 30% to 100%, much less the retroactive impact. Strikes followed. The banks went on a slowdown, cashing one check per hour which is about one fourth their normal rate. The water workers and electrical employees walked off the job. Even the night soil men threatened to "down buckets" if their complete Udoji demands were not met. If you have ever been to Lagos, you realize that a strike of even a few days of the night soil men would be a far worse catastrophe than being without light and water.

The army intervened and restored a semblance of order. As could be imagined in a military regime, whether of the right or left, the army is not gentle with strikers. At the electrical power station in Lagos the army confronted the striking workers with rifle butts raised. When the strikers did not budge, the officer in charge of the soldiers gave the order to swing around from rifle butts to rifle barrels. The electrical workers, finding themselves looking directly into 150 rifle barrels, retreated and went back to work. The government then ordered the electrical company to sweeten its offer and the strike was settled.

The strikes and wage negotiations were all settled within a month and the net result was that all wages in the private sector went up from 30% to 100%. This produced a second tidal wave of additional money flowing into the economy, and prices went up again. The inflation rate in 1975 is expected to be about 70%. There was a strange irony in picking April Fool's Day for the retroactive date of these wage increases. The results, nine months later, verify the very negative and tragic impact of attempting to suddenly improve everyone's standard of living by making more money available.

The people hurt most are the lower paid. The price of staples, cassava flour, yams, and tomatoes have gone up 100%. Eggs have gone up from 8 cents to 20 cents each. Scrawny chickens which sold for $2.70 last year are now selling for $6.00 each. Bus fares have gone up from 15 cents to 50 cents. The government has tried to force the bus prices back down but is having difficulty. Most of the buses are one-man businesses and as there are fewer buses than the demand for rides, the owners can do pretty much what they please and it is hard for the government to control them. When these buses pass, they look like a college prank as it seems each bus is trying to claim the record for the most passengers, with arms and legs are hanging out in all directions.

The inflation, however, is only one of the elements of public discontent in Nigeria. The traffic situation in the capital city is a second major problem and the traffic keeps getting worse. It seems that Lagos is just one big traffic jam. Often cars are at a standstill for 15 minutes at a time and when they move, they barely move. There are no traffic lights and most of the streets are very narrow and barely wide enough for two cars. It is sufficient for one car to stop for any reason, and you get a tremendous jam. The car in back pulls out to pass the stopped car and comes face to face with a car coming from the other direction. The cars coming in the opposite way, seeing a gap, pull out to pass and find themselves looking headlight to headlight into the car that was stopped. In 30 seconds, you get two lanes of cars facing each other backed up for four blocks. Extrication is agony and takes forever.

There are just too many cars in the city in proportion to the roads. To make matters worse, all goods coming into Lagos harbor must be trucked through the middle of the city on their way to all other parts of the country. One day I ate lunch at my hotel three miles from the office. The driver picked me up after lunch and by the time I got to the office it had already closed for the day. Another time, I got out of the car to walk the remaining distance and made it to the office half an hour before the driver - at 5:30 pm. I met an Italian engineer from Fiat at the hotel who said he had spent seven hours in traffic jams that day.

During the rainy season, traffic is worse than normal. With six inches of rain dropped in a matter of three hours and with the sewers already inadequate, some of the city streets become raging torrents. It is not uncommon to find cars moving slowly through the water, running board high and at times higher. On some of the side streets the force of the current can be dangerous for children playing. With these rains you do get a flushing of the sewers, which are open ditches alongside the road. But the flushing results in an overflow of the sewers up on to the streets. The sewer contents then become beached on lawns and sidewalks, somewhat akin to the Nile overflowing its banks and depositing rich silt on the shores. This annual flood may explain in part the lush green foliage of Lagos. Many Nigerians walk barefoot with pant legs rolled up during the rainy season. If the expatriates would follow suit, they would save considerably on their cleaning and shoeshine bills.

A third chaotic element in Nigeria is the Lagos port. On my first trip to Lagos in October 1974, there were 32 ships waiting outside the harbor for a berth. In February 1975, this number had increased to 75, in July it had jumped to 250, and by October there were 375 ships waiting to dock. This is three times the number of ships involved in the Normandy Landing and over twice the number of ships in the Spanish Armada. Two thirds of these ships are loaded with cement and the 1975 Nigerian cement problem will undoubtedly go down in the record books as the biggest scandal of the 20th century. The numbers involved are enormous. In the five-year plan published in 1974 the government identified the need for 20 million tons of cement during the coming five-year period. Of this, 20 million tons, eight million were to be produced locally. Since there had been some cement shortages in the past, and to make certain that cement would not be a bottleneck in the coming 5-year plan, 20 million tons were immediately ordered from companies outside of Nigeria and delivery was requested within 12 months. In this haste several major factors were "overlooked."

One of these factors is the inadequate cement unloading facilities at Lagos harbor, which could handle 2000 tons per day. Assuming cement can be unloaded during the rainy season, which is unwise, it would take them 28-1/2 years to unload 20 million tons of cement. Even with the crash program to increase the port capacity tenfold by the early part of next year, it will still take almost three years to unload the cement ordered.

A second factor is the effective life of cement. Assuming all the cement does get landed within three years, it still represents five years of consumption assuming no local production of cement, or about eight years' consumption along with Nigerian cement production. In so far as cement has a normal shelf life of about six months before it loses its strength, at best only about one eight of the 20 million tons of cement ordered could really be used. Then comes the cost question.

As cement plus freight charges to Lagos comes to about $50 a ton, on the surface it appears that the financial commitment of the Nigerian government for 20 million tons is about one billion dollars. But in so far as the Nigerian Government takes title to the cement on shipment, any waiting charges must be added to the cost of cement. As waiting charges average about 40 cents per ton per day, if a ship waits four months, the waiting charges come to about 50 dollars, so the effective price of the cement is doubled. If the ship has to wait for one year, the landed cement will cost 200 dollars rather than 50 dollars per ton. As it will take a minimum of three years to offload the cement, at the unloading rate that is expected to be reached shortly, unless some other drastic action is taken, the cement ships will have an average wait of one and a half years giving an average cost of cement of about 300 dollars per ton. That means that unless other instructions are given to the ships, the one billion dollars' worth of cement will cost the Nigerian Government a total of $6 billion

Rumor has it that all the pressure to get these 20 million tons of cement delivered within 12 months was influenced by a commission of one dollar per ton to be paid in Switzerland on behalf of one or two officials rather high up in the Nigerian Government. If true, their enrichment would amount to about 20 million dollars. The criminality of a few officials lining their pockets with 20 million dollars of public money becomes insignificant in comparison to the five billion dollars of potential waste of taxpayers' money. In actual fact, the Nigerian Government can probably take some action to reduce their total loss. But the actions are unusual. One action would be to tell 200 of the ships to dump their cargo in the sea, and another fifty to sail to other West African ports and offer the cement as a gift from Nigeria. One action being considered by the Nigerian Government is to buy a Greek cement factory, close production, and supply the customers from the ships waiting outside of Lagos harbor. Whether a customer would accept bags of cement that have been sitting in the hold of a ship in the humid tropics for four months remains to be seen.

Apart from the cement bottleneck, the other ships must still wait five months outside the port unless their ship has a priority. This port congestion brings with it some colorful as well as tragic episodes. You can imagine the boredom of the sailors waiting five months outside of Lagos harbor, in the humid heat or under heavy monsoon rains. We heard there had been two suicides and one murder on the waiting ships in the past month. The only diversion for the sailors is a trip to the nearby beach. On Sunday morning it appears that a United Nation Army is about to invade Nigeria as longboat after longboat, full of sailors, each flying their own flag comes sweeping shoreward. When we were there, we saw Norwegian, Danish, Polish, Russian, English, Italian, German, Chinese, Malayan, and even a Swiss longboat. We asked the sailor how there could be a Swiss ship. He said that it was Swiss-owned and Swiss-registered but had its home port in Hamburg rather than at Lake Lucerne.

There is a little bar and restaurant at the back of the beach shaded by palm trees. It is called "The California" and does a booming business with all these bored and thirsty sailors. They also pick up substantial foreign currency from three rooms which they rent out for short periods of time.

There has been some attempt to relieve this port congestion by unloading ships at other West African ports, such as Cotonou in Dahomey (now Benin), or Lomé in Togo, and even as far as Accra in Ghana, but this solution creates other problems. The ports in these countries are also rather small and the roads through the jungle from these countries to Nigeria are not built for heavy traffic. It won't take very long before a flow of trucks will break them up. In addition, every time there is the whisper or rumor of a coup, the borders of these countries are closed, and the trucks could be blocked in transit for some time.

Just a few months ago we had a truck full of equipment blocked in Dahomey when the Premier had one of his top ministers arrested and shot under the charge that had been caught in bed with the Premier's wife. As a consequence, the border was sealed for five days. After a thorough search revealed that no other ministers were hiding in closets or foot lockers in the Premier's house, the border was reopened. In spite of the delay caused by an amorous Dahomey minister, the merchandise still reached Lagos via Cotonou, quicker than had the ship waited its turn outside Lagos harbor.

The solution to the under dimensioned Lagos port is complex and will take years to improve. Not only are the number of births insufficient but the unloading equipment is old-fashioned, and much unloading is still done by hand. In addition, there is not enough warehouse space at the docks. Most of the docks are on an island and the road to the mainland is narrow. This narrow road passes through the center of Lagos, itself blocked with traffic jams. A ring road is being built to solve this last problem and better unloading equipment is being ordered, but improvements progress very slowly.

At the same time, the expanding economy, and the attempt to build an infrastructure in a country which produces very little itself except petroleum, palm oil, and cement, means that all heavy equipment and building materials must be imported. The actions required to expand the infrastructure create new rings of bottlenecks upon existing bottlenecks which choke future expansion and progress comes very slowly.

A typical problem is the electrical supply. There is insufficient electrical power in Lagos and the docks need more power to run the present, much less future, unloading equipment. The power company wants to increase their electrical capacity and has the money for it but in order to increase their power output they need steel, cement, and equipment which must be imported through the clogged port facilities. To bring additional materials away from the port, roads must be expanded which in turn requires more steel, cement, and equipment. When you stir in the expansion needs of the other basic services of a developing economy, such as communications, water supply, airports, schools, and hospitals, the logistics and priority problems become very complicated.

Although Nigeria is fortunate to be in an ample hard currency situation, the inability to spend this hard currency fast enough is a source of frustration with so much work to be done in the country. With the inflation, dreadful traffic and port problems it is no small wonder the country was ripe for a change, which in most of Africa means a coup. Lydia and I had the opportunity to partake in one of those unforgettable experiences, an African coup d'état. Fortunately, it was the most peaceful one they ever had in Africa in the past ten years and there was no loss of life or even shots fired.

General Gowon, chief of State and eight of his principal ministers including the Head of the Army were in Kampala, Uganda for the annual Organization of African Unity (OAU) meeting as well as to admire the unveiling of a new statue of Field Marshal Ida Amin. Many of the other senior army officers were in the north of the country at Kano playing polo. The day of the coup we had planned to visit a maintenance site at Port Harcourt and arranged to be picked up at 5:30 am to take the early morning plane. As we approached the airport, we found the road blocked with barbed wire and three soldiers. They said the airport was closed. I got out of the car and went up to talk to the officer in charge to get more information. He did not know for how long it would be closed or the reason. He had his hand firmly on his submachine gun and it was pointing at me, but he was very polite.

As unusual things happen at the spur of the moment in Nigeria and as it is customary for the roads and hotels to be cleared when visiting dignitaries come, we did not give this incident as much importance as you would in most other countries. Also, the military is always very much in evidence in Nigeria. Since we were already out of town and past the worst traffic, and as I had also planned to visit an earth satellite station we were building 150 miles north of Lagos, we decided to shift plans and drive up-country to the satellite station, rather than wait for the airport to open. As we passed through various towns everything was peaceful and people were going about their normal business. After a two-hour drive we came upon a roadblock.

Five soldiers with submachine guns were manning the roadblock and they waved us down. They asked us to get out of the car and they looked through our luggage. Then they told us very politely to proceed on our way. As they each carried submachine guns, I thought it better to proceed when they said to proceed, rather than ask them to explain why they were checking cars and if there was any connection between their action and the fact that the airport was closed.

Up until this time the idea of a coup seemed remote. However, after passing this roadblock we did begin to wonder if there was something major going on and whether there might be a coup taking place. But nothing else seemed out of the ordinary and at the earth satellite station things were peaceful. There were always two or three soldiers on guard at the entrance to the site and they did not even ask us for identification as we drove up. Our white faces must have been sufficient identification as expatriate technicians and engineers come and go continuously.

Once at the site the Nigerian engineer in charge asked if there was anything strange going on in the city. He said their telephone communication was cut off with Lagos and they were unable to call out of Nigeria. When we told him the airport was closed and there was a roadblock halfway to Lagos, a grin of illumination spread over his face. I began thinking about what the manual says regarding the various steps to take in making a coup. Close the airports and frontier, cut off communications inside and outside, set up roadblocks, and a grin of illumination also spread over my face. As we sat grinning at each other a truck load of soldiers drove in. and our grins were confirmed. The corporal in charge said they had orders to double the guard, and everyone must show their ID on entering and exiting the site. After the soldiers left, the chief engineer suggested we leave soon and get back to Lagos before dark. We agreed that was a good idea and asked if he would mind giving us a letter stating we were on official business and who we were. He agreed willingly and we felt this letter plus our passports should get us through any new roadblocks that might be in the process of being set up.

Prior to returning to Lagos, we had a fine meal at the site. On my last trip we had left the choice of the lunch up to the steward. This was a mistake. When we arrived at 1:00 pm he served us something which had the texture of rubber with the aroma of chicken. After that meal we asked him where he had gotten the chicken. He replied that he was sitting on the step outside the house trying to figure out what to serve us and the chicken just happened to pass by. He grabbed it, killed it, plucked it, cooked it and served it, all within an hour. By comparison, the meal this time was a masterpiece. It was prepared by a new houseboy, Marcello, who had come two weeks before from Dahomey, an ex-French West Africa colony. Marcello cooked in the French style. He served us ham, but I'm sure it was not from a little pig that just happened to be passing by before lunch.

While at lunch, our site manager told us about the invasion of snakes they were having. During the rainy season the snakes come down from the hills. One of these is known as the 2-step viper, a small snake about 12 inches long that often lives in the banana trees. Its venom attacks the nervous system and there is no known serum against the poison. According to the natives, if you are bitten, you have time to take only two steps before you drop dead. For this reason, many of the men you see in the region who make their living picking bananas have one or two fingers missing. If they happen to reach up for the bananas and the snake comes out to bite their finger, a quick stroke of the machete to whack off the finger is the only cure. If you hesitate for a few seconds, it might be too late. Going through life one is faced with many situations requiring a decision but none probably requiring as quick a decision as this one, "to chop or not to chop, that is the question."

The reaction of the natives is automatic and probably based on the philosophy of "if in doubt chop". While this policy results in a few fingers unnecessarily cut off when bitten by a less lethal variety, it is one of those calculated risks, and a good one at that. Encounters with snakes are not limited to the banana pickers. One of our installers was reaching his hand up to straighten some cables on an overhead rack and in lifting one of the cables between his two fingers, felt that although the cable had the right diameter, it had an unusual consistency, He was also surprised to find it was not attached very firmly, in fact it was not attached at all. At this point he froze. Then, ever so slowly, he raised his hand up and brought it back.

"There is a snake up there," he screamed.

The other fellows of the crew came running and one of them had a knife and hammer. This time instead of reaching up into the cable rack, a ladder was brought so one could see. What was seen was a small brown snake moving slowly down the cable rack. Two sharp blows of the hammer, and it was dead. The fellow was still shaking. "I don't think he bit me, at least I did not feel anything," he said. But five minutes later his forearm started to swell, and it became twice its normal size. He was rushed to a car, the dead snake was thrown into the trunk, and they drove off to the nearest dispensary. Luckily, it was not the two-step viper, but one of its benevolent distant relatives, and the proper antidote was available and applied.

Another snake found in the area is the mambo. This little fellow spends part of his time in trees, and if he feels irritated at your intrusion into his part of the jungle, he will drop out of the tree onto your back and bite you on the back of your neck and hang on like a mastiff. The poison of this particular mambo is not usually deadly which I imagine is some sort of a minor consolation, as you go running to someone to get that snake off the back of your neck.

Fortunately, reptiles are not the only wildlife in this area and there are many wild monkeys living in the nearby rocks. One monkey was tied to a tree in the village like a pet dog, and I went up to greet him. He was very friendly and shook hands. He was also very curious and, slowly and gently, he reached out to touch and twist the hair on the back of my forearm. Then he looked at me and reached out again very slowly to twist my arm hair. At first, I thought it was my white skin that was so different from the black skin he was used to that had aroused his interest. But then as I looked around at the natives, I realized that they had virtually no hair on their arms. As the monkey looked closely into my face after examining my arm hair for the third time, I almost felt him saying "You must be my long-lost cousin. Look, we both have hair on our arms.'"

After this touching reunion, we drove back to Lagos and were surprised at how uneventful our return was considering a coup was in progress. We stopped at the roadside stand to buy some bananas and to allow our driver to negotiate for 30 pounds of cassava flour and 10 huge yams. The final negotiated price was less than half of the Lagos price and provided our driver with staples for three weeks. There was one roadblock about halfway to Lagos, but this time we were not even asked to get out of the car. Once we reached the outskirts of Lagos, life seemed to be going on as usual. All the small storekeepers were busy hawking their wares, and women, as usual, were carrying big loads on their heads with their babies strapped to their backs.

However, there was one thing unusual - the lack of traffic. Our road forked off from the airport road, just out of the city, and normally from this point into the city you have up to two hours of bumper-to-bumper stop and go traffic. This time we flew along the road. There were virtually no cars and on the Apongbon bridge we were the only car. It usually takes 15 minutes to cross this half mile causeway.

Back at our hotel we heard the radio announcement of the Colonel in charge of the Lagos regiment. He told the population that, due the general deterioration of living conditions and citing inflation, traffic congestion and the unsolved harbor problems, General Gowon ceased to be the Head of State. The Army (which was already in charge) was taking over, and a new chief of state would be named shortly. The colonel announced that all airports, ports, and borders were closed and there would be a rigid dawn to dusk curfew until further notice.

The next day business activity resumed as usual, and the population accepted the change calmly. In fact, most Nigerians, I spoke with, felt that nine years were enough time with the old rulers in office and the change should be positive. When reached at the African leaders' meeting in Kampala for comments, Gowon quoted Shakespeare philosophically. "The world is a stage, and the actors make their entries and exits."

Although one of the reasons cited by the new government for the change was the Lagos traffic situation, the traffic in Lagos the next day was the worst I have ever seen. With the curfew, the normal 4:00 pm to 7:00 pm traffic had to be compressed into half the time and traffic came to a standstill. I walked out of the office at 5:00 pm and realized I would never make it to the hotel by the 6 pm curfew time, if I went by car. The hotel was three miles away, so I walked. I got back before dusk, but most of the cars were still at a standstill two hours after sunset.

We made several futile trips to the airport in trying to leave Nigeria. We drove to the airport on the first day the radio said the airport was open, but no one apparently told the guards on the airport road about it, and traffic was turned back. On the following day, the radio said the airport was open and we drove out again through the two-hour traffic jam. When we got there, we found the airport was open but only for domestic traffic. On the third day, the radio announced all flights were going but this time it was only Nigerian airline flights going out of the country.

With all the crowds at the airport, we thought we would have a better chance to get out by taking an airline to a neighboring West African country, which had normal international traffic, rather than fight the crowd of Europeans for spots on the few planes going to Europe. On this particular day we had the choice of a Nigerian Airlines to Abidjan stopping at Accra, Ghana, on the way, or a Ghana Airlines plane that went to Accra and then on to Abidjan. There did not seem any strong argument favoring one of these airlines over the other, but because maintenance is quite a problem in West Africa plus the confusion created by the coup, we thought there would be a better chance of the Ghana Airlines making it to Abidjan. The planes left within two hours of each other. The Nigerian airlines made it to Abidjan, but the Ghana airlines did not.

Just after we hooked up our seat belt at Accra, after landing to discharge and take on passengers for the next leg of the trip, we were told to get off the plane. We wondered if there was now a coup taking place in Ghana. The problem was not quite that bad, but our flight was cancelled. The next day our Ghana Airlines plane did get off and made it to Abidjan.

We decided to do a bit of sightseeing in the Ivory Coast before flying back to Europe. We had heard that the mountainous region in the north of the country was attractive and had the longest Tarzan type vine bridge in the world. That was the place to go and see before returning home. We found there were two planes per week to Man, the capital town of this area and one of these two had left the day before. The alternative was to rent a car which was frightfully expensive or go by public bus transportation. The public bus won the debate, and we went down to the main station at 7:00 in the morning. There were no regularly scheduled runs by bus companies that went to the town of Man, but there were individuals who owned small buses and when they had full load they departed. We found one that was going to Man and got two good seats on the bus. It was a half open vehicle slightly larger than a Volkswagen bus. There were three people in the front seat and in back there were four rows of seats with place for five on each row. Fully loaded, it carried 23 people. While each person had a seat, it was a bit tight. There was no problem of ventilation as the sides of the bus were open, closed occasionally with canvas when the intermittent rains came, but for the most part the ride was breezy and fresh.

While buses in Europe and in the U.S. are supposed to make a pee stop every two hours or so, the buses in the Ivory Coast make regular prayer stops. There is a mid-morning prayer stop at 10:00 and a mid-afternoon prayer stop at 4:00. Our bus was more than 50% Muslim and one of the passengers was very religious. He reminded the driver when it was time for the first prayer stop and was the first to start and last to finish with his prayer ceremony. He carried his own carpet, as did many of the others, and a tea kettle of water. The water was used for the ablutions (washing hands) before starting the prayer. One other item in addition to a tea kettle of water and a carpet that is needed to be a good Muslim must be a compass. I did not see anyone with a compass, but someone must have had some kind of a Mecca direction finder as the carpets for the 10:00 am prayers were lined up at an oblique angle to the road. At the 4:00 pm prayers the oblique angle was different. There was a lunch stop for an hour at a medium-sized town on the road. We stopped near an open-air cafeteria with wooden benches made of mahogany, and the menu was dried fish, okra, and lettuce. We decided we would lunch on French bread and bananas. We had not had any stomach trouble so far and wanted to keep our record clean.

One incident that happened after lunch was disturbing. It concerned the police blocks on the road which are very common in the Ivory Coast, and this one was particular. We had already passed through two police roadblocks before lunch. At each block there were two policemen beside a small shack. One policeman had a whistle with which he stopped the cars, and the other policeman checked the papers of the driver. At each block, our driver stopped, got out of the car, and carried a large wallet with licenses and registration papers to the policeman. At each stop the checking took no more than three minutes and we were on our way again.

At this particular check point there were five vehicles stopped going in our direction. Our driver pulled up behind the last one and got out with his papers. Five minutes passed, then 10 minutes, then 15 minutes. He came back and talked to the fellow in the seat next to him, who seemed to be the administrator of the bus. They both went back to the policeman. After we had been there half an hour I got out and stretched my legs and in the best French I could muster asked the driver what the problem was. "The policeman wants money" was the first reply I received.

"What for?" was my naive question. "Is there something wrong with the papers? Is the license expired?"

"No, the papers are all in order, but the policeman wants money."

"Aha, so it's a shakedown."

I did not know the French equivalent of the word shakedown, and my attempt to translate shake and down into French did not work very well. Even though they did not understand my question, I now understood what was going on. Several other vehicles came along the road and the policeman with the whistle flagged them down also. We now had about eight vehicles stopped and no one seemed to be doing anything. I walked over to the shack and tried to understand the conversation going on and heard the policeman emphatically say to one driver, "You must pay me."

I spoke to the driver of the bus ahead of ours. He was distraught. I asked him if his papers were in order. He said everything was correct, but "The policeman just wants money."

"What he is asking for will eat up all the profit on this trip for me, but what I can do. My passengers want to be off, and I can't leave until I pay."

This was a case of highway brigandage with the toll being extracted by the one responsible for keeping law and order. My sense of righteousness was rising, and I wanted to do something, if at all possible, to fight against this abuse. Lydia and I were the only Europeans in all these vehicles, and I wondered whether our presence and intervention would make any difference.

"Do you think it would do any good if I talked to the police officer? He might be afraid I would report the incident to higher authorities," I ventured.

"I appreciate your interest, but this is West Africa and I doubt your assistance would help, au contraire," (on the contrary).

I was torn. Maybe my intervention could make a difference and if it would, I should not sit back, but rather do something. On the other hand, we were guests in the Ivory Coast, and should we meddle in internal affairs? Even though we do not agree with the customs of the land, should we try to change them?

If the Ivory Coast were still controlled by France, the threat to inform the authorities could be all that was necessary to dissolve this "knot in the road". On the other hand, all of the Central and West African countries have gained their independence from France, England, and Belgium fairly recently and the thought of a white man flexing some muscle might not be the proper way to improve this situation. In any case, I decided to test the reaction of the police officer to see whether I could detect a trace of apprehension at having a European in his midst who might report an incident of blatant corruption to the authorities in Abidjan. If I could see even a hairline fracture in his sense of assurance, I would push ahead with more force.

With as much military manner as I could muster, I walked crisply up to the police officer and in my best French I asked him what the problem was. As a face of black granite turned slowly towards me, I realized there was absolutely no crack in his sense of assurance. This was emphasized all the more, by his slow reply to me.

"I don't owe you any explanation."

At this point, I thought of the experience of our construction manager who had gone in Dahomey to clear some material that had arrived at the Port of Cotonou. He had been picked up by the police while he was there and was taken to the jail for questioning. He was detained only an hour as he spoke French and could explain who he was and what he was doing. On his way out he saw two white faces in the jail. He asked who they were and why they were in the jail. He was told they were two Englishmen who had come into Dahomey without a visa. They had been in jail for three days already and no diplomatic office had been advised of their retention. Fortunately, our man was able to obtain their freedom. They were extremely grateful and said

"I appreciate your interest, but this is West Africa and I doubt your assistance would help, au contraire," (on the contrary).

I was torn. Maybe my intervention could make a difference and if it would, I should not sit back, but rather do something. On the other hand, we were guests in the Ivory Coast, and should we meddle in internal affairs? Even though we do not agree with the customs of the land, should we try to change them?

If the Ivory Coast were still controlled by France, the threat to inform the authorities could be all that was necessary to dissolve this "knot in the road". On the other hand, all of the Central and West African countries have gained their independence from France, England, and Belgium fairly recently and the thought of a white man flexing some muscle might not be the proper way to improve this situation. In any case, I decided to test the reaction of the police officer to see whether I could detect a trace of apprehension at having a European in his midst who might report an incident of blatant corruption to the authorities in Abidjan. If I could see even a hairline fracture in his sense of assurance, I would push ahead with more force.

With as much military manner as I could muster, I walked crisply up to the police officer and in my best French I asked him what the problem was. As a face of black granite turned slowly towards me, I realized there was absolutely no crack in his sense of assurance. This was emphasized all the more, by his slow reply to me.

"I don't owe you any explanation."

At this point, I thought of the experience of our construction manager who had gone in Dahomey to clear some material that had arrived at the Port of Cotonou. He had been picked up by the police while he was there and was taken to the jail for questioning. He was detained only an hour as he spoke French and could explain who he was and what he was doing. On his way out he saw two white faces in the jail.

they did not know when they would have gotten out if our man had not come along. The situation was serious as they were running out of money because in many of West African countries the prisons do not provide the prisoners with food. Instead, the prisoners either have to pay the guard to bring food or have relatives nearby who will come to the prison with food.

As we did not have much money with us and no relatives within 3,000 miles, I decided it was best if our bus driver resolves his own problem. This was undoubtedly not the first nor would it be the last time he was shaken down on the road, and it was just one of the many difficulties with which a bus driver in the Ivory Coast had to learn to cope. We were passengers and would have to accept the ride for the money we paid with all of its adventures and delays. We just hoped the delay would not be much longer. Besides, in a little town in the middle of the jungle, the local police chief is probably a king in his own right and could probably keep a foreigner in jail for many days on his own authority, particularly if he did not like his looks or thought he represented a threat or danger to his lucrative business activities. While putting an American in jail could be eventually dangerous for the police chief if diplomatic sources had to become involved to obtain his release, but I wondered how could we make the American Consulate aware of our situation with 200 miles of jungle separating us from Abidjan?

The negotiation between the drivers and the police chief proceeded. The fellow in the bus ahead of ours was evidently not a good bargainer as he paid 30 dollars to be able to proceed with his busload of passengers. Our driver apparently had more skill as he got away with only a 10-dollar toll.

I did manage to do something anyway. I took down the badge number of the police officer and have since written a letter to the Minister of Tourism and Minister of the Interior informing them of our enjoyable trip to the Ivory Coast, marred by this one incident and giving the number of the policeman responsible. I have not heard from them yet, but I am hoping I'll get back a reply thanking me for my interest and advising they have fired that police officer.

The afternoon drive from there to Man was uneventful except for the 4:00 pm prayer stop and another police roadblock five miles before reaching our destination: This was another three-minute routine check so a second letter to the Minister of Interior was not necessary.

At the hotel in Man, we met a young boy from the area who spoke a little English and he offered to be our guide to the vine bridge and make all arrangements. It was 90 kilometers away on a bumpy dirt road and we hired a taxi for the day. As we approached our goal, we realized that both our guide and taxi driver had never been there before, and we were lost. After asking several people we finally got off the trail that cuts off from the main dirt road. It was not marked and unless we had been well instructed would have gone right past it and on into Guinea whose southern border was just a few miles ahead. The trail was two tracks cut into what looked like impenetrable jungle. After a mile on the track, we found our way blocked by a fallen tree. A half loop trail was beaten down around the tree, but as it was the rainy season it was too muddy to get around.

It was hard for us to determine how far away the bridge was. We asked several people who lived in the area who were walking past on this trail. One of the natives said the vine bridge was not very far away, just past the village ahead, but when asked how many miles or how much time it took to walk there, he did not know. The next person to pass along the trail said it was very far away, but he was also unable to put the distance into either a mileage or time framework. Our guide was all for giving up and going back home, but as we had come this far, we were determined to see the bridge. So, we started out on the trail by foot, unsure whether we would be walking for one hour or three hours.

We were both very pleased that the car could not make it as the walk through the jungle on this path was beautiful. It was not too hot, and the foliage was fascinating. There were some huge trees, which I believe were mahogany. The trunks were enormous, and they rose up four times as high as trees I am used to seeing, with no branches until the very top. They seemed as tall as the redwoods in California. At the top, the branches came out like an umbrella. There were many banana trees, coffee, and cocoa trees and lots of vines hanging down from the taller trees. We came upon a little village of about 30 huts and several men had just killed a goat and were skinning it as we approached. We paid a little boy a toll for passing through the village and he took us to the river where the vine bridge was.

The bridge is shaped like a V and has three large vines the diameter of my wrist that form the main bridge. These three vines which make up the load bearing structure are fastened to two large trees on either side of the river. The mid-point of the main vine is at the level of the water which was running very fast. As one walks on the main vine at the bottom of the V you hang on to the two vines at shoulder level. Between these three main vine cables are woven smaller diameter vines which make it look like a net. However, in some places the size of the holes is big enough for a body to slip through.

Lydia took off her shoes and climbed up into the tree where the main vines were attached and started across the bridge. I followed. It was very scary, and the bridge was beginning to sway a little with our weight on the main center vine. The fast current of the river was pushing the main vine that was somewhat in the water. As I stepped onto the bridge and looked down into the water, I got a very dizzy feeling. It felt as if the whole bridge was moving sideways up the river. I proceeded slowly, looking ahead rather than down, and placed my feet very gingerly, the heel of one foot touching the toe just behind it and feeling very carefully that the forward foot was right in the middle of the vine before putting my weight on it.

As I inched my way closer to the center and near the point where the bridge begins to dip into the water, a combination of the rapids pushing plus my weight tilted me and the bridge at about a 10-degree angle from vertical with my feet pointing downstream and my head pointing upstream. As I worked my way closer to the center, the angle of the tilt kept increasing and as my foot touched the fast water, my body was now making at least a 20-degree angle off the vertical. I had the crazy feeling that the bridge was going to tip over like a hammock, but I assured myself that it was only an optical illusion. And besides Lydia was ahead of me and had already passed the mid-point and the fast-flowing water was only up to her ankles.

She was much lighter than me. I decided to wait for a few minutes and let her move up completely out of the water before I got in deeper. I was concerned that our combined weight would be enough to have the bridge flip us both out.

She made it across, and I proceeded to place my feet even more carefully, one ahead of the other. As the water swirled past, reaching halfway to my knee, the angle of the tilt kept slowly increasing. As I reached the mid-point I felt as if I was almost in a position at a 45 degree to the water. The force of the water had loosened and untied some of the smaller vine netting in the middle of the bridge and if my foot slipped off the main vine I could easily plunge into the water. My fingers held the two guide vines tightly and the knuckles looked white. Each hand slipped ahead six inches at a time. All of my sense of awareness was concentrated in the souls of my feet and toes, and I have never felt such a strong desire for a prehensile big toe as I did at this time. Once past the mid-point, the bridge slowly began to right itself and as my feet came out of the water. At that point I felt more in control of the situation. The return trip from the other side was a less frightening than the trip across and Tarzan and Jane came skipping back like veterans of the jungle. Our guide preferred not to make the crossing and was content to watch us.

Our trip out of West Africa, after a coup in Nigeria, a forced stay in Ghana, roadblocks in the Ivory Coast, and a voyage across a vine bridge near the Guinea border would not be in complete character if there was no difficulty in our departure. We had a midnight Alitalia flight from Abidjan to Rome, and three hours before departure time we heard that the flight was cancelled because of a strike. Fortunately, there was an Air Afrique flight leaving an hour later for Geneva, and we managed to get on that one. The only thing we missed on the trip, was a stopover in Timbuktu. We will have to save that visit for a later time.

SIXTEEN

1976: Jordan to Timbuktu

1976 has been a milestone year for both Lydia and me. It included a trip to my 25th Harvard college reunion, a change of jobs, an ambitious financing program to construct the American School in Milan, and a trip to Timbuktu. It was also an extremely busy year for Lydia as she was president of the PTO at the American School.

At David's Harvard 25th College Reunion

Although very time consuming, and at times exhausting, Lydia did an outstanding job of organizing the mothers into the many committees needed to have an active and effective PTO. While I look at the matter from a biased standpoint, Lydia's energy, and enthusiasm, plus her ability to encourage the parents to give their time, was a major force in creating an exceptional group of events sponsored by the PTO this year. Lydia also learned a great deal about diplomacy in the process and found that the best way to silence a vocal complainer was to saddle her with some responsibility. She also discovered that many of the habitual complainers are all mouth and no action.

The American School has also been a focal point for me this year and my major project has been the building of a new school. My participation started two years ago when I was asked to join the Board of Trustees and was given the job as Treasurer. The school has been in existence since 1962 and has had a rather unusual beginning. It was founded by a man who was running a language school in Milan and who wanted to offer an alternative to the International School of Milan and the German School.

The first year of the school was a lively one with 17 students ranging from kindergarten through high school. Halfway through the year the newly hired headmaster ran off with the wife of the founder of the school and they took the cash box with them. While the headmaster followed the call of the flesh and the cash box, the small, devoted teaching staff closed ranks and, despite no money for their paychecks, continued with their calling. Inspired by the teachers, the parents decided to give additional support to the infant school, forming a new corporation, and carried on. The school was fortunate to have the Gilioli family as participants of the school. Dan Gilioli was a prominent lawyer with both an Italian and a US license to practice law and served as the lawyer of the school from the start. His brother, Enrico Gilioli, was his law partner and was married to Rita Gilioli, one of the high school teachers.

1976: JORDAN TO TIMBUKTU

Valeria, Lydia, Robin and Gary celebrating the U.S. Bicentennial while in Milan

From the 17 original students when the school started, the American School of Milan has now grown to 400 students. One of the members of the kindergarteners of that initial group was Enrico Gilioli, the son of Dan Gilioli, who went all the way from kindergarten through the high school and is now a lawyer in New York City specializing in petroleum law.

While the academics of the school have been good, the facilities had been a constant problem. For the past seven years, the high school had been renting the 5th floor of a bank in the very center of Milan and the lower and middle schools had been renting space from a Catholic church run by Don Aldo in the western outskirts of Milan, eight miles from the high school. Both the bank president and Don Aldo were anxious to get us out as they need the space. The Italian real estate laws protect occupants from cruel and oppressive landlords, whether these landlords be fat bankers or lean ecclesiastics, and we have been able to continue our occupancy at rents blocked at 1968 price levels. In spite of these favorable economic factors, the space was inadequate for the growing number of students and completely without athletic facilities.

A project to build our own school had been under study for some time. With our enrollment at 400, and expected to reach 500 students, the design included a gymnasium, a large library, and a cafeteria-theatre area. The total project was estimated to cost $2.5 million or an investment in the facility of $6,000 per student excluding the cost of the land. We wanted a piece of land large enough to include outdoor sports fields and hoped to be able to build a high ceiling gym. However, finding a suitable piece of land in the Milan area with those specs was a major challenge.

About the time I came on the school board, a real estate developer descended from heaven and announced that he was willing to give us nine acres of land on the outskirts of Milan in his new apartment development complex. Were we to buy this land it would cost us about half a million dollars. The angel explained that while he was very pleased to help us, we should not consider his donation to us entirely altruistic as by zoning requirements he had to assign a certain area of his land for public service use and a school qualified. The presence of our school in his complex should also help him to rent his luxury apartments.

While it did not take us long to accept his offer, the formal approvals took quite a bit of time and the Italian bureaucracy had to have its chapter in the project. As we are an "Ente Morale," or a nonprofit organization, donations in the form of land must be approved by the appropriate government authorities. In our case the proper government authority was no less than the President of Italy. It took a year to get his approval. Once in possession of the land we went to the banks to borrow money for the construction of the building. We met numerous rejections because the school had no net worth.

Our first angel had appeared as a real estate developer who saw a market in this area outside of Milan for a large apartment complex with an adjacent American school. Our second angel appeared dressed as a banker. We obtained a mortgage loan from a large Milanese savings bank, "Cassa di Risparmio della Provincia di Lombardia" (Cariplo). At the mortgage signing ceremony, the General Manager of Cariplo told us that, from a strictly business standpoint, any bank would be crazy to make a loan to an undercapitalized private school with zero net worth. But Mr Nezzo, the Bank President, found a way to justify granting a construction loan to the school.

In 1975 this bank was the largest savings bank in the entire world. It was founded about 1850 by the Austrian governor General Radetzky who had defeated the former French rulers of the Lombardo-Veneto area of northern of Italy. This area of northern Italy in 1850 was underdeveloped. General Radetzky admired the intelligence, ingenuity and work ethic of the northern Italians and he thought a savings bank was needed to build up the economy of this area of Italy. By charter, this savings bank had been dedicated to the development of the economy of the City of Milan. A school contributes to the development of an area by drawing skilled businessmen with their families to the Milan area. In addition, there was a clause in the charter of this bank to allocate one half of the bank profits for "worthwhile social purposes" and for the growth of the local economy. We could not have picked a better partner for our long-term financing of the building of an American

School. The board members, parents, and students of the American School of Milan should stand when the march composed by Straus and dedicated to the Austrian General Radetzky is played.

At that time there were ten American banks already operating with branches in Milan that were eager to participate in the growth of the Common Market. Most of the American banks had chosen Milan as their Italian Headquarters and had moved their residences to Milan. I invited the ten American executives of those banks who were currently living in Milan to a meeting. Most of them had children at the American school. The purpose of the meeting was to get their advice on the best way to put the financing of the school on a firm long-term financial basis. These American bank executives were anxious to provide their input, recognizing it was to the long-term advantage of their bank to have an American School during the many years it takes to develop an Italian executive bank cadre.

Most of the American Bank Managers currently working in Milan were enthusiastic of the idea of building a modern school building. Some of their wives were already on our school board. Nine of the ten American banks with branches in Milan agreed to contribute a grant to the school of $25,000 each. Once that verbal financing was agreed to, a contract was awarded to the Austin Company to design and build the new school which had ample land for school sports teams. Within a year, the custom-built school was ready.

This was the year of my 25th Harvard college reunion. At the time of my graduation, I was curious to see what some of my classmates would be like 25 years after graduation, which of them would still have their sense of humor and which of them would have interesting experiences to share. The reunion was a family affair, and Gary and Valeria joined us at Harvard. They spent five days in a day camp run by the Harvard Reunion Committee and their program included visits to the Harvard campus, games and activities and a trip to Boston. They were both very enthusiastic about the program and both said they wanted to go to Harvard for college.

I found the renewal of acquaintances exciting. One thing that struck me was the difference in the aging process that had taken place among my classmates. The majority looked almost exactly as they did when we graduated in 1951. There were about 20% who looked well past 60 and were almost unrecognizable. What was it that caused this group to age with such acceleration? Would the many youthful and optimistic fellows remain young looking for the next 25 years or would they age suddenly, as one emerging from the valley of Shangri-La? I look forward to my 50th reunion to get the answer to these questions.

The Harvard Crimson newspaper described our class as a mediocre with no outstanding personalities. By contrast the class of 1950 had both Henry Kissinger, Secretary of State and National Security Advisor under Presidents Nixon and Ford, and James Schlesinger, Secretary of Defense under Nixon. In the 1,100-page class book with the autobiographies of most of the classmates, I read that many of them have led interesting lives, and a few have made substantial contributions in their area of expertise. I was surprised that those in business and industry represented about 20% of my classmates. The opportunity to converse with renewed friends over a five-day period was very enjoyable. I was also amused at breakfast time seeing the children of classmates in the food line. Many of them looked like caricatures of their fathers.

We were assigned accommodations in Winthrop House, my college dormitory. Our suite was next to the room I had as a freshman. One thing that surprised me was the rapid growth of the trees in the lawn between my dormitory and the next dormitory. These trees had just been planted when I was a freshman and were saplings about my height at that time. Now they were over five stories tall and formed a cathedral-like path between the buildings. While long conversations, the aging process, tall trees, caricatures, and nostalgia was the reunion for me, for Gary and Valeria Harvard means jumping on the trampoline in the Harvard Yard and the Harvard band playing loud and rousing music at the drop of a hat.

One of the consequences of this trip to the United States was a new nose. It all started one day when I wanted to show Gary and Valeria how to swim underwater. I took them to a pool in Atlanta and first explained long distance underwater swimming theory.

"Your strokes should be slow and powerful, and you should wait until your forward motion is completely stopped before taking the next stroke. You can watch the bottom to see when your forward motion stops. You can also hold your breath much longer than what you imagine. It is a matter of training and practice," Once the theoretical part of the lesson finished, I moved to a demonstration of what I had just pontificated.

"Watch me, I'll swim the width of the pool underwater".

After taking four powerful strokes I thought I should be close to the other side. Beginning to feel the need for a breath I decided to take a particularly powerful last stroke. When I reached out my arms to make the last powerful stroke, my fingers must have been just inches from touching the edge. Needless to say, my last powerful stroke surged my face, led by my nose right into the concrete side of the pool. I heard a crunch. My first thought was, "What a stupid thing to do!"

The second thought was, "My underwater swimming strategy must be modified." ·

I surfaced and only then realized the extent of my wound. Blood poured from a gash on the bridge of my nose, the swimmers were told to get out of the pool, and I was rushed to a hospital. Upon arrival at the emergency entrance the nurse took one look at me and said she was going to call the plastic surgeon immediately. While waiting for the doctor she staunched the flow of blood and took an x-ray. After stitching up the skin as best as he could the doctor examined the x-ray and said, "You have broken your nose, but it is not a difficult task to reset. I'll be able to give you back the nose you had with an operation that shouldn't last more than half an hour."

When I told him I had to fly to Europe the next day he decided not to do the operation. "With the tampons in your nose you could get an ear infection from the change of pressure from flying. As the nose bone will stay moldable for three or four days there is time to have the broken bone reset when you get back to Italy."

When I got back to Italy, I went to see a plastic surgeon. He admired the fine stitching job and then looking at the x-rays of the broken nose he asked me if there had been a bump on the bridge of my nose.

"I'll be glad to reset your nose bone as it was, but quite frankly if I leave it as it is now you will have a more attractive profile. In fact, I have done many nose operations to remove such a bump as you had, and I would recommend doing nothing. You must have hit the wall of the pool at just the right speed and at just the right angle, to create that new nose line. I doubt you could repeat that feat, but it is the best job of do-it-yourself plastic surgery I've ever seen." I'm now walking around with a fine Greek nose.

Speaking of things Greek, at the time of my birth an oracle predicted that I would have two major careers. She said nothing about two noses. I don't know whether that is good or bad. Anyway, a change of jobs as well as a change of noses was a major milestone for me this year. After 15 years with GTE in Milan I was made a job offer I couldn't refuse. Fortunately, it was not a Mafia boss making the offer but another multinational company. The new company is Rheem Manufacturing, a subsidiary of City Investing, a large U.S. holding company which has many activities including a factory near Milan, Italy in the steel business.

They make 55-gallon steel drums, the kind used in the Caribbean for making calypso music. But the major use of these drums is for storage and transport of oil and chemicals. They also make small steel pails for paints, along with steel parts for shelving for factories, warehouses, and also hot water heaters.

Rheem was looking for a managing director for their Italian operations. This company and approached me through a headhunter. They made me an offer and I accepted. The size of Rheem-Safim, the Italian subsidiary company, is to my liking with an annual sales volume of $25 million and 700 people. This is about the same number of people at GTE in Milan when I first came to Italy in 1961. That company has since grown to 7,000 people and had become much more bureaucratic.

What was particularly attractive to me about the Rheem company was the small size of their head office in New York. Consequently, with only a handful of people they don't have the headquarter resources to bother you with time consuming headquarter staff problems, most of which add no profit to the company. The GTE head office in New York was about this same size when I started with them in 1961 but unfortunately their headquarter staff grew a great deal since that time. I hope the parallel stops here and no similar clouds follow at a 15-year interval.

The growth of headquarters staff is a general multinational problem. As the companies grow, all kinds of new and largely useless staff functions sprout up as spontaneously as mushrooms after a fall rain. These new staff groups include centralized insurance, legal, personnel, audit, safety, planning, cost reduction and overhead analysis, task forces, and marketing. Each group is a ravenous devourer of information and once the information starts flowing on a periodic basis, the periods become shortened. What the headquarters groups do with all the information gathered remains a mystery.

Another mystery I have read about recently concerns the "black holes" in space, where the gravitational pull is so strong that even light cannot escape once it becomes sucked in. There is a certain similarity between these "black holes" and U.S. headquarters groups because once information gets sucked in you never hear about it again.

Naturally the consequences of this "black hole" management are twofold. First of all, you have the cost of maintaining an expensive head office staff and secondly, and of much greater cost, is the erosion of the time of the managers on the front line. They waste away as if consumed by stomach cancer. The time they should be spending on the basics of organizing and dimensioning their company to manufacture and sell more efficiently gets absorbed in an ever-growing vortex of reporting requirements to the black mouthed god. While "black hole" management may be endemic to some of the large big-name multi-nationals, it is even worse in governmental agencies and could be the cancer that proceeds the fall of western civilization.

Although the employment level of my new company of 700 people is comfortable, and the New York headquarters staff is small, we have many problems to address. Rheem Safim lost a lot of money in 1975 and there are still too many people on the payroll for the present sales volume. In addition, the company is undercapitalized, Consequently, our financing costs are high, particularly because interest rates in Italy are now running at 21%, three times the U.S. level. With the Italian political situation as unstable as it is, it is difficult to convince stockholders to invest more money in the country.

One of my objectives is to develop export markets for the shelving division of the company. We have very good automatic equipment and a good product line but not much had been done so far to export these products. With Italy's ideal geographic position with respect to the Mediterranean basin countries, North Africa and the Middle East as well as its proximity to the Eastern European countries, exporting into these areas would seem logical. If we are successful in obtaining new business from these export areas this additional business plus normal turnover would solve the overstaffing problem within a couple of years. In this connection, I have started to travel to some of those areas.

One of the first trips was to Jordan where we exhibited our products at a trade fair in Amman. We generated quite a bit of interest and appointed an agent for our products. We were also approached by a potential agent in Oman. I had to look at a map to remember where Oman was. It is on the toe of the Arabian Peninsula and is about the size of England. In our conversations, the agent told us a little bit about the history of that area.

For a long time, Oman had been ruled by a royal family under the protective wing of the British. In the early 1950's, the sheik in power decided he would send his son to England for his education. The cold weather there must have affected his mind because the son came back after several years abroad and began telling his father that they should build schools, roads, and hospitals in Oman for the people. His father, convinced that the son had gone crazy, put him in prison. He chose prison because at that time there were no mental hospitals in Oman (or maybe because the mental hospitals were all full of political prisoners). In 1970 there was a revolution in Oman, the old sheik was overthrown, and his son was given the throne. He started building roads, schools and hospitals and it seems that the country is beginning to thrive. If we get some orders from there, I will have to take a trip to visit Muscat and see for myself how they are progressing.

Another contact was made at the Amman trade fair with a person from Saudi Arabia who has a frozen food business. He has large frozen food lockers in Jeddah but no shelving in these lockers. Consequently, the last merchandise in the locker is the first merchandise out. He feels that some type of shelving in his large freezing locker would give him a better flow of merchandise. He is also anxious to find out what is on the very back wall of his locker. It has probably been there for years.

In my free time during the trade fair, I managed to visit the city of Amman and found it to be a fascinating place. During the time of Alexander the Great around 300 B.C., Amman was a flourishing city known as Philadelphia. It has had its difficulties since then and at the end of World War II had only 15,000 inhabitants plus numerous Bedouin tribes moving in and out of the outskirts. That old town now has half a million people. To the north of Amman, one finds very attractive hilly countryside which is quite fertile. Wheat is grown there, and the terrain resembles the rolling countryside of Western Nebraska.

To the northwest is the well-preserved Roman town of Jerash. The theatre is virtually intact and has splendid operatic acoustics. There is an oblong forum, somewhat like a miniature Saint Peters Square in the Vatican City with columns surrounding the forum. The main paved Roman road running down the center of the town has temples on both sides and a part of the original Greek wall, rebuilt by the Romans, can be seen surrounding parts of the city. A short way from Jerash is one of the castles built by Saladdin in the 12th century. It is a magnificent fortress perched on the top of a hill and on a sunny day Jerusalem can be seen from it.

Another place of great interest in Jordan is Petra. Petra is about two thirds of the way between Amman and the Gulf of Aqaba and is a beautiful mysterious place. You enter it on horseback through a narrow gorge in countryside that resembles a miniature Grand Canyon. On the side of the gorge up on one wall can be seen an aqueduct built by the Romans to bring water to the town that once was Petra. The water supply for this aqueduct comes from a nearby spring and this spring is supposed to be the one that Moses created by hitting the rock with his staff. I tasted the water, and it is still fine 3,000 years after its discovery.

As you ride your horse on the trail through the narrow canyon to reach Petra there are places where you can touch both sides of the wall with your outstretched arms. Fig trees grow out of cracks in the rocks. As the canyon widens you find a clearing and the first of many temples directly in front of you. This temple is carved into the soft red sandstone rock and Greek-style pillars are also carved from the rock as part of the temple. Behind the pillars is a perfectly square room that must be seven stories high. The ceiling is perfectly parallel with the floor and smooth. The room had been completely chipped out from the stone.

Directly in back and deeper into the rock is a second main room still enormous but about two thirds the size of the first room and off of the main temple room are smaller rooms to the left and right. One can achieve a wonderful resonance singing in the main room and I can picture Egyptian priests calling "Radames, Radames". This area was developed by the Nabateans and was a market center for them. The temples were built a few hundred years before Christ. The area is still a trading area, but the sheep, camel, silks, amber, and precious stones traded here in the past by the Nabateans have been replaced by Bedouins selling beads, post cards, and Coca Cola.

One curious thing I found in Jordan is the vast range of skin color of the Jordanians. They range from fair haired blonds to various shades of brown and, in the southern desert, I saw some Bedouins whose skin was as black as the Buganda tribe in Uganda. A major source of the blond strain, in addition to the many Norman crusaders who settled in Jordan, comes from the Circassians. At the time of Alexander the Great, the Circassians occupied an area just north of the Black Sea for many centuries. As Mohammed and his followers swept east and continued these Circassians became converted to the Muslim religion. In the 1860's, the Czar of Russia wanted to convert all Muslims in Russia to the Russian Orthodox church. This change was difficult for most of the Circassians, and they were persecuted severely for their Muslim religion. Large numbers of them that would not convert to Christianity were killed. To avoid this persecution a first wave of Circassians immigrated in 1870 to what is now Jordan. A second group came to Jordan at the time of the Russian revolution.

The more recent arrivals in Jordan are the Palestinians. I had the opportunity to meet several and it was the first time I have had the chance to have a conversation with people who have fled Palestine. These conversations have given me quite a different outlook on the Israeli-Arab conflict. One of the people I spoke with was from Haifa. His ancestors had lived in Haifa for hundreds of years. In 1947 his family left Haifa because of repeated Jewish sniper fire coming from various concealed locations. Many children of prominent Arab families were killed by this rifle fire. A second Palestinian I spoke to was a newspaper man from Jaffa. One day a Jewish gang made an attack on his family house, and his uncle was killed in the attack, he himself was shot in the stomach and they were ordered out.

A third Palestinian told me his story. They came from Jerusalem where their family had lived for centuries. He was not ordered out but left of his own accord because when the Israelis took over as business activities were hindered for those of non-Jewish faith whether they be Muslim, Armenian, Greek Orthodox or Catholic and those who remained were treated as a second-class citizen. In all cases the property of these people was taken over and no compensation was offered.

A fourth person with a story left the West Bank after the most recent Arab-Israeli war. He comes from the town of Nablus. He has many members of his family still living in Nablus. In the recent demonstrations in the West Bank, I noticed from the newspaper that a 17-year-old girl of the same last name was killed by Israeli soldiers. I wondered if he was related to this girl. When you know some of the people involved in this situation and see how logical and decent they are, it brings the tragedy of the Middle East conflict into focus when stories of families displaced and terrorism on both sides are told. It is unfortunate that the Palestinian cause has been taken over by such a radical terrorist group who hijack airplanes and shoot Olympic athletes in Munich. With the poor press created by these Palestinians terrorists, the other side of the story is obscured and the chances for reconciliation are blocked.

Even though the Jordanian Palestinians whom I met are bitter about their loss of land and home, they still seem prepared to put an end to their dispute with Israel. While compensation by the Israelis to those Palestinians who have lost their property is a poor substitute for their lost ancestral land, it still is an offer that should be made and certainly costs less than the arms and lives lost in an ongoing war. One curious thing I noticed is that bitter as the people are against Israel, there is still a much stronger feeling against the Turks. In so far as the Turks left the area over three generations ago their domination of the area must have been awful to have left such strong feelings against them.

While the Turks were pushing into Arab lands and dominated Arabia for the past 600 years, the Arabs were extending their trading routes south into the Sahal area and black Africa, proselytizing for the Muslim religion in the process. The result of their missionary work was more extensive and successful than Christianity. In most African countries there seems to be a higher proportion of Muslims than Christians.

Mali is one of the countries where the Muslim influence is more visible than Christianity and, on my last trip to Nigeria, I managed to pass through Mali and visit Timbuktu. I first heard about Timbuktu in grammar school and at that time considered it as a fictitious place in the middle of nowhere. But Timbuktu does exist, though it is, in fact, in the middle of nowhere. The Bambara is the principal tribe of the country, and the capital city is called Bamako.

My trip to Timbuktu had to start in Paris for several reasons. The first being that Paris is the only place in Europe where one can obtain a visa to Mali and Timbuktu. The second is that flights to Bamako from Europe only start in Paris and Marseille and flights from Paris to Bamako are infrequent. There are three trips per week from Paris and two of these are handled by the Mali National Airline. This isn't because of French protectionism so that the French can dominate and profit from the large and lucrative travel from Europe to Bamako but due to the volume of travel from Europe to Bamako which is neither large nor profitable. This cost and the mystery of this far off, scarcely populated country, was more apparent to me as I boarded the 120-seat jet plane in Paris with eight other passengers, two stewardesses and a steward. Three of the passengers and the steward were in first class and five tourist passengers and two stewardesses occupied the coach section. Consequently, we coach passengers had a better passenger stewardess ratio (2-1/2 to 1) than the first-class passengers and we were treated like tribal kings.

We flew south across the Sahara for hours and it is unbelievable to think of anyone crossing this vast waterless space on foot or camel. On approaching Bamako, you see the first signs of life as the Niger River snakes its way across the desolated countryside. The Niger River was the first river the Arab traders came upon when traveling south across the Sahara. Both Bamako and Timbuktu are on this river which starts in the hills of Guinea and Senegal and flows east across the lower part of the Sahara marking the boundary between the Sahara Desert to the north and the jungles of west Africa to the south.

At Timbuktu, the river is at its farthest northern point and from there it bends south to run through the countries of Niger, Upper Volta (now called Burkina Faso), and Nigeria. In the last leg of its journey, the river passes through the former Biafra area of Nigeria before emptying into the Gulf of Benin and the Atlantic. In Bamako the Niger River is at least one mile wide and about 50 feet deep, full of a tasty fish species called Capitaine. In Mali this large fish reaches 100 pounds. The people of

Bamako have a secret tradition for smoking this fish and it takes on the flavor and color of smoked salmon. It is not quite as dry as salmon and I am told it is delicious. With the present price of salmon this fish could be an excellent export item for Mali. However, distribution in general, much less refrigerated export distribution of fresh fish, is extremely rudimentary in Mali and we understand this delicious smoked fish can only be found in Bamako and nowhere else in Mali.

Regarding the transportation system in Mali there is a railroad that comes to Bamako from Dakar in the Atlantic coast. The rail line continues east from Bamako for 60 miles and then turns south to Ouagadougou in Upper Volta. There are a few roads, paved for part of the way, which cross the country in an east-west direction just south of the Niger River but there are virtually no roads north of the river. For those brave enough to venture north into the Sahara there is a trail – two tracks in the sand - that goes the 1,000 miles to the southern border of Algeria. From this border it is another 800 miles before you are off the desert. By camel this 1,800-mile trip would take about 45 days.

There are two other means of transportation inside Mali, a river boat up and down the Niger River and Air Mali. Air Mali has one two-engine propeller Russian plane with a high wing, similar to the small Fokker short-haul Dutch plane. This plane is kept busy making three trips a week from Bamako to Gao, stopping at Mopti, Timbuktu on the way. The day I took this flight, the plane was rather full. There were two goats with their heads sticking out of burlap bags as passengers in the seat behind me. It was probably their first trip as they bleated during take-off and landing. As the plane flies low and follows the river up country, you can get a fine view of the landscape.

The river boat on the Niger is probably the best way to travel through this country. They keep the goats in steerage and don't let them mingle with the first-, second- or third-class passengers. It takes five days by river boat from Bamako to Gao and only three and a half days if you want to get off at Timbuktu. The boat is a cross between the African Queen and a Mississippi paddle wheeler. I met the American Consul from Liberia in Timbuktu who had just taken this trip with his family and found it most comfortable and interesting.

One major problem in Mali is the changing of money. In every foreign country I've ever visited so far there has been a change window at the airport. Not so at Bamako, and the bank in Bamako has very limited hours. The taxi driver took me directly to the bank from the airport. It was 2:30 pm when we arrived, and they had already closed for the day. My plane to Timbuktu left at 6:00 am the next morning and the bank opened at 7:00 am. I thought I could make do and change money in Timbuktu. No bank in Timbuktu. The plane back from Timbuktu the following day arrived at 11:30 am and the Bamako bank closed at 11:00 am for the day. It was now Wednesday afternoon and, from my arrival in the early afternoon of Monday, I had been unable to change into local money. The plane left Thursday morning, but I had to be at the airport a half hour before the bank opened.

I had written to the Director of Tourism to inquire about trips to Timbuktu. Unfortunately, he was just leaving for an audience with the Minister, so he turned me over to a capable assistant, Mr. Alfa Osman Ouologum, who was nice enough to pay for the hotels and transfers in local currency while I was in Mali in exchange for some of my travelers' checks. I also managed to borrow some West African francs from a Senegalese girl that was acting as a tour guide for two American couples on the same plane. With these funds I was able to purchase a sword from a Tuareg blue man whose camp we visited on the desert outside Timbuktu. I also bought a silver ring for Lydia which was being made in a father and son workshop in a mud hut in Timbuktu.

At the motel there was a French couple with a 3-year-old child who were making a good living buying used Peugeot cars in France and driving them across the Sahara to Mali where they could be sold for five times the price. This profit gave them enough money to buy their airplane tickets back to France and a nice amount in addition in order to repeat the process again and again. There seemed to be no problem of selling the car. When they arrived at the motel, they let it be known they had a car to sell and within three hours the deal was completed. The cash was obtained the next morning from the bank (open between 7:30 am and 11:00 am) and they were on their way back.

They showed me the route to take if I ever cared to drive across the Sahara. They indicated there is a nice detour to be made in southern Algeria where you can take a three-day camel ride around this high desert mountain range. There are traces of a Neolithic Iron Age civilization in evidence here. Many people have car breakdowns and die of thirst every year trying to cross the Sahara. I was told which trail had the most traffic and also learned about the distances between gasoline and water stops.

The next morning my plane was to leave Timbuktu at 6:00 am. It was delayed because the pilot was in the habit of having his breakfast at the airport and as someone had forgotten the key to the restaurant. He couldn't leave without his tea and bread. Someone finally arrived with the key, and the pilot and I had breakfast together. We were both ready to leave by 7.00 am.

In the passenger manifest there were five Americans, four goats, and 40 Africans in white gowns with face covers. I felt out of place without a face cover and no white gown. We had two 30-minute stops at two the villages on the way to Timbuktu. At one of these villages, an American missionary couple met us. They were waiting for a replacement and gave me a letter to give to the missionary who they said would be meeting the plane at Timbuktu.

I usually like to take a seat by the window to view the scenery and this small 40 seat plane flew at a low altitude, so I had a great view. As I fastened my seat belt, I looked up and there was a large man all in white coming down the aisle, leading a small goat. He saw the empty seat next to me on the aisle and smiled. I motioned to him that it was free, please take it. He led his goat to the seat, lifted the goat up, set him down on the seat, and attached the seat belt. Then he proceeded to take a seat for himself in the next row. As the plane gathered speed, I looked at my goat seat mate and the goat looked at me. When we rose in the air the goat said "Baa", a little nervously. I responded "Baa", with a voice as calm as I could. I believe the goat felt more secure with my response. I saw that the goat was looking out the window and seemed more comfortable as our airplane flew quite low over the river on its way to Timbuktu.

Timbuktu looked as I would have imagined. The sand-colored buildings were square and no more than two stories high. Many of the houses shared a common wall, presenting a fort-like appearance on the side of the street. The streets were made of sand and the two floors of the houses were constructed out of tightly packed sand. The first mosque in Timbuctoo was built in 1200 and is still standing. The hotel where we stayed had been the French Military headquarters. The rice and mutton meals in the hotel were not exactly French cooking but adequate. The bread did have that good French appearance and aroma but, unfortunately, it was uncomfortable to eat as it contained little grains of sand. Gritty bread is the curse of Timbuktu, a town at the edge of a vast desert.

When we landed at Timbuktu I was met by a guide, a thin-faced man with deep set eyes and slate black skin. He had an aquiline nose and thin European lips. He told us he was of the Tuareg tribe, and he introduced himself as Mohamed Ali. He spoke good French and some broken English. We were amazed to hear he was only 30 years old. He looked like he was over 60. Mohamed Ali walked around the city with us and told us a some of the history of this city.

When the Moors swept into Spain in the 800's, another group of Moors driven by religious fanaticism with their objective to obtain converts to their Muslim religion, went south into Africa and reached Timbuktu, which at that time was a small native village. These Moors made it their desert capital. When the Ashanti tribe from Ghana came north about the year 1200, they were stopped by the Arabs at Timbuktu. No European appeared at Timbuktu until 1827, when a solitary English Major crossed the Sahara and reached Timbuktu very thirsty. The Arabs gave him water, and then killed him as they didn't want any interference in their salt, gold, and slave trade. For over 1,000 years, the Arabs had been coming down from the north in camel caravans with precious cakes of salt and exchanged these products for gold and slaves with the African slave traders coming up from the south. A French company of 200 soldiers appeared a year later and their firepower was too much for the Arabs. When the French came, the town had a population of 100,000. Today in 1976 the population is 6,000.

I hired a driver to explore the desert to the north to visit some Tuareg camps. The Tuaregs raise goats and move about following the few tufts of grass that grow sparsely in the desert. There are some low trees in this area no more than eight feet fall and some prickly bushes which provide a bit of shade as well as firewood and fencing material for corrals for the goats. An occasional chicken is also seen in the desert. While most of the soil is sand there is some cultivation. We saw a little corn and some watermelon plants. But instead of red flesh these melons had a white flesh and tasted more like cucumbers.

We came upon an old water well that was 90 feet deep. A Tuareg man, wearing a typical blue gown, had the rope of his bucket over a pulley at the top of the well and it was tied to two donkeys. His 10-year-old son drove the donkeys to pull up the pail full of water. The pail was a goat skin bag, and the muddy looking water was emptied into a wash tub beside the well. From the wash tub, the boy had a wooden ladle that he used to scoop up the water and put it into two goat skin bags that were hanging from another donkey standing patiently. The water was then put into his family store of water. We went to visit his camp, a half mile away. The top of his tent reached to my belt and the bottom of the tent was one foot above the ground. This design he explained provided good ventilation.

There were woven straw mats on the floor and his wife, and two smaller children were sitting in the tent. His wife was sewing. She was extremely beautiful; her dark hair was straight and kept in a braid. Her smile was gentle and full of contentment. The children were extremely attractive and looked at us with large round eyes of surprise.

This Tuareg desert dweller returned from his water gathering chore and, in hospitable Muslim fashion, offered us tea. He spread a straw mat in front of the tent, still shielded from the sun by a few scrub trees and we sat down cross-legged. His wife brought a wooden bowl with water and the small tea glasses which were not much bigger than whisky shot glasses. Our host washed those glasses with only his right hand, according to the 1,400 years thousand years of Muslim tradition. The right hand is used for handling food and used for carrying food to one's mouth, and the left hand is only used for post toilet cleaning. Anyone who reaches into the community food bowl with his left hand immediately becomes a social outcast and is never invited back for a meal.

His wife had brought a small brazier with some burning embers and the small tea pot was placed upon it. The tea pot seemed to be half full of tea leaves and our host then poured half a bowl of sugar into the small pot. There didn't seem to be much room left for the water. Our host then poured out a glass of tea holding the tea pot a foot above the glass and didn't lose a drop. In fact, as the stream of tea came out of the spout and, with a stream of tea connecting the pot and the glass, he raised the pot still higher above the glass. As the glass reached half full, he brought the tea pot slowly down over to the glass level and tipped it back to stop the flow. Still, not a drop was lost. He then poured this glass back into the tea pot and repeated the performance twice more to mix the tea, the water, and the sugar thoroughly.

We were offered the tea graciously and sipped in silence. It was hot, strong, and less sweet than I would have imagined with all the sugar he poured in. It was thirst quenching in the hot desert. This ceremony was then repeated twice more. Three cups of tea are apparently the minimum for a good host to offer his guests, and any guest that leaves before the third glass is consumed is considered rude.

After the tea we did some business. He had a nice-looking sword with a black sash, and I asked if he would be willing to sell it to me. I explained I had a collection of swords from different places in my travels as decorations for the wall of our apartment in Milan and we didn't have a Tuareg sword. The guide translated, as the Tuareg spoke only his own Tuareg language along with Arabic. He agreed to sell the sword and asked 10,000 Mali francs for it ($25). I countered with 7,000. He answered that it had belonged to his father and his father's father before and, unless he could get 10,000 for it, he wouldn't sell. We compromised on 9,000 Mali francs. That sword with its black sash is now hanging in our living room.

Just after sunset and before dinner I returned to the desert, this time for a camel ride. Many camels were sitting on the sands in a sphinxlike position, and each had a precarious looking wooden seat upon their single hump. Even though they were sitting on the ground, I had to climb up to get on the wooden seat. The Tuareg camel driver crossed my ankles halfway up the neck of the camel. He coaxed the camel to stand up, but the camel objected loudly in an irritated and rasping voice. It sounded as if he was shouting "no, no, no" at the camel driver. As the camel driver pulled the rope around his neck to the left and right, the camel tried to bite him. Finally, the camel got up, but he almost threw me off in the process. The seat was already on the back side of his hump and when he got up on his forelegs, the seat jerked backwards, and the seat tilted so far back it was parallel to the ground. The camel, after extending his forelegs fully, lurched up with his back legs, catapulting me and the seat sharply forward. This time I almost shot off the seat over the camel's head. We then set out across the desert.

The camel's walk was very stiff legged and the seat which had no padding jerked forward and backwards. I could feel every step and I think the resentful camel was doing this on purpose. When the camel started to run the rhythm got smoother and was nicely undulating. We journeyed out for about an hour and saw the glowing wooden embers of many Tuareg families camping on the sand. Our guide knew one of the fellows and we stopped to have another session of tea drinking.

Returning to Timbuktu from our desert ride it had now become very dark, and the stars were beautiful and clear. The air was balmy and there was a very light breeze blowing. While hot during the day, the air temperature and humidity of the desert at this time of night was the most comfortable I've ever known. We were told that the camel caravans travel at night, averaging about 50 miles per night and sleep under their tents during the heat of the day. I can see the enormous appeal of travel across the desert at night, picking your course by the constellations.

Back in Timbuktu, after a supper of mutton and rice at the Foreign Legion Hotel, with cans of pineapple juice from the Ivory Coast as our beverage, I set off for an evening walk in the town. The schools were open and older students of 12 years and over were in the classrooms writing and studying. As I continued my walk through the town, I found clusters of men sitting in groups in the marketplace playing cards, checkers, and backgammon. Small gas lamps illuminated their play. Even though it was after 11 pm, small boys were still up playing vigorous games of soccer. One of them about 12 years old, detached himself from the game when he saw me and extended desert hospitality. He said he knew a woman who didn't have a husband and would I like to be her husband for the evening. Although my curiosity was aroused, I declined.

I got up early the next morning to see the village awaken and started my walk just before dawn. While the night before I had seen mostly men and boys up and around, in the predawn of the morning I only saw women. The women were very busy tending morning fires and baking their daily bread. There were numerous beehive mud ovens about five feet tall scattered throughout town. Good fires were glowing in many places. Some women were selling breakfast bread, and some were selling burning embers used to start other morning fires. A thin flat metal scoop was used as a shovel to collect a small number of burning embers to sell to another woman to start her morning fire. The credit rating of those purchasing embers must have been good as I saw no money change hands. I was curious as to whether payment was made weekly or monthly or whether reimbursement was made in barter of some kind. I never got the answer to that one.

SEVENTEEN

1977 - Business in Saudi Arabia, Vacation in Sardinia, and the Houseboat Adventure

In spite of continued political unrest and economic problems in Italy, the family is thriving. Lydia is painting and has sold a number of very attractive pictures of Tunisia following her trip there in the spring with members of the American School of Milan. She continues to make presentation charts for me, both for various company reports as well as for my volunteer treasurer's position on the Board of the American School of Milan.

After two very active years as Vice President and President of the PTO of the school, Lydia is now a saleswoman for the advertising of a book being prepared for the 15th anniversary of the school. Last but not least, she is again a room mother and one of the library assistants at the school. Robin is now three and has started at the Milan Montessori School. Her vocabulary is expanding rapidly, and she is using her new words to ask lots of questions. For example, "who is the moon's mother and what does the moon eat?"

Valeria is eight and in the 3rd grade. She enjoys her ballet class which we feel has also given her excellent balance for her skiing. She goes racing down the expert trails and just doesn't fall. She has shown an interest in other languages and has started to study German. At this rate she will probably be speaking three languages next year. Gary is 11 and in 5th grade. He has also started German. He has won an orange belt in Judo and can handle the expert ski trails better than me.

Both older children are enjoying the new school. The construction has been completed and the ample sports fields are finished. All parents that participated in this project are proud of the completion of this piece of the American School in Milan. Our only remaining problem is to pay for it. From a financing standpoint the school is in good shape as we have a long-term mortgage and sufficient lines of bank credit which will be repaid as the major multinational companies, whose children use the school, make payments on their pledges. While even the Japanese companies using the school have paid their share of the construction cost, there remain three major U.S. multinational companies that have failed to pledge their fair share. One of these companies has been using the school continuously for the past 10 years. These are not the kind of companies one would expect to see sneaking out the back door to avoid paying their lunch check.

Regarding the question of political unrest and the economic problems of Italy, I am beginning to feel that except for a few minor interludes, political unrest has become endemic to Italy since the end of Pax Romanus. As far as the economic problems are concerned, it is the large companies that are having most of the difficulties. Many of the smaller US companies are doing quite well, and those that have less than 50 employees are doing exceptionally well. The Italian labor movement doesn't feel companies of that size are worth the trouble of unionizing and, consequently, those companies benefit from the creativity, energy, and hard work of the Italian entrepreneur and factory worker.

Our plan to slowly lower our head count, while at the same time

1977 - BUSINESS IN SAUDI ARABIA, VACATION IN SARDINIA, AND THE HOUSEBOAT ADVENTURE

increasing production, is proceeding according to plan. In the two years since I joined City Investing, the manufacturer of steel drums and steel shelfing, the company has been able to reduce our labor force by 10% and increased our production volume by 15%. The Italian market for our product line, large steel containers, and steel shelving has been rather static, so we have increased our export business. We have found new clients in some Eastern European countries, North Africa, and the Middle East.

In Eastern Europe we are selling our products to Yugoslavia, Bulgaria, and Hungary. They have been good customers and pay their bills more promptly than our Italian customers. We had our first major project in Algeria this spring and some interesting business prospects in Libya. In the Middle East we have established a distributor in Jordan, Kuwait, and Saudi Arabia, and our products are beginning to be sold in each of these countries.

The most interesting of these countries from a business standpoint is Saudi Arabia where government development programs are enormous. I have made several trips to Saudi Arabia this year and Lydia joined me for the last trip there. Women are not usually admitted in Saudi and Lydia came in as our company interpreter.

Apart from several good-sized orders that were generated on this last trip, the highlights for Lydia and me included a couple of swims off the coral reefs of Jeddah in the Red Sea. We went snorkeling during the long lunch hour (1:00 to 5:00) about 30 miles north of Jeddah and it was like swimming in a tropical aquarium. I've never seen so many fish while snorkeling and the many-colored coral formations which provide their playground and hiding places were beautiful.

At the end of the reef there is a vertical drop off of about 30 meters to the ocean bottom and along this vertical wall, composed of various colorful coral formations, live the large fish. Large groupers sometimes reaching 500 pounds hide in caves in the vertical walls. When they open their mouths, they could swallow a human being. We heard of a Saudi man of small stature that was sucked into the mouth of one of the groupers. He had the presence of mind to push his way out the side gills of the enormous fish and lived. At such time when their oil runs out, Saudi Arabia has a marvelous untapped tourist resource in their coastline for underwater enthusiasts.

During my trips to Saudi Arabia, I've managed to piece together some of the interesting history of the area. The Turks occupied the Arabian Peninsula for many hundreds of years. After the First World War, the Turks were pushed out by Bedouin tribesmen with the help of Lawrence of Arabia. Then a struggle for power followed to determine which of the three principal tribes would become dominant in this enormous land, the size of the entire common market. The Sharif of Mecca controlled the area in the west, Sheik Al Rashid controlled the center area with his capital at Riyadh, and the eastern Arabian Gulf area was under the leadership of Sheik Abdul Aziz Saud.

An inconclusive war was waged between these three sheiks for about eight years. Then, one night in 1919, a small band of Bedouins led by Abdul Aziz Saud arrived at the walls of Riyadh after a long camel trek across the desert. They came from an area near Dammam, not far from where Aramco, the Arabian American oil company has their drilling headquarters. The followers of Abdul Aziz scaled the walls of Riyadh and attacked the garrison of Al Rashid. Abdul Aziz killed Al Rashid in this battle.

I understand from one of the relatives of Al Rashid that he was a cruel and unjust man and his followers willingly joined Abdul Aziz, increasing the number of his warriors, allowing him to become the major political force in central and eastern areas of Arabia. After killing Al Rashid, Abdul Aziz then married one of Al Rashid's widows. There are those that claim that this particular widow was extremely beautiful and others that claim that this matrimony was prompted by reasons of state to reunite the tribe of Al Rashid with that of Abdul Aziz. Whatever the motives the marriage took place and did have the desired political affect.

The first son of this widow, Abdul, Rahman Al Malouf became one of Abdul Aziz's favored warriors and fought bravely by his side in conquering the Sharif of Mecca. This was the last of the battles among the tribes and the country became united. Abdul Aziz Saud then became king and gave his family name to the country which became Saudi Arabia. He ruled as king until he died in 1953. Abdul's first son Mohammed wasn't interested in government affairs and the throne went to his second son Ibn Saud. I was told that Ibn Saud used most of his energy taking care of a large harem and had little energy left for government affairs. He was deposed by his brothers in 1963. During his 10-year rule he had managed to squander the income of the government, consisting mainly of oil revenues from Aramco. The country was running a negative balance of payments and was virtually broke.

Faisal, the third son of Abdul Aziz, replaced Ibn Saud and under Feisal's rule the economy of the country was strengthened and reserves began accumulating. Even before the sharp increase of petroleum in 1973 from $2.50 per barrel to $10 per barrel, the country was well in the black. Faisal was unfortunately assassinated by the son of one of his many brothers and Prince Khalid, another son of Abdul Aziz became king. The prolific Abdul Aziz had many sons and most of them became active in the government and in finance.

Next in line to the throne after Khalid is Crown Prince Fahad. The other brothers in the government include Prince Abdullah, Minster of the National Guard, Prince Sultan, Minister of Defense and Aviation, Prince Majid, Minster of Municipalities, Prince Mite, Minister of Housing and Prince Naif, Minister of the Interior. Two nephews of these brothers, sons of the late king Faisal, are also part of the government. One is Prince Saud Al Feisal, the Foreign Minister and the other is Prince Mohamed, Deputy Minister for Education. With all of these sons and grandsons of the great Ibn Saud holding important positions in the government, it becomes even more appropriate that the country be called Saudi Arabia.

In spite of the current nepotism, the country is well run. Saudi Arabia exercised good restraint on the last round of oil price increases and fully understands the explosive impact of oil prices on the political stability of many western European countries. As Saudi Arabia is capitalistic, both for religious as well as for economic reasons, they feel uncomfortable with the proximity of the communist countries. If a few of the Western European countries move down the path of Socialism and eventually Communism, and in the process, change the balance of power in Europe, a very dangerous situation could be created for the rich oil producing countries in the Middle East.

Regarding the general price of crude oil, it still seems low to me at $12 per barrel, particularly when you realize that a barrel of Coca Cola costs about $100. Gasoline is about the cheapest liquid one can buy in Saudi Arabia and gasoline at the local gas pump costs 15 cents per gallon. Bottled drinking water costs about $4 per gallon. The minister of Water Resources in Saudi Arabia is afflicted by the curse of Midas. Every time he sinks a well looking for water, he hits oil.

A few figures might help to put the richness of Saudi Arabia into perspective. For example, in 1976 Italy ran a negative balance of payments of about eight billion dollars. In the same year Saudi Arabia ran a positive balance of payments of 19 billion dollars. This surplus is likely to grow because the country is unable to spend their oil revenues as fast as they earn them. In 1977 their oil revenues are projected to be 40 billion dollars and other revenues about three billion, most of which comes from pilgrims visiting Mecca. Over one million pilgrims came last year. In comparison to the total of 43 billion dollars of revenues, both the government and private sectors were only able to spend about half of this amount.

Since Saudi Arabia does not want to become dependent on oil as the only source of national income, the Saudi government has embarked upon a long-term program for the development of industry. For the next five years they have earmarked 150 billion dollars for the development of industry roads, ports, and infrastructure, a figure that is twice the amount Iran has ear marked in their five-year plan. One of the development projects is the Al Jubail Industrial Area where a town of 200,000 people will be constructed. The industrial complex will include two oil refineries, one large steel mill and four petrochemical complexes. This project has been assigned to Bechtel for overall planning and design.

There are other riches in Saudi Arabia that have not yet been tapped, including large quantities of minerals, such as bauxite, tin, copper, and uranium. With a stable political environment and sufficient capital, they could become a major raw material source for the world. Although the minister of Water Resources has his difficulties, there are large amounts of water under the desert. Once tapped and irrigation develops, the desert could bloom again as it probably did several thousand years ago. Saudi Arabia could be the land of tomorrow.

While Saudi Arabia is moving into Tomorrowland with great speed, the Arabian Peninsula has more of yesterday land than of any country I have yet visited. The first thing that strikes a visitor is the Saudi women, or lack of women in the towns and cities. Although I have spent two weeks in Saudi Arabia, I have never seen the face of a Saudi woman. They all wear veils when out in public and also in private if guests are around. These veils are not just covering the nose and mouth but the entire face, eyes included. This veil which fits over the head like a small tent is made of a fine knit black gauze. The veil blends into the other black garments which fall shapelessly from the head down to the toes and gives the distinctly unprovocative appearance of a pyramid sitting upon a cylinder.

One Saudi explained to me that there is a sound practical reason for keeping the Arabian women so covered. The Arab is hot blooded and given to feuding. Because of the close extended family tradition, feuds can explode into small wars and can go on for a long time. As the possession of a woman's charms are often the cause of dispute among men, temptation is largely eliminated by keeping the women veiled and the possibility of arguments, feuding, and bloodshed is diminished. The selection of a marriage partner is then not a matter of attraction and individual choice, but a serious family matter.

Most marriages are arranged by the parents and while the prospective bride has already managed to see the face of her future husband, the groom has no idea of what his bride looks like until the day of the engagement, which is the first time he is permitted to see her face. The moment in which the future bridegroom gets to see the nude face of his fiancée at a time he is already committed to marry her might be a rather traumatic moment for both parties and both families. If the young man doesn't particularly like the face of this girl as his future wife and manifests the slightest disappointment, or not sufficient enthusiasm, the scars can run very deep. If by chance he takes a dislike to what he sees and wants to back out of the arrangement, the matter can become very sticky. Here you place the reputation of the girl and the girl's family at stake. If she is refused by the prospective groom, she gets a reputation, and it would be extremely difficult for her parents to arrange a marriage with another family. "What could be wrong with her?" the others may ask. Since no one but family have or can see her, imaginations can run rampant.

"Does she have pimples all over her face?"

"Is she ugly?"

"Is her nose too big or her mouth too small?"

"Does she have bad teeth?"

Unfortunately, in these circumstances the presence of the veil impedes the nuptial aspirations of young women. One 24-year-old Saudi told me "We young men all have different tastes in women, and one man's perfume may be another's poison. If some young man has already backed out of the marriage arrangement in spite of pressure from both families, the unknown face behind the veil takes on a sinister aspect. Your aunt's assurance that Khalilah is really attractive even if Abdul backed away after he saw her face, can be puzzling and discouraging if direct visual verification of the beauty, or lack of, the young girl is not possible. Consequently, after the unveiling, even if the girl is not particularly appealing to the young man but is still within tolerable limits, he will go ahead with the arrangements just to keep the two families from getting at each other's throats. This is why men are currently allowed to have up to four wives in Saudi Arabia. If your luck was bad in your first draw, maybe your luck will improve in the second draw.

We met one 26-year-old gentleman from a powerful Saudi family. His wife was two years younger than him, and they had a 10-year-old son. I asked him if he was considering looking for a second wife. He said he had been thinking about it. It is not that he and his wife were not getting along well. On the contrary, they got along very well together, as she was a fine woman. But every so often they argued, and it was unpleasant to come into a house where the smoke of dissension hangs heavy. Therefore, a second wife would provide good relief. When the first wife is moody the husband could be comforted by the second one. This relief would allow the first wife to calm down at her own speed. When she is calm, she may greet her husband with open arms. It could be best for all concerned.

The question of whether and when to take a second wife is one of the difficult decisions facing the Saudi man. We have heard that occasionally it is the first wife that helps the husband pick out the second wife. Knowing his personality, shortcomings, and temperament, the first wife can often help her husband make a good match for the second wife. Also, since in many cases the wives live in the same house, the second wife becomes a sister to the first wife, and if you can influence the disagreements or other subjects that arise, it is better to have a compatible rather than an incompatible sister. It is also nice for the women to have some extra company, particularly when most of their life is spent in the house.

As could be imagined, family life is very important in Saudi Arabia, and becomes even more important when one realizes there is no public entertainment. When I was there were no public theaters in the entire kingdom. On the other hand, there are shops where movie films and projectors can be rented. Most of the movies one sees in Europe or America, as long as they are not X-rated, can be rented. The rental cost is about $100 per film. One family I met indicated that among their relatives they had about one showing per week, alternating between the houses of uncles and cousins. While one is aware of the strict rules governing the Saudi women, their unusual dress and clandestine habits, and their complete absence is strange. I became acquainted with a Saudi who had four daughters and three sons aged 10 to 22. One evening he invited me to dinner and the sons were present at dinner. But during the four hours I was in his house there was neither sound nor sight of a woman or girl.

Another unusual item in Saudi Arabia is the absence of women in offices, airlines, and shops. Even if it were customary for Saudi women to work in offices or stores there would be many practical problems created by veiled secretaries or store clerks. It could be difficult to take accurate dictation behind a veil, particularly if the boss mumbled. Correcting typing errors might even require lifting one corner to the veil to see better and this could be misinterpreted. Trying to read flight

1977 - BUSINESS IN SAUDI ARABIA, VACATION IN SARDINIA, AND THE HOUSEBOAT ADVENTURE

numbers on airline tickets thru two layers of the black gauze of the veil could result in many pieces of luggage sent to the wrong places. Saudi women are allowed to work as schoolteachers and nurses. For the large American and European companies in Jeddah you do find a few western women in the offices.

While being somewhat behind the West with respect to women's liberation and communications, Saudi Arabia is also way behind the West when it comes to crime. There is very little delinquency in Saudi Arabia and crime does not appear to be very much a part of everyday life. This doesn't mean there are no criminals among the seven million inhabitants, but when a crime is committed the criminal is rapidly apprehended and justice is swift and harsh.

The trials are held outside and open to the public. I was at one trial when two culprits were led out from a paddy wagon and a judge dressed in the robes of a sheik read the crime and sentence of the first one. The judge announced he had stolen a car. As this was his first offence his sentence was one year in jail and 50 blows of the cane. The soldiers laid him on the ground, face down spread eagle. Four soldiers were around him, each holding a foot or arm to keep him immobile. Then on both sides were two whippers. There was another person that held eight canes which looked like they were made of bamboo. He handed a cane to one of the whippers who began beating the criminal as hard as he could. After about the 10th strokes the cane broke, and the cane man gave the whipper a new cane. After the 25th stroke the first whipper was exhausted, and the second whipper took over. His cane lasted until the 45th stroke. He threw that cane aside and received a fresh one to finish up the job.

The culprit was then raised to his feet, supported by two soldiers, and brought before the judge. The judge told him in a loud voice that could be heard by the entire crowd of hundreds, that he would now spend a year in prison for his crime. Beware, if after he served his sentence and was ever brought back before the court again, he would pay for his second crime by placing his hand upon the block and the sword of Allah, in the hands of an officer of the court, would chop it off. The police dragged him back to the paddy wagon and he was off to prison. Then came the second offender. This man had tried to rape a woman. He was also married. I thought we would see some blood for this crime. However, the judge only sentenced him two years in jail and 100 blows of the cane. I asked the Arab standing next to me, why the sentence was so mild. He explained that it was his first offence and trbesides he hadn't succeeded in the crime. It was only an attempt. After having received his 100 strokes of the cane, this criminal was dragged up to the judge to hear the warning before being sent off to jail. He fainted as the judge warned him of WHAT he would order to be chopped off if he tried that crime a second time. Unfortunately, my translator had wondered off, so I'll never know exactly what the judge said.

Public beheadings still take place in the main square in Jeddah, Riyadh, and Dammam, and hands are chopped off frequently for stealing. One Saudi told me that while I may feel their punishment is cruel, virtually all Saudis approve of this harsh justice and the public is protected. If the crime has repulsive moral overtones the punishment is harsher. Last December, during the annual pilgrimage to Mecca, a robber stole from a pilgrim at knife point. Not only was the hand of this robber chopped off, but a foot was also chopped off since the crime was committed during the pilgrimage. Another incident recently was the case of the four Saudis who raped a woman during Ramadan. As three of the men were married, they were guilty also of adultery. When you add adultery to rape that is about as bad as you can get. The single man, guilty of only rape was beheaded, but the three married men were stoned to death, more painful and takes longer than a beheading.

Foreigners are not exempt from the arbitrary, swift, and harsh Saudi law. While I was there, an example of severe Saudi punishment for a mere whistle occurred. This example of swift Saudi justice was told to

1977 - BUSINESS IN SAUDI ARABIA, VACATION IN SARDINIA, AND THE HOUSEBOAT ADVENTURE

us by a British engineer who was staying at our hotel in Jeddah. He had just arrived from Dammam that morning, a small city on the East coast of Saudi Arabia on the Persian Gulf. Large deposits of oil had been found in that area and the Saudi Kingdom had a large project expanding the port of Dammam. They had contracted with a South Korean engineering and construction company to increase the capacity of the port and the Korean company had sent Koreans engineers and skilled construction workers for the project in Saudi Arabia.

The English fellow told us he had a second-floor room in a hotel on the main road in Dammam and while he was looking out his hotel window, he saw two veiled Saudi women walking on the road beside the hotel. At that moment four Koreans passed by and whistled at these women. There were four Saudi policemen who saw what happened and must have considered whistling at the woman as an assault. Apparently, several Saudi gentlemen on the road were also outraged at someone whistling at a woman. The Saudi policemen intervened quickly and luckily apprehended the 4 Koreans, apparently saving them from a lynching by the crowd of Saudis that were very angry at this lack of respect for women. However, the senior officer of the police squad decided to be judge and jury and motioned to the four Koreans to get down on their knees with their hands behind their backs. At a sharp command the four policemen drew their sabers and four Korean heads rolled into the street.

When the news got back to the Korean labor camp, the Korean workers rioted. They pushed their construction equipment into the sea and stormed into the town smashing everything in their way. The Saudi army was called out; the rioters were surrounded, put in a Saudi camp, and sent back to Korea. According to the Korean version, the four Korean victims may have been fresh or joking trying to chat up the veiled women, but the women were not touched.

Visiting customers in Jeddah can be difficult and it is a major problem in finding their office. In many sections of Jeddah there are not only no street numbers on the buildings but also no street names. One morning I had an appointment with an American contractor in Jeddah and the directions I received were that his office was in a sandy colored building just off the Mecca Road and within three blocks of the Swedish Embassy. Fortunately, the Swedish Embassy has a tall flagpole, and I spotted the Swedish flag. But as most of the buildings were sandy colored it took 15 minutes searching for the road that leads to this building. With the Swedish flag as my center point and three blocks as the extend of the radius, I made many forays to all points of the compass before I found the proper building, about 300 meters and in a south-western direction from the Swedish embassy. I must bring a compass and tape measure on my next trip to Jeddah and hope the people I am to visit have a good sense of distance and direction, as well as a good landmark nearby, preferably an embassy with a tall flagpole.

While business drew me to the Middle East, our vacation was far from the parched deserts of the Arabian subcontinent. The first part of our vacation was spent on the coast of Sardinia, at a place called Costa Dorata. There are many small, isolated beaches on this coast, ideal for nudists and families looking for privacy. We had been to Sardinia before, but I hadn't been aware of the nudists then. Now the number is substantial. Gary was the first one to notice the nudists, probably because he has the best eyesight in the family. Gary and I were out one day with our rubber boat scouting for a good beach we planned to take the whole family to the next day.

"Gary" I said, "that looks like a nice beach ahead. Let's have a look at the fineness of the sand." As we passed the promontory, Gary shouted out, "there is also a nice beach over there, but there are some people on it and the women have nothing on." The boat swerved to the left, and I said, "Since we are this close let's have a look at the sand on the beach before we decide on this one".

1977 - BUSINESS IN SAUDI ARABIA, VACATION IN SARDINIA, AND THE HOUSEBOAT ADVENTURE

The nudists - probably Swedish, took no notice of us as we pulled our boat up on the beach. Several of them were in the water swimming and some on the sand. I put on my mask, snorkel and flippers and went in the water looking for marine life. I saw a few small fishes. There must have been a slight current, or maybe it was the tide, because before long I found I had drifted among the nudists. Nice as colorful fish are seen through an underwater mask, a young nude female figure swimming in the water is even more attractive, particularly if she has long hair. It is unfortunate underwater masks were not known at the time of the renaissance painters. I would love to see a painting of the three graces of Botticelli swimming nude through the clear Sardinian waters as viewed by the artist through his face mask, looking upwards in the depth of about one meter.

For this trip and future exploring among the islands, we purchased a 13-foot rubber boat called a "gommone" which are becoming very popular in Italy. One of our friends is the President of a company that makes such boats as a sideline business, and we purchased one from him that was designed for eight people. He and his family also came to spend a week with us at the large house we had rented on the coast of Sardinia.

You can imagine our collective chagrin when, after the second day of normal usage, the boat began to come unglued. One of the carrying handles came off completely in his hand the first time he helped us haul the boat from the beach into the water. In addition, one of the oar locks came off while he was rowing - you can imagine his embarrassment. We both felt it was much more interesting for him to be out in one of his boats with a few faults than be in a perfect one.

During the rest of our vacation, I overheard Bill muttering the things he would say to his production and quality control manager once he returned to the factory. In spite of his mutterings, I felt encouraged by his presence. It would have been uncomfortable to go back to the company that made our boat and ask them to repair the faulty gluing of the components and have them reply. "You must have mistreated the boat to cause this damage. We have never had anyone complaining about this problem before."

We enjoyed a different kind of fishing this time in Sardinia. We found a knee-deep pool of sea water just behind the beach. It was formed by a tired stream that didn't have quite enough flow to make it to the sea. The last rain had fallen several weeks earlier, and the water was evaporating. Thousands of finger-length fish that must have swum in from the sea now found themselves trapped. When the fish were excited, they would dart all over the place and it was impossible to get close to them. But if you were slow and deliberate you could stand over them, put your hands slowly into the water on either side, make a quick clasp, and catch one sometimes only by the tail. These small fish are then fried, and you eat head and all, leaving only the tip of the tail. We caught about 100 of these fish and had a fine grilled meal of them.

On a second trip to this dried-up river several days later, the evaporation had lowered the level of the water to ankle bone depth and the skull of a sheep of fairly recent mortality protruded above the water. That day we caught many fish but decided not to eat any.

While Sardinia was one part of our summer vacation, a houseboat trip on the canals and lagoons of the Veneto region was the other part. We became aware of the houseboat possibility from an advertisement in the newspaper. The description read: sleeps six people, easy to handle, no driver's license required. Relax and enjoy the scenery along the canals and lagoons between Aquileia and Venice.

We sent for the brochure, and it had a picture of a boy of about ten driving the houseboat with his parents taking the sun on the roof deck. We convinced our friends from Berlin, Peter Ludwig, and his wife Josi, to come with their two boys Holgar and Axel.

1977 - BUSINESS IN SAUDI ARABIA, VACATION IN SARDINIA, AND THE HOUSEBOAT ADVENTURE

According to the brochure there was a completely equipped kitchen. This was partially true. The two-burner gas stove worked well. The small refrigerator was only a box that required one to put in coolant at frequent intervals. Small plastic bottles that hold cold for 12 hours were provided to us at the starting port and it was suggested that when we stop for the evening, we find a deep freezer where we could deposit our cooling bottles for refreezing. This system worked fairly well for the first 12 hours after leaving the home port. However, the lagoon area is sparsely populated, and it is not easy to find people in general, much less someone who can refreeze our plastic bottles.

The kitchen sink was small but sufficient. It had a pump for sucking the water out of the tank and this worked. But having transferred the grease from our pots and pans into the sink, the elimination of this greasy water was often a problem. The drain was temperamental, had a propensity for collecting air bubbles, and required frequent coaxing before we heard that welcome gurgle of water exiting. There was a small toilet on board, and it worked well. The boat had a 25-horsepower inboard motor, and the driving was easy, but the stern swung sharply when turning the houseboat and it felt as if the stern was trying to catch up with, and pass. the bow. It was useful to have helpers at the back ready to fend off any boats, canal markers or docks that got in the path of the arc we describe as we make our turn.

Our first day out we went up a nearby river. About lunch time we came upon a farmhouse. Hammered to a tree beside the river was a sign announcing grilled fish. We stopped and the farmer's wife started a wood fire, pulled some coals out of it, and grilled some eels for us. They were delicious. As we continued upstream, we explored some of the smaller tributaries of the river. Some plants got tangled up in the propeller and cut our speed. Using mask and snorkel, I dove under the boat, cleaned out the propeller and shaft, and speed returned to normal.

The next day we stopped on the lagoon side of a deserted island with the Adriatic Sea on the other side. We found many small crabs and the kids caught them with their fishing poles. The crabs didn't swallow the bait but grabbed ahold of it with a claw. With one claw holding on to the bait tightly, the crab had the other claw free for us. And this free claw went snap, snap, snap, as the crab was pulled out of the water swinging like a pendulum as we lowered him carefully into a can. Getting the can under the swinging crab was the most exciting part of the maneuver and no one wanted to hold the can. Even though we weren't at a dock we thought there would be no harm in parking at this pleasing protected place for the night. We had been told at the starting place that we must always park tied to a dock. We were soon to learn the reason for this. The wind was blowing in from the sea. We put stones on top of our anchor to make sure it would not drag. After this careful bit of seamanship, we went on the beach, gathered firewood, made our big bonfire, and grilled our fish. The wind died down as we retired for the night to our bunks aboard ship.

About 2:00 am I was suddenly awakened by our boat lurching 20 degrees to one side. Robin fell out of her bunk. On my upper bunk I found myself saved from a fall by the two ropes that attached my bunk to the ceiling. I stepped down and groped my way out to see what the problem was. As I slid open the door a full moon illuminated a scene of desolation. Both boats were sitting on mud completely out of the water, and the nearest water was 30 yards further out. While we had taken great care to make sure the anchors didn't drag, we had completely forgotten the tide. To make matters worse, the wind must have come up from the opposite direction after we went to bed. The anchors held but the boats were pushed closer to shore at the very top of high tide. I had serious doubts that the water would ever come up high enough to refloat us. And if it did come back there was a second serious problem because our boats were extremely close together, each sitting on the mud at different angles, with our boat somewhat under that of the Ludwig's. The returning tide would probably push our boat under theirs and I could visualize an awful crunching of hulls as

1977 - BUSINESS IN SAUDI ARABIA, VACATION IN SARDINIA, AND THE HOUSEBOAT ADVENTURE

our three-ton monsters begin to right themselves. As there was nothing we could do, so I climbed back to my tilted bunk. No sooner was I settled than Robin called:

"Water please, Daddy."

I swung myself down off the bunk and with one foot on the wall and the other foot on the floor I made my way to the ice box. As I opened the door, all the contents came tumbling out. I attempted to put the stuff back in and tried to close the door, but with the tilt of the boat this was not easy. Something was always sliding out before I could get the door of the ice box closed. When I opened the door enough to put the meat back, the butter slid out, and when that was put back, a piece of cheese slipped out and so forth. While it probably took no more than three minutes to get everything back into the ice box and its door closed, it seemed like 15 minutes. As dawn arrived, I could hear a wonderful sound, the soft gurgling of water as it came advancing across and up through the mud on which we were stuck. We only became buoyant at the very top of high tide and it was a wonderful feeling.

About halfway back to home base Peter's boat stopped. We went back to find out the trouble and Peter announced that he had lost steering control of the boat. As he remained tied to the wooden canal markers, we cruised back to the main port to get a tow boat. Peter's boat was towed back to port, taken to the crane, and lifted out of the water. We saw that the hood surrounding the propeller which provides the steering was missing. It must have dropped off in the water or is still mired in the mud at the island where we spent the night. The next morning with a new rudder, the two boats went out for new adventure, this time towards Venice. The canals through which we travelled had tall reeds growing on each bank and from time to time a fisherman appeared between the reeds.

We approached the first draw bridge over the canal and squeezed under without requiring it to be opened. We made it by about four inches, very slowly. At the next bridge we decided not to extend our luck and honked for the bridge man. No one came. We honked again. Still, no one came. I got off the boat and left the driving to 11-year-old Gary and went searching for the bridge custodian. I found the nephew of the bridge operator who had just come back from fishing, and he invited me into their house by the side of the canal for a glass of wine. He explained that his aunt, the bridge caretaker, was off to the grocery store. After we finished the wine of Merlot, the bridge mistress arrived. She stopped the car traffic, opened the gates, and we went through.

The next bridge was two miles upstream. As we approached, I saw a man leaning on a fence who appeared to be the bridge custodian. When I asked if he could open the bridge for us, he jerked his head towards the right. I looked to the right, and no one was there. I asked again and again he jerked his head to the right. I then realized he was not the gate keeper but a man with a tic just watching the canal. The bridge operator appeared after a couple of honks of our horn. After putting down the road barriers, he slowly cranked the bridge around, and we continued our journey.

We stopped for lunch at an island where the canal parts and, again, didn't think about the tides. We must have tied up just at high tide and by the time we finished lunch the tide had gone down enough to ground us. The attempt of the other houseboat to pull us off ground, plus a rope thrown to us by a passing motorboat was not sufficient. We just had to wait for the tide to rise again.

Farther ahead we found a big rusty sunken canal dredge parked at the side and I thought this would be a secure place to tie up for the night. There was plenty of space along the side and the dredge had iron hooks to which we could attach our ropes. The two houseboats tied up close together but we fixed our ropes so we could not bump into each other during the night. At 1:00 A.M. a bump woke me up. I

1977 - BUSINESS IN SAUDI ARABIA, VACATION IN SARDINIA, AND THE HOUSEBOAT ADVENTURE

went onto the deck to check the ropes and found we had not bumped the other houseboat. Rather, our bow had bumped up against three wooden poles standing as a tripod in the water marking the channel. I shortened the ropes so that our bow was a good four feet back from these poles and went back to bed. Half an hour later another bump shook our boat. "Oh, good grief", I said to myself, imagining that one of the ropes must have gotten loose, so again in a half sleep, I went up to the deck of the dredge to fix the rope. I tightened it again and went back to bed.

Twenty minutes later there was another thump. As I went out to review the situation for the third time, I realized that the dredge was not sitting on the bottom of the canal but was floating and moving gently back and forth with the current and was taking our two boats with it, stopped only by the thump of our bow against the wooden poles. As we didn't have enough rope to tie the dredge to the canal bank, I returned to bed, to sleep as best as I could between thumps. An hour later, I was awakened by loud voices.

"What is this boat doing here?"

"Oh, my goodness, the police" said Lydia, "I know we shouldn't have parked our boats here"

"I'd be surprised if the police came to this canal at 4:00 am to make certain people don't tie their boats to some rusty dredge in the canal." I replied.

I got out of bed to have a look at the guests we may be having. There were two men standing there holding fishing paraphernalia.

"Good morning" I said as I poked my head out." Is there anything the matter?"

"No, we are just coming to fish" said one of the men.

"I hope our boats are not in your way," I replied.

"Yes, your boats are in the way, but we can manage" the fellow replied.

There is an old Italian proverb "if you can't fight them, fish with them," which is exactly what we did at 5:30 that morning. I put out a line.

The next day we reached the Piave river before turning back. On our return we had a problem with one of the bridges. It was Sunday and the road traffic even on these small country roads was fairly heavy. As we approached a bridge that had to be opened to let us pass, the bridge master told me to turn around and approach the bridge from closer to the left side of the river. Peter and his boat waited further upstream to make a run past his bridge. There was a bit of a current and I had difficulty turning around. Then the bridge master told me he couldn't open the bridge just then as it was Sunday and there was much traffic waiting to cross the bridge. We would have to wait a while. I explained that we had to turn in the boats in the early afternoon and our friends had to proceed to Yugoslavia, and wouldn't he please open the bridge for us.

"All right" he said, "but come through quickly as I can't interrupt the traffic for long."

"Okay" I replied and tried to maneuver into position to be ready to shoot through.

Just as he was starting to crank the bridge around so we could pass through, a police car came up with his sirens screaming. He came to a stop right at the barrier, turned off his siren and waited patiently. The bridge swung open, but I was still maneuvering, trying to get the boat turned around. Every time I turned out into the current, the current swung the stern downstream or the whole boat floated broadside to the current. I don't want to go through the bridge backwards.

1977 - BUSINESS IN SAUDI ARABIA, VACATION IN SARDINIA, AND THE HOUSEBOAT ADVENTURE

I went back and forward, turned right and left, put on full throttle, cut back to half throttle, but was unable to line the boat up property. With the bridge closed, cars began backing up behind the barriers on both sides of the canal. Many of the impatient drivers began honking. Others got out of their caress and seemed to be sprouting horns as they came up to the edge of the bridge, agitated and irritated to see what the cause of delay was.

Peter Ludwig who was driving the other boat with his wife Josi and their two sons Holgar and Axel, stayed way back from the bridge. There he determined where he wanted to be before going through the narrow opening under the bridge. Once he was lined up, he headed to the space with good speed which gave him the headway to glide through the open way. The drivers of the cars waiting to cross over the bridge, applauded when he his boat cleared the bridge and came through at the other side. Then it was our turn. We were not as well lined up and our boat started out with the current pulling the boat parallel to the bridge. There was not enough room to go under the bridge sideways. Four drivers had left the cars and came on the bridge to watch us go through. Four were coming from the left side and six were waiting the right side.

"Go under on the left side" the first on was shouting. "Give it full throttle and turn the wheel to the left."

The second driver was hanging over the railing of the bridge and he was waving his hands providing the opposite instructions from the first driver. The third driver had his hands over his eyes. The fourth driver was very impatient and threw both hands in the air forming a V. He was probably a semaphore expert signaling the word vexation. The policeman was writing something in his pad, probably taking the number of my boat. Another person was out of his car and leaning over the bridge shouting "svelto, non-posso aspettare tutto il giorno." (Quick, I don't have all day.) None of the suggestions from those on the bridge worked. I was unable to get the boat pointed in the right direction and with the tide getting stronger it did not have enough power to overcome the speed of the water which was drawing it to one side.

When I approached the opening under the bridge, I ended up at a 45-degree angle and was being pulled in the direction of the river flow. If I was unable to change course our boat would bang into the concrete supports in the middle of the canal. I tried to take the boat out of the current and go through the open space straight on. But the current overcame my steering, and we were on a course to bump the brick wall of one of the openings under the bridge. Finally, the cranky bridge master, who was standing almost directly over me with his crank in his hand shouted.

"Throw me a rope and I'll hang you"

While I heard the first part of his sentence clearly there was shouting, and the second part was partially drowned out. I asked him to repeat and was relieved to hear him say a second time.

"Throw me a rope and I'll help you"

We threw him the rope and he pulled us past the concrete pillar. When the stern was free, the boat passed under the opening at a 45-degree angle. All of our fans hanging over the bridge clapped and waved to us. "Bravo". As we approached the next bridge, less than a mile away, we saw that bridge master already on the bridge and, acting like the flight manager of an aircraft carrier, was motioning to use to approach from the left side of the canal. We were convinced that the bridge master we had just passed had telephoned ahead to his colleague, advising that there were a couple of landlubbers coming towards him who should never have been given a boat in the first place, and who didn't know how to steer. They need assistance to be able to handle the fast-exiting current.

1977 - BUSINESS IN SAUDI ARABIA, VACATION IN SARDINIA, AND THE HOUSEBOAT ADVENTURE

After we passed under that last bridge, the remaining few miles were uneventful, and we turned in our boats. The chief of the boat station probably closed his one eye as he inspected our houseboat for damages, and we got our full deposit back. After a week's experience with tides, currents, and bridges we all felt confident we could face another houseboat trip with pleasure and a certain sense of expertise. It would make a nice trip for Gary's Boy Scout troop or Valeria's Girl Scout troop.

EIGHTEEN

1978: Lydia becomes an American, Claridge's Hotel, and Yemen

One of the major events of the year was the winning of Lydia of her American Citizenship. Lydia was the only one of the family not a citizen of the United States and we decided to do something about it. Normally for aliens, a residence of five years in the U.S. is necessary before citizenship can be obtained and naturally, during those five years, you have to be on your best behavior. As Lydia hasn't had any serious run ins with the police in the past five years, we thought she could easily pass that part of the requirement. We were pleasantly surprised to find that American law waives the five-year U.S. residence requirement for spouses (either male or female) whose work with American institutions may keep them overseas.

Therefore, we proceeded with all the legal formalities from Italy. Lydia obtained the handbook on citizenship prepared by the Daughters of the American Revolution (DAR) and proceeded to study. After a few weeks, she knew more about the Bill of Rights, the Constitution of the United States, and the amendments than I ever knew. I'd find questions rifled at me at all hours of the day. I'm embarrassed to say that most of them drew an "I don't know" from me.

1978: LYDIA BECOMES AN AMERICAN, CLARIDGE'S HOTEL, AND YEMEN

The legal procedure involves a large packet of documents, proving who you are, that you are married to an American citizen, that you are not a communist and never were, and are not currently a prostitute. You also have to provide a list of all countries you have traveled to in the past five years. Fortunately, her trip to Moscow was eight years ago. Then comes an interview with a member of the Immigration Department and finally, if all of your documents are in order, your frequent trips to East Europe don't make you suspect, and your closet full of furs doesn't raise other suspicions, you move to the swearing-in ceremony.

I read through the booklet prepared by the DAR for future citizens and, while I appreciate their efforts in helping immigrants understand the American government and philosophy, it contains an America first, isolationist tone, reminiscent of the far right in the 1937 period. While some updating is in order, the cost of updating these booklets would cost the taxpayer millions of dollars per year, especially given that the government is already operating overbudget. I prefer to have a few white-haired ladies continue with their volunteer efforts even if their views may be a few decades behind mine.

Lydia studied diligently and passed her interview with flying colors. The man at the Atlanta office said he rarely met anyone as well prepared. However, her green card had been misplaced and when she came to the swearing in, the judge made a disturbing preamble. First, he said he usually handles deportations. Secondly, there were several of the applications that were being refused. Lydia was in a cold sweat until it was clarified that those being refused weren't because they had been careless with their green card but because they hadn't shown up. We now have all the same color passports!

The other three blue passport holders, Gary, Valeria and Robin are maturing faster than we had realized. Gary, now in the 6th grade, carefully combs his hair before going to school and Valeria, our 4th grader, has been asked by a 5th grader to go steady. She was both flattered and puzzled by the invitation. I hope she was not feigning puzzlement. Gary doesn't approve of the 5th grader. Robin, the 4-year-old, now joins the other two at the American School of Milan and is starting nursery. She corrects Lydia's English and my Italian and tells the porter at our apartment building that her father doesn't speak Italian very well. To polish up her English and to pass Robin's critical ear, Lydia has become secretary and purchasing agent of a book club in Milan. In addition to a full suitcase of Wheaties which I bring back on my return trips from the United States, I now carry back 15 pounds of books each time.

The enrollment at the American School of Milan is now virtually at capacity and in some grades, we aren't able to admit all who apply. Financially, it is on a sound footing. Lydia ran the Christmas bazaar and art show at the school this year and good earnings were produced from this venture. Her pictures of old Milanese scenes continue to sell well.

Following the major project of the summer, which was Lydia's citizenship, we took the two older children to see something of the southwestern United States. This included a peaceful stay at a New Mexico ranch, riding and hiking in the Grand Canyon, and swimming in the rapids in Zion National Park. A brisk sailboat ride in San Francisco Bay, a cold ride on a cable car, and a swim in the Pacific were the extent of the children's exposure to the west.

I had the opportunity of taking both Lydia and Valeria to London on my last business trip and prior to departure, Valeria wrote to the Queen of England and asked if she could come to the palace to meet her. We didn't get an invitation from the Queen but did receive a nice answer from a lady-in-waiting explain that she had been commanded by the Queen to answer Valeria's letter and the Queen's schedule unfortunately was rather tight. She said the Queen usually receives visitors only on the recommendation of Ambassadors. I was impressed by the detail and personal quality of the letter which was a full page in length.

1978: LYDIA BECOMES AN AMERICAN, CLARIDGE'S HOTEL, AND YEMEN

In spite of the Labor government and all the problems that England has, there is still a delightful Victorian flavor that persists. This flavor comes through strongly at Claridge's, an old-style hotel near Grosvenor Square. Our company traditionally holds its European meetings at Claridge's and, apart from our group, the hotel guest list is usually very distinguished. While we were there, Gianni Agnelli, Henry Kissinger and Prime Minister Trudeau shared the hotel's impeccable service with us.

The musty tradition starts at the door where the doorman is in a top hat and long frock. You pass the concierge desk, and he is standing proudly with his red waist coat, 1850s style. The registrar clerk is wearing black tails, and his assistant, who precedes you down the long-carpeted halls to show you to your room, is also wearing tails. The elevators are not automatic but are commanded by proud whitehaired gentlemen dressed as if they have just come in from a fox hunt.

The first morning at Claridge's, I had the opportunity of savoring the old English mastery of diplomacy and understatement. I left my room at 7:00 to take a morning run and my running suit was a bit on the ratty side. As the white-haired huntsman opened his elevator door, his head moved back, and his eyes widened. I could picture him saying very precisely and calmly, "service personnel take the service elevator." Eventually he recognized me as a guest. He maintained his composure and welcomed me into his elevator with a well-controlled "Good morning, sir." There was a haughtier tone in his voice than when he first took me up to my room the day before wearing a suit. The meaning he conveyed was quite clear: "Our gentlemen guests do occasionally engage in athletics, but I can assure you they are quite properly dressed for the event." I'm sure he would have felt very embarrassed and partly responsible if, on our journey from the fifth floor to the lobby, one of the guests of the hotel were to call the elevator and find him with me in his elevator.

As I passed the desk of the concierge, I could see that his surprise at seeing a ragamuffin emerge from the guest elevator. The sight of me loosened his jaw muscle and his chin dropped ever so slightly. I had a nice 20-minute run in Grosvenor Square and returned with a good sweat. The doorman greeted me with dignity, but the concierge ignored me as I passed. The elevator man bowed slightly and said only "Good morning." His omission of "sir" was deliberate and calculated and, had I been English, this omission would have been devastating. The elevator stopped on the second floor and a very well-dressed gentleman got in. I thought I saw his eyebrow arch, but it could have been my imagination. His ride was short, and he got out on the 3rd floor. After the elevator door shut and we were alone on our way the 5th floor, the haughty fox hunter turned to me and said slowly, "That was our manager."

I have a strong suspicion that it wasn't chance that brought the manager to ride the elevator with me in my running suit. I have the feeling that someone tipped him off and the reason he took this ride was to verify for himself what was really happening. After hearing the story, Lydia bought me a new running suit, which I now call my Claridge's suit, to be used when I travel to the better hotels in Europe.

Last year, my travels to Saudi Arabia produced good economic results and this year we should reach one million dollars of sales volume. With our flag firmly planted and producing revenue in the Kingdom of Saudi Arabia, I decided to push our business frontiers southward and went to Yemen to see if there might be some possibilities in this very old country just emerging from its cocoon of isolation.

Yemen is the country of the Queen of Sheba and is on the southwestern heel of the Arabian boot, just across from Ethiopia and Somalia. It was known by the Romans as Arabia Felix because of its abundant food supply, content, and intelligent people. It is also known as the Arabian Tibet because of its rugged topography. With the exception of the coastal regions, most of the interior of the country is a high plateau surrounded by rugged mountains. The capital of the country, Sana'a is at an altitude of 7,000 feet above sea level and the mountains of Yemen reach 12,000 feet. Much of the mountainous area is highly cultivated and there are terraces running all the way up the sides of the mountains to the 11,000 feet level. Because of the fertile soil, the area has always supported a rather large population and, because of its high and inaccessible location, has had less than its share of ravaging wars through the centuries.

It wasn't only the inaccessible location that has kept foreign invaders out of Yemen - the Yemenites are wiry and tough. They were ardent followers of Mohammed and a large part of the Muslim army that moved across North Africa into Morocco and from there into Spain came from Yemen. As soldiers they were as good on defense as they were on offense and when the Ottoman Turks expanded into Europe and south into Arabia, they were unable to dominate Yemen. The best they could do was to maintain a few garrisons in some of the coastal towns. The English didn't do much better. They captured the port of Aden, which protected their flanks on the route from Egypt to India but were unable to penetrate farther inland.

The country has been ruled for centuries by Kings or Imams. The last Imam ruled until 1962. Neither he nor his predecessors allowed foreigners into the country except upon his invitation. I met a German who had received an invitation from the Imam and had been an advisor to him before the Imam's overthrow. At that time, there were no telephones, no electricity and roads were goat paths. The trip from Sana'a to Taiz, about 200 miles across the mountains, took six days and a guard of 50 soldiers was recommended.

The way of life in Yemen in 1960 could be compared to feudal Europe in the Middle Ages. The Imam was a complete autocrat and his subjects had to approach him on their knees. After the audience finished, they had to back up on their knees and could not get up or turn their back until they were out of view of his highness. Heads were cut off for minor offenses and hands were chopped off frequently. Another punishment still common in 1960 was to be condemned to wear chains. One ankle, one wrist, one year, was a typical sentence and, in the Sana'a marketplace, seeing men walking around in chains was not uncommon.

Powerful as the Imam was, his control was not complete. While the various tribal chiefs gave their allegiance to the Imam, they were relatively autonomous. The Imam's method of maintaining central control was to keep one of the sons of a tribal sheik in his palace in Sana'a or Taif as a hostage and behead the guest if his father became rebellious. I heard of this custom from the distributor whom we appointed in Sana'a, a man of 37. His father was the ruling sheik of the northern province of North Yemen, an area with a population of about two million people. He had been a guest at the Imam's palace in Taiz and fortunately received permission to return to his father in 1958. In early 1959, his father was invited to Taiz by the Imam and subsequently killed because the Imam thought he was behind some rebellious movements. This was, in fact, true and three years later, the actual rebellion took place which overthrew the royal family.

The Egyptians came in on the side of the Republicans in an attempt to spread a Nasser-brand of Arab socialism and the Saudis supported the royalists. The Egyptians lost large quantities of manpower and material, and the war was an enormous drain on the Egyptian economy. The Republicans finally won but when they realized the Egyptians wanted to run their country as a colony, the Egyptians were kicked out. When peace was finally made in 1972, the southern and eastern sections of the country broke away and formed what is now called People's Democratic Republic of Yemen – known as South Yemen – with Aden as the capital. The ruling clique in South Yemen fell under the Soviet wing and the country is in a disastrous economic situation. The regime is extremely repressive toward its population, and it is a dangerous place to visit. Contacts with strangers can be punishable by death. One foreign businessman I know who worked for a U.S. multinational company, was imprisoned for two years in Aden on charges of being a western spy. This was not true. He was only released (or ransomed) following the completion of a large aid package by several countries.

The Yemen Arab Republic – known as North Yemen – is in the western camp. Kuwait and Saudi Arabia are supplying economic assistance, and the country is taking a capitalistic private enterprise approach. From a political standpoint, it is rather typical in the Mideast to have a one-party system and a president appointed by a ruling clique. While in Syria, Iraq, Algeria, and Egypt, the presidents have been in power for quite some time, the term of office of the president of North Yemen has been rather short. Three presidents have been assassinated in the past 18 months. The circumstances surrounding the assassination of the last two were rather dramatic.

The assassins took advantage of the special considerations towards women in Yemen. No one would dream of lifting a woman's veil, nor would they dare to frisk her. The two armed assassins dressed as women and managed to walk past the presidential guards. As the president and his brother had a reputation of being libertines and had the habit of relaxing in sheik-like fashion in the afternoon after a hard morning spent on affairs of state, these habits of theirs made it easy for the two veiled "women" to pass the guards. Both the president and his brother were surprised by the assassins as they were entertaining two French models and were shot dead. The assassins escaped out a back window.

While the assassination was undoubtedly politically motivated, the extenuating circumstances of the president being found with the French girls permitted the motive to appear as religious outrage. Unfortunately, in the sequence of events, the two French models were pulled out of the palace and were stoned to death by the crowd. Rumors circulated afterwards that the assassination was provoked by the Saudis as they were afraid the president was moving towards the left.

The assassination of his successor last June was allegedly planned by the Russians as they saw an alliance developing between North and South Yemen which would pull South Yemen out of the Russian orbit. There had been a series of talks between the presidents of North Yemen and South Yemen on unification and it supposedly included a plan to kick out the Russians. Unfortunately, their plan was discovered by the Russians and in a rapid series of moves and errors, the presidents of both North and South Yemen were killed within a day of each other.

An envoy was sent from South to North Yemen and at the South Yemen border, the envoy was intercepted. A new envoy was substituted and given a new attaché case with a revised secret message from the South Yemen president to be delivered personally to the president of North Yemen. The guards were suspicious because they didn't know the envoy, but the young president said to let him in. The envoy entered, opened his attaché case to pull out the envelope and a bomb inside killed both the president and the envoy. The next day, army officers in South Yemen loyal to the Russians attacked the presidential palace and killed the president. After the dust cleared, the new president of South Yemen is considered pro-Russian, while the new president in North Yemen is considered pro-western.

With a private enterprise approach in North Yemen, the economic pace is quickening but the public services of a biblical era hamper rapid economic growth. The telephone system is under dimensioned, but progress is being made. There were no telephones in the country prior to 1962. The only method of communicating past shouting distance was with the key telegraph. Now there are some telephones in the country, but they rarely work. The main exchange in the capital city of Sana'a was a present from East Germany. The system works pretty well except when it rains. I never fully appreciated the convenience of a telephone until I had to spend 14 dollars for cab fare and an hour of time to make an appointment that I can usually do with a three-minute 25 cent phone call.

1978: LYDIA BECOMES AN AMERICAN, CLARIDGE'S HOTEL, AND YEMEN

Another public service yet to be developed in the capital city of North Yemen is the sewer system. In Nigeria, I was very much aware of the open sewers. But at least there were sewers. In Sana'a, there are no sewers. Consequently, rainwater doesn't go away very fast. After ten minutes of rain, many of the roads are anklebone deep in water. Returning to my hotel after a rain, a riverbed which had been dry half an hour before was now a raging torrent. Several men with their skirts hoisted above their knees were pushing a stalled car to the other side of this raging stream. Fortunately, my taxi was a land rover, and it forded the stream without assistance.

Speaking of men lifting their skirts above their knees, Yemen is one of the few countries along with Greece and Scotland where men wear skirts. The difference is that the Yemen men wear their skirts at a modest ankle length, The Scots at the knee and the Greeks have a mini skirt. It is the Yemeni women who wear pants. But when you ask the question, "Just who wears the pants in the Yemeni family?", the somewhat contradictory answer comes back, "Why, the men, of course!"

The Yemen men are more heavily armed than any national group I've seen so far. Many men carry rifles and all men of 16 years or older wear a curved dagger on a wide belt. The dagger is worn right in the middle of their stomach and the handle is just over the belly button. The dagger is a national dress and not worn for protection. However, with the weapon so close at hand, quarrels end up with a dagger drawn. The laws in this respect are stiff. Anyone who draws his dagger in public gets sent to prison.

One custom peculiar to Yemen, as well as Ethiopia, is the chewing of Gat. Gat is a local bush whose leaves are chewed by most Yemenites. It is supposed to make you feel both relaxed as well as alert. Much of the Yemen social life is centered on Gat and almost every afternoon, men gather together for a Gat chewing session. Once I was invited. For those of us who were wearing pants, skirts were passed out by the host. I took mine and followed the motions of the others, stepping through the top of the skirt and then tucking in the excess material around the waist. We sat down on carpets and leaned against the pillows. The skirt was wide and roomy, reached the ankles, and felt much more comfortable for lounging than pants which had been removed.

A large water pipe was placed in the middle of the room with two long tubes. Then our host came in with an armful of branches and these branches were passed out. Each guest picked a leaf, put it in his mouth and chewed. I followed their example. The green leaf tasted rather bitter, but I smiled at the others as I chewed, trying to look as pleased as I could in spite of the bitterness. After chewing the leaf into a pulp, I wondered what to do next. The others were ahead of me and already had a wad of Gat slightly bulging out their right cheek. The guest to the right picked off a small leaf with a young sprout attached. He offered this to me. I accepted it graciously and chewed. It didn't taste much better than the leaf I picked off my own branch, but I guess it takes a while to get used to the taste of Gat. As the offering of a young sprout to your neighbor seemed to be the polite thing to do, I studied my branch carefully trying to find a tender sprout, plucked it off, and offered it to the person on my left. He took the sprout with a smile, looked at it, then looked back at me without a smile. He chewed my sprout with more an expression of duty than pleasure. I decided I had better learn which are the choice leaves before I begin offering them to others.

Part of the Gat chewing ritual includes puffs on the water pipe and sipping of rose water. With the rose water, it is necessary to pour it out on a saucer and slurp it up. Somehow, if you drink it without slurping, it doesn't generate the same sociability. In the background, there was soft Yemeni music with a sing-song Indian pattern. We sat there and chewed Gat for three hours and I must say it was a relaxing and pleasant experience. I'm not sure to what extent it was the effect of the Gat itself, the slurping of rose water, the puffs of the pipe, the reclining on soft pillows, the skirt, or the company. Now I can understand the social ties it creates and I'm sure it is hard to be angry with someone with whom you have spent the afternoon chewing Gat. An acquaintance becomes a friend once you have chewed Gat with him. I can hear two Yemenites playing the game "Do you know?" "Do I know Abdullah? Why yes, I chew Gat with him."

The part that Gat chewing plays in the economic life of the country raises some interesting questions of business ethics for U.S. companies operating in Yemen. I know of the sales manager of a U.S. multinational company there who invited one of his potential customers to his house for an afternoon of Gat chewing and put the cost of the Gat on his expense report. This expenditure was not reported to the SEC in connection with shady business practices and I think it should have been. Is it possible that offering green backs to a customer is bad and offering green leaves is good - particularly in Yemen where these particular green leaves are expensive and almost considered legal tender?

It seems to me that his company should have informed not only the SEC but also the Food and Drug Administration as well as the Surgeon General, because of the suspected narcotic effect of chewing Gat. Trying to buy a contract is bad enough but doping the purchasing agent seems even worse. A business lunch is not considered corruption and does not have to be reported. But what happens if the client is invited to your house for lunch and you happen to have some Gat handy for after luncheon relaxation and it is offered as one were to offer a cigar and brandy? Maybe that would be all right. On the other hand, if lunch is not involved and one is offering a customer Gat by itself for a whole afternoon session of chewing that would probably be frowned upon by the SEC. Some guidelines should be developed to avoid misunderstandings. In the guidelines, it would be well to specify what kinds of green leaves one can and can't offer the client and under what circumstances. We don't want to eliminate salad from the businessman's lunch nor have an outcry from the California lettuce grower's lobby. Incidentally, he got the contract.

To get a better view of the country and its economic potential for our products I took a trip to visit the major towns and cities. The itinerary chosen went from the capital city Sana'a to Taiz in the mountains to the south, then to Moka on the coast, the town from which the word Moka coffee comes. Then along the coast to the major Yemen port of Hodeida and then back up to Sana 'a. Our trip from Sana 'a to Taiz took us across a high plateau at an altitude of 7,000 feet and we were surrounded by mountains on all sides. There is rich farmland on this high plateau and little villages of about 20 houses each dotted the countryside. These houses are very solid and are made of one-foot square stone blocks: They are about four stories high and look more like towers than houses. Many of the farm areas are surrounded by 6-foot-high mud fences and round watch towers are at the corners of the property. Many of the small villages were built on excellent defensive positions and on hill tops and rocky ridges. We would see a phalanx of these stone houses making an imposing front to any invading band of bandits or soldiers. Many of these small stone villages date back to before the time of Christ and the farm equipment and techniques are also of the epoch. We saw wooden plows pulled by both oxen and camels and the threshing of grain was done with long flat boards resembling cricket bats. Donkeys were used everywhere.

We stopped at the town of Thabet for lunch. My chest brushed against the skinned carcass of a goat hanging by one leg from the ceiling. Various servings of dinner had already been carved from the carcass but there was still a good amount of meat left. While I was looking forward to having a traditional Yemenite meal, my two companions, Dan Gilioli and my brother Dante, walked into the restaurant and passed the hanging goat like two wide eyed boys entering a spook house. Our host, Mohammed, studied the hanging goat and after finishing his examination said, "We will eat here." There were a few flies buzzing around but apparently, they didn't like goat meat (or were already full of goat meat) because they didn't alight very often on the corpse. Our host explained that it is customary for the Yemeni people to examine their meat at a restaurant before committing themselves to a meal, to make certain the meat is good and fresh. Not having had much experience studying hanging goats, I gladly took his word for it. Dan and Dante weren't sure they wanted meat for lunch, or lunch at all. At the back of the restaurant was the hand washing area. The owner ladled fresh water over our hands.

Our meal was a real feast. After the curry soup came a bowl with pieces of okra, potatoes, and a few other unidentified objects. Another course was a blend of tomatoes, eggs, and peppers. The large flat bread served as our spoons and forks, and we cut off pie-shaped segments and dipped it into various dishes. The meat course was one large chunk of goat meat in a dish. I tried at first to get a piece off the chunk of goat meat by using my pizza bread as a tool. I thought that if you knew how to do it correctly you would end up with a piece of meat inside your bread like a sandwich and wouldn't leave your fingerprints on the meat for the next guy. But the bread blunted the cutting edge of my fingers. At the risk of being gross I used my fingers like a crab and pulled off a nice piece. It worked and my host did the same. At first, I thought he may have copied what I did not to make me feel awkward. My younger brother Dante never had much of an appetite when he was little, and I guess patterns established in childhood remain with you all your life because he picked at his meal like a bird. However, he liked the soup and asked for more.

Proceeding from Thabet to Taiz, we crossed the mountain pass. We climbed up to 10,000 feet and saw the terracing work that must be many thousands of years old. Virtually all of the mountain land is terraced and cultivated. A series of fields of various sizes and shapes march up the mountainside following the contours. Every possible inch of land is utilized and is neatly planted in curved rows. The vertical drop from the mountain pass to the valley below is immense and certain areas look like the Grand Canyon. As far down as your eye can reach to the canyon floor you can see the pattern of these contoured step-like fields. Watch towers command the high points overlooking the road. At the highest point on the pass there was a little village and in this place the Gat is supposed to be particularly good. Mohammed stopped to negotiate with the Gat dealer. His shop was one bed wide and two beds long and the Gat keeper was probably eating up his stock as he had a blissful expression while reclining comfortably in his small shop. On the other side of the pass little boys were also selling Gat and the range of prices for equivalent quality was from one to three.

The road down the other side of the pass to Taiz passed a number of other watch towers perched on top of hills. Taiz itself was well situated from a defense standpoint with a large mountain at its back. Until recently the mountain was filled with bandits. The jail of the Imam was also halfway up the mountain and very inaccessible. The Imam's palace in the center of Taiz has now been turned into a museum. There are pictures in the main entrance of people being beheaded. These were some of the martyrs who opposed the king. The king watched these beheadings from his palace overlooking the square. He sat in a porch behind a wooden lattice so that he could watch the proceeding while not being seen by his subjects. However, the removal of these heads was not enough to suppress the revolution.

The interior of the palace was less opulent than I would have expected. His main sitting room had Persian carpets and silk cushions and a large Turkish water pipe in the center of the room. There were a number of other rooms for special purposes. There was a gift room filled with all the gifts he had received from foreign potentates including a watch from Harry Truman. He had a room for hats only. This room was filled with hats on shelves. He had 35 fancy hats with tassels for state occasions and 135 everyday bowl type hats.   The king must have been a hypochondriac as he had one room reserved for medicines. He was also partial to perfumes and the shelves full of perfumes seemed to be a 50-year supply for him and at least 20 wives. He had two bedrooms and liked to be rocked to sleep. One bed was suspended from the

1978: LYDIA BECOMES AN AMERICAN, CLARIDGE'S HOTEL, AND YEMEN

ceiling and the other was built like a swinging lawn chair. There was a small motor to provide the rocking movement. The rooms of his wives had a more refined color scheme and more dainty appointments but still fell far short of the grandeur I expected.

The sanitary facilities were rudimentary. The bathroom looked more like a laundry room and the toilet section was two non-slip treads over a hole in the floor. In one of his rooms, he did have an upholstered toilet seat with a chamber pot underneath. There was a secret room in the palace and rifle slits on either side of the entrance. A heavy door with a large wooden bolt kept out the intruders and further back, there was a secret passage that led to an exit in the garden and a second exit several blocks away. The description on the door indicated that his secret service would advise him to seek refuge when there were rumors of discontent among the population of the city. He would then sit in this room until his secret service chief came to tell him the troubles had passed.

From Taiz we drove to Moka. The road crosses a plateau that looks like an ancient lakebed. At the far end of the plateau the road follows a river, and the vegetation becomes richer as you approach sea level. Date trees are abundant along with papaya and mangoes. Between the small villages were encampments of nomads. While the Yemeni village women usually covered their faces, the faces of the nomad women were without cover. They also wore more colorful dresses. The asphalt road gave out about halfway to the coast and we drove across an area which looked like an African savanna. The dwellings were also similar to African villages with round mud-like houses and thatched roofs. Six houses formed a circle enclosing a central open area and thorn bushes provided a fence between the houses. Goats, sheep, camels, and chickens shared the compound with the people.

The port of Moka was small and capable of handling only fishing boats. However, it is a major port for smuggling, and this is the main entrance into Yemen for contraband beer and whisky. Prices in Moka reflect the proximity to the source. A case of Heineken beer in Sana'a costs about 100 dollars while the same case can be purchased in Moka for 25 dollars. We found the smugglers area and bought some beer.

After a swim in the sea, we decided to proceed up the coast. Our driver did not want to take the sea route. He told us that when the tide was up, water covered the road. This was not a logical explanation for us, and we decided he just didn't feel like taking the coastal road. After we had beaten back the argument, he added that where the road crossed the rivers and dried-up riverbeds, we could not get through unless we had a jeep. Having at first had one illogical argument, we felt this second reason was also not the real reason and so insisted that we at least start. If we ran into difficulty, we could always turn back. So, we started up the coast road which amounted to two tracks over rather hard packed sand. Frequent ruts made progress slow. As we passed through the date groves, we came upon occasional travelers, some on foot and some on camels. It began to get dark, and we still had not reached the first town where we thought we might bunk down for the night.

As it got darker, we saw no lights, but our headlights illuminated a camel coming toward us. We hailed the camel and his rider and asked directions. We were told the village we were looking for was "just ahead" but, as camel drivers measure distances by day of travel and not by hours or miles, " just ahead" could mean another half day's journey. We drove on and came upon a land rover. Our driver asked the name of the head man in the next village. His name was Amahl, but he was in jail at the moment in Moka, probably for smuggling, and the village was "just ahead". We were also told we couldn't make it as the river had washed away the road and we would sink in. Our driver was right! We turned around to go back to Moka.

Unfortunately, we began to stray from the sea. The tracks in the sand weren't very distinct and frequently there would be forks. Our driver seemed to be partial to the left and our course began slowly curving away from south to something to the left of south. We stopped the car to scan the horizon for lights and saw a few in the distance. It appeared that we had swung 90 degrees from the direction we should have been headed and were now going parallel to the road we had thought to hit though we weren't sure. A few times the path softened, and we had to get out to push the car. We saw some lights behind us in the distance and managed to intercept the path of the other vehicle.

It was a land rover and the driver said he would lead us out to the main road. He told us to go ahead, and he would follow. After about 15 minutes of driving the land rover signaled to us. We stopped. He said that in following us he lost the fork he was looking for and he was also lost. He was going to drive back to try to find his fork but told us to go straight ahead and we would probably hit the asphalt road. He drove off. Even though we were lost, it was a beautiful balmy dry night. We had two plastic bottles of mineral water which we nursed from time to time. The pleasure of a swallow was one of the real joys in dry Yemen. If that plastic bottle of mineral water were not nearby, I would get panicky. It didn't matter that it was warm. Just knowing we had safe liquid to drink was an immense satisfaction.

We saw a light in the distance and drove to it. It was a village, and the men were sitting on the ground in three rows - each row was about 10 men deep. They were smoking from large Turkish pipes. They all had expressions of being in a dream world. Maybe it wasn't tobacco they were smoking. As we get out to ask directions the chief of the village came forward and offered us water and directions. We thanked him for the directions but declined the water. After another hour of driving, we came to the main road and found a truck stop where there was a motel. In Yemen, a motel is a place where bunks are rented, and you sleep outside. The bunks we were offered were 20 feet from the road and the lights of passing vehicles were disturbing. We wanted a quieter place, and I found a depression in back of the shacks that lined the road. I started to take my cot down, but the owner shook his head. I was decisive. He again suggested that we would be less comfortable in the depression; he didn't seem to understand that there was less light and noise down there.

He reluctantly helped us carry the beds to where we wanted to sleep. As advancing dawn swept away the streaks of black in the sky and dimmed the stars, we heard a new sound. A braying donkey. This donkey awoke a few dogs who added their voices to the new sounds and they in turn woke the chickens. By.4:30 A.M. we had a full barnyard chorus. This woke Dan. As he opened an eye, he saw a large vulture hovering over his bunk. When the vulture saw that Dan was alive it flew off. As I rolled over, I saw to what purposes our selected dormitory area was dedicated. This was the place for certain daily needs of men and beast. With the dry climate there wasn't much odor, but we had to watch our steps as we carried our bunks back to the motel. Hot aromatic tea and bread was served by our motel owner before we proceeded on our journey.

Our next stop was the town of Zabid. This is the place where Pasolini produced many of the scenes from his movie "A Thousand and One Nights". The town is a few miles from the sea in a fertile area growing date palms, grain, and vegetables. The old wall of the city enclosed a large area and the watchtowers at its perimeters were still standing. The Turks occupied this area for some time. As we walked in the gate of the fort, I had visions of the adventure novel and movie, Beau Geste.

Two schoolboys came over to talk to us. They were bright and intelligent and led us through the fortress. At one corner of the fortress was a mosque with a very tall minaret. There was a corkscrew stairway inside the minaret leading to the balcony at the very top. As we started up, small birds came streaking down between our heads and the low ceiling of the narrow passageway. We had come upon the Muslim equivalent of bats in the belfry, which is bats in the minaret. At the top we found the masonry crumbling and a few gaps in the wall. The boys told us the wife of a German tourist tumbled over the breach in the wall a year ago while backing up to take a picture. The authorities weren't entirely convinced it was an accident. "Back up a little more, dear, now to the left, now two steps back."

Coming down from the minaret the boys asked us if we would like to visit the mosque. They led us to the pool of water, took off their shoes and washed their hands and feet, and we did the same. We then followed them into the mosque barefooted. In another corner of the fortress opposite the mosque was the prison. We saw several prisoners in the courtyard and two of them had chains on their feet. As we came out, the two camels that had been resting were being loaded with merchandise by the camel drivers in white skirts and with daggers on their belts. A veiled woman passed in front with a jar of water on her head, and the scene, framed by the walls of the fortress entrance appeared as if out of the Old Testament. This biblical atmosphere continued as we walked through the marketplace.

At the mill, which was the size of a large living room, was a camel with blinders walking around in a circle. He was harnessed to a large stone wheel which was grinding wheat. He walks for an hour and then another camel takes his place while the previous one rests. The camel seemed to fill the whole room as he plodded around.

A short distance from the camel mill was the butcher shop. This was a public area where the various butchers gathered, each with his respective carcass, goat, sheep, camel, or cow and each had a knife in hand while negotiating with his client. When the price was agreed upon, a piece was cut off the carcass, weighed, and wrapped up. As we remembered from the restaurant, the Yemenite likes to see his meat on the animal. The mincemeat maker was sitting cross-legged in front of his butcher's block and with a long sharp knife was chopping and mixing pieces of meat and pieces of spice together into a reddish blob. Flies were interested in his work and occasionally a curious one with slow reflexes fell beneath the guillotine and got mixed together with all the other ingredients. Our driver stopped to talk with the sheep butcher and purchased a handful of fine sheep's liver. He opened his palm to show it to me and his smile told me he had made the deal of the month. He then took his liver to the restaurant across the path and asked them to cook it for him for breakfast. I wanted eggs for breakfast, but this restaurant just does the cooking, you have to provide the food. So, we bought some eggs at the market, and they were cooked along with the liver. I never ate sheep's liver before, but our driver offered me some to taste. I couldn't refuse. It was really very good, cut into thin French fry size pieces with onions. I'm pleased our driver didn't buy the mincemeat.

As we were leaving the marketplace, we came up on the freight terminal. Three camels were waiting patiently to be unloaded while a fourth camel just unloaded was being led away. Dante wanted to take a picture of the camel and the driver offered to give him a ride. The camel knelt for him to climb aboard, and they trotted off. As they returned, the camel lurched forward on his front knees to let Dante off, and Dante was shot ahead. He managed to stop himself with the pummel, but he said he came close to breaking his wrist. The people at the marketplace were very amused by the show and Dante was pleased to have provided them with the day's entertainment. At the next village we also contributed to the day's entertainment as we were both given rides on the small donkeys. We hope we did not make asses of ourselves.

Hodeida, the main port of North Yemen, was our next stop. In late May we found it a hot dusty town without much character. On the waterfront there were some old buildings constructed by the Turkish customs collectors and an old Turkish fort. The beach was lined with dhows and fishing boats. The main port was to the north, and we counted over 80 ships waiting to unload their cargo and a mile-long line of trucks. The cost of unloading freight in Hodeida is unbelievable. It runs about 50 dollars per ton as opposed to about 15 dollars per ton in the port of New York City. With this room for improvement, our distributor in Yemen has a project to unload the ships with a small blimp. The blimp is on a cable with one end of the cable attached to an anchor in the sea and the other end anchored on the shore. The blimp has a hook and picks up a container from the ship and carries it in the air to the shore and drops it on to a flat bed of a truck. His joint venture partner is an engineer from Princeton. The first tests were a bit of a disaster as the blimp was not filled sufficiently with helium and a wind tore it open. They lost all of their helium. Once the blimp gets repaired and they receive the new helium, they think they can offer unloading service to the ships at a price of 25 dollars per ton and make a good profit in the process.

Driving back from the beach at Hodeida we saw a most curious sight: a railroad engine of about 1910 vintage half buried in the sand. North Yemen has no railroad tracks. In fact, the nearest railroad track is about 1000 miles north which is the end of the line of the Damascus-Medina Road which the Turks built in the early part of the 1900's and which Lawrence of Arabia and his Arab friends severed in many places during the liberation of the Arabian Peninsula from the Turks. Apparently, this engine was brought to this location by sea when the Turks still controlled the port of Hodeida. It may have been part of an ambitious program of the Turks to extend the rail line from Medina all the way down to Hodeida. It could have also been part of a project to connect the inland capital of Sana'a with the port of Hodeida. At that time, the Turks controlled the ports of Yemen but were unable to extend their rule into the interior. Perhaps the building of a railroad into the interior of Yemen was part of their military plan for control of the area. As the Turkish governor has long since died, we can only speculate on the Ottoman strategy in connection with this engine. The wind from the sea passing between the rusty flakes of its cast iron boiler produces whispers advising the sand crabs of the grandeur it can have when the tracks arrive. Generations of crabs have heard this message and are no longer impressed. They merely watch as drifting sands cover and expose different parts of this enormous black intruder on their deserted beach.

After leaving Hodeida we drove up into the mountains towards Sana 'a, and our driver told us of a beautiful waterfall and pool where we could take a swim and wash off the salt and sand from the hot coast. He added that it was fresh, clean water you could drink and a perfect temperature for swimming. We found the stream, the waterfall and pool. As we hadn't had a bath for four days, we brought our soap with us and had a delightful swim and wash. We saw a few fish in the pool, and they must have been famished as they nibbled gently at our toes. I'm glad we had a chance to thoroughly enjoy our swim and bath before we talked with the two Englishmen who had been there the day before. That evening, as we reached the village of Monakah, we met two young men from Manchester.

"We enjoyed the view of the pool and would have loved to swim as we were hot and dusty. We looked for and saw the poisonous snake we were told lives in that pool. Did you see it?"

Our lodging in Monakah was in a five-story tower house and we had a room on the top floor. There were Persian carpets on the floor, and around the walls were pillows of various colors and sizes. A square low table about hand high was in the middle of the room. This was our sitting room, dining room, smoking room, and bedroom. You sleep on the pillows around the wall in a "U" formation, that is, head-to-head and toe-to-toe. This house has its own electric lights and a generator. It has also an indoor toilet, and a flush toilet at that. However, there is no central sewage system in the town and our house did not have its own septic tank. There was a shallow hole next to the house at the foot of one of the walls, directly below the bathroom. A groove on the outside wall plus the slight tapering of the house channeled the waste products from the flush, down the wall to the hole at the foot of the house. I thought a railroad type sign would be appropriate, "Don't flush toilet when train is at station or people are walking below."

The water for the flushing does not come from a central water supply but from a large steel barrel in the bathroom itself. You are supposed to fill up the flushing bowl with a ladle and someone else fills up the barrel. The cavalier guest refills the bowl for the next guest. My predecessor had not. Along with a sign stating, "Look out window before flushing," should be added, "refill bowl for next user."

The service in the inn was excellent and we had our dinner in our room. We sat around our table on pillows with legs crossed and ate rice, eggs and tomatoes, beef, lamb, vegetables, and soup. The tea was strong, aromatic, and sweet. We were advised to drink the tea after our meal to aid digestion. We went to sleep slightly after nightfall and woke up about dawn. While the sewage, electrical, and water systems had not yet become public services, the sound system in Monakah was a working public service. The Muezzin had a main loudspeaker at the mosque connected to 20 other loudspeakers throughout the city. He could be sure that when he trudged up those steps at 4.00 in the morning to start his wail, he would be heard in all corners of the town. One of his loudspeakers was attached to the side of our building and we heard him clearly. In fact, this loudspeaker was just outside our window and so close we heard his breathing between wails.

When we got up at dawn, I found the woman of our house was already up. She served some delicious pancakes with honey. I wandered up to the main square in the village and saw many women gathered at the community waterspout. The water supply for the village comes from a large cistern that is fed from pipes that go further up the mountain branching off to different springs and collecting pools. This was the end of the dry season, and the flow of water was only a dribble. Pails being filled represented the daily usage of water for all purposes for a family. The dress of the women was colorful. While black was the most common color for the baggy pants of the women, the shirt or blouse was usually blue, brown, or green, and the headgear had a length of extra black cloth that covered the nose and mouth. While the veil of the Saudi women covers their eyes as well, the Yemen women only cover their nose and mouth and must seem forward and brazen by comparison, showing their naked eyes for any man to see. As I approached, I saw that many of them had let down their guard and I could see their naked faces. One of the women must have seen my curious stare and warned the others as she quickly covered up. In two seconds the only female skin visible was the small piece above the bridge of the nose and the eyelids of the more modest. The more curious among them penetrated me with their laser-like brown eyes.

I left the village well and walked through the upper end of the town and came upon the slaughter field. At the edges of the area many dogs roamed, yapping, and snapping for position and waiting for stray pieces of meat to be tossed aside to them. One of the butchers threw a handful of fat to the outside and a dog darted in to get it. Then came the growling and fighting as the other dogs tried to share his breakfast with him. Fortunately, the path I was on went above the butchers' field, so I got a good view from the top as a pre-med student in a surgeon's amphitheater and the accompanying odors were not that overwhelming.

Three large logs in teepee form supported the animal suspended head down and the butchers and skinners were busy at their work. After the skinning, the choppers took over and, with large axes cut, the beef into its two half sides. A small wiry man placed himself under the teepee in a football stance and the two choppers slowly lowered one half of the beef onto his back. In this bent forward position, neck and back almost parallel to the ground, the porter carried this half carcass to the marketplace about a quarter of a mile away. Shortage of refrigeration recommends that meat be eaten the day it is killed. Aged meat is not considered a delicacy in Yemen. If the slaughterer judges his market correctly all meat should be sold before noon.

In the marketplace we found a few small boys who were offering berries on large green leaves half the size of this sheet of paper. They looked like large blackberries but had no seeds and were part red and part black and had a very good tart flavor. While in the market, we came to the courthouse and, after taking off our shoes, looked in. We met the chief judge and a defense lawyer and were offered drinks and a chat in their chambers. Dan, our lawyer, asked about the judicial procedures in this court and the judge explained to us through an interpreter that most of the time he listens to both sides and tries to get them to understand the point of view of the other and arrive at a compromise. Land boundaries, who owns the fruit of a tree, and other questions of property are the majority of matters brought before the court. Criminal matters are rare, and he explained that punishments involving the loss of a hand or head must be sent to Sana'a for approval and don't happen very much anymore. We did see the prison and one of the prisoners had shackles on his ankles. It was explained that he was a hot head who had unsheathed his knife.

We left Yemen with our appetites only whetted. On the next trip, we want to see Mareb, where the queen of Sheba had her capital, Rada, the area from where our agent comes, and other mountain villages.

NINETEEN

1979: Are there crocodiles in Lake Como?

There were many different high spots for the family this year. For Gary, it included earning his Tenderfoot badge, getting a fish while spearfishing, and his first dance party. Valeria, who is 9, made an unassisted double play in Little League baseball, was an active Girl Scout, authored a book and opened a savings account. Robin, our 4-year-old, learned to ride a bicycle and swim. Lydia keeps selling her pictures. She has taught part of a home economics course at the school, traveling the 16-kilometer roundtrip to school and back on her bicycle, is a Girl Scout assistant, a chief buyer for the Christmas bazaar of Asian objects, and in spite of the heavy schedule, she cooks gourmet meals for us. As for myself, the high spots were being nominated as President of the Italian operations of Rheem, getting a fish while spearfishing, and a trip to South America.

Valeria open a savings account at oldest savings bank in the world in Cariplo

Valeria, Gary and Robin on Lake Como

As far as work is concerned, my de facto job as president of the two Rheem companies in Italy for the past year was made official and I was given the title of President of both Rheem Safim, the drum and shelving company, and Rheem Radi, the water heater company. The first of these two companies is now making a profit and the task is to figure out what levers to push or pull to make the other company turn from a loss into a profit. Luck has as much to do with improved results as does wise guidance, and it is sometimes hard to differentiate between which of these two factors has been most responsible.

In spite of sporadic strikes during the six-month negotiation for the new National Labor contract and the influence of the petroleum crisis on our customers and on our costs, we made higher profits at Safim in 1979 than in 1978. Our joint venture project for building the first and, we hope, only shelving factory in Saudi Arabia is proceeding and we expect to have it in operation by the end of 1980. The idea of selling shelving in Saudi Arabia to save space seems silly at first glance, with so much uninhabited desert. However, the cost of real estate in the Saudi cities is much higher than in most European cities. For example, land ten miles from the center of Jeddah costs $60 per square foot. Consequently, it does pay Arabs to invest money in our shelving so they can better utilize their cubic meters available. We are continuing to receive requests for know-how and turnkey projects from communist countries and although the decision process is slow, we expect to have something going in a communist country before too long. Whatever project develops will likely make good material for a future report.

In Italy, one of the major customers of Rheem Italy is the large chemical company Mont Edison. They purchase steel drums from Rheem for shipment of their chemical products to many countries. They have been selling their chemicals to China for many years and in their China business they exchange their chemicals for hundreds of drums filled with powdered Chinese eggs in payment rather than dollars. Mont Edison resells those powdered eggs to Italian bakeries for making the delicious Italian Christmas cake Panettone. This barter arrangement allows them to avoid exchange control.

One of my friends is the Mont Edison purchasing agent. He told me that China does not have any heavy equipment for making the 55-gallon steel drums necessary for export of many kinds of products. He noticed that our Milan factory had an extra drum line that we were not using and asked if we would consider selling it to China. This employee of Mont Edison makes a business trip to China every year and said he would be glad to introduce me to the appropriate purchasing persons in China that could make the decision to purchase our extra the drum line. As Lydia and I had taken a fascinating trip to Russia a few years earlier, we both looked forward to visiting emerging China and seeing the comparison.

What we saw in Communist China in 1979 was far different from what we saw in Communist Russia in 1970. Rather than a grey sad country with an apathetic and dispirited population, our impression of China was of a vigorous country with wide awake and purposeful people. In China our impression was of an enthusiastic population with a strong desire to improve their country. While the living standard is extremely low, we saw a dignity and optimism in the people we saw. There were many we spoke to that told us of great differences between the old China and the new China. They are convinced that they are much better off now than before. They were aware that the main problem for the Chinese for the past 3,000 years had been basic survival and famine. Due to the frequent and major widespread famines, many people died from hunger every year. The basic food problem had never been solved by the emperors and rulers of the past.

One of our guides, Gu, a man of 24, focused this problem of food for us through the eyes of his family. His father's family came from north China where his grandfather was a street vendor selling wheat cakes for sale in the marketplace. The government at that time was very corrupt and civil servants stole from everyone. Soldiers would come and help themselves to the freshly fried cakes that his grandfather produced and sold daily. If he asked for payment the soldiers would slap him. Sometimes the soldiers ate up his whole day's earnings and there was nothing he could do about it. Most of these episodes took place during the fat eight months of the year, and during the lean four months of the year, while waiting for the new wheat harvest, the family nourishment consisted of tree bark, leaves, and roots. At the age of 11, his father left the family and joined Mao's army. There he met his wife, and both were convinced that there was a better way to organize society and the communists addressed some of the problems of China. According to Gu, the problem of basic nourishment has now been solved for the first time for the Chinese people. What we saw were slim, well-proportioned people, taller than I would have expected.

A second element of basic survival is shelter and less progress has been made in this area. People live very close together. Young couples must wait a long time before they can have a place of their own. Once they get a place, it is miniature by western standards. A family of four has a total of twenty square meters, which is the size of our bedroom at home in Italy. We visited what was supposed to be a typical home in a farming community near Canton. It was for a family of five and consisted of two rooms and a courtyard. The living room was about 15 square meters and the sleeping area for the entire family of five was about ten square meters. There was an alcove for the bed of the parents and a loft above where the three children slept. These parents were fortunate to have such privacy as we saw other houses where entire families slept together in one very small room.

The kitchen was in the courtyard with a brick oven in one corner and a cast iron box with a grill for boiling water and vegetables was in another part of the courtyard. There was no water faucet in the house and fresh water was obtained by a trip to the nearest well. Water from the well was not to be drunk without being boiled first. Each group of houses have their community outhouse and here privacy is limited. You take your place in single file straddling a trench. Being one behind the other conversation is limited to an occasional remark cast over the shoulder. The habit of reading when on the toilet has not yet reached China. In fact, I've never seen people move in and out public toilets as fast as in China.

While there are community bath houses we understand that most of the washing is done at home with a small pail of heated water. Dishes are washed outside on the street. On an early morning walk we saw many people with a cup of water brushing their teeth just outside their door. Ice boxes and refrigerators do not exist in most of the houses. Even if they could be purchased there would hardly be any space for them. A table, a few chairs and a sideboard take up most of the living room area. Using the present rule of thumb in China of five square meters of living space per person we should share our apartment in Milan with 21 other people. While people don't have as much living space in China as compared with the West, we saw no one sleeping on the streets as we did in India and other parts of Southeast Asia, and in many metropolitan cities in the West.

A third element of survival less compelling than food and shelter is the winter temperature which drops below freezing. The most common dress is the famous blue jacket and blue pants, but this is not the only color. We saw green and several shades of grey as well. Many people wear different colored jackets and pants as one would wear slacks with an unmatching sport coat. The dress is unisex, and women wear exactly the same clothes as men as the clothing doesn't define the basic anatomical differences between men and women. Long braids still worn by many women helps in the identification of sex. In all the time we were in China our eyes must have seen over a million people in the overcrowded cities, but we saw no women in a skirt.

An area where great strides have been made in the past thirty years is in schooling. Ku, a second guide of ours of thirty who came from a poor peasant family, told us that before the revolution it was completely impossible for the children of a peasant to attend school. At that time schools were private and were missionary schools that educated less than five percent of the population. Now, in virtually all of China, ten years of school are obligatory, and illiteracy is nil below the age of thirty. University is available to many more but is still very restricted. Our guide told us that admittance to university is now based strictly on merit rather than on the politics of the parents. He said before the Gang of Four was thrown out in 1976, there was favoritism in school admissions based on the position of one's parents, but he added that this unwholesome "Russian-like" practice has now been eliminated in China.

As far as employment is concerned, China still has a major problem. The economy is not providing enough jobs for the population. Many people work in street cleaning brigades and the streets are very clean. Many others are sent out to agricultural communes. He estimated there were still about 30 million unemployed Chinese. But he said that in China, this represents three percent of the total population of the working population which he assumed was similar to many Western countries. He said the major unemployment problem is now far lower than in pre-Mao days.

Our entry into China, as well as the whole visit, was very positive. From Hong Kong we took a train through the new territories of Kowloon to the frontier. On the Hong Kong side formalities are crisp and rapid and commanded by a magnificent species virtually extinct – the British colonial officer – complete with moustache and swagger stick. It seemed strange leaving the British passport desk to see a sign with an arrow that merely said, "To China".

You then walk across a covered railroad bridge over a low muddy river with an unimpressive barrier between bustling, industrial, capitalistic Hong Kong and agricultural China. The tension of armed guards and security that exists between Austria and Hungary or East and West Berlin is far different from the atmosphere at the Hong Kong-China frontier. There were only two soldiers on the Chinese side while there were no soldiers on the British/Hong Kong side.

Once across the bridge we were met by a guide whose job was to take our group through the Chinese border formalities. In addition to checking our yellow vaccination card, we had to fill out a form and declare, among other things, whether we had had any glandular swelling in the past half month. We continued to the customs area to fill out a declaration that informed us which items taken into China we were required take with out with us upon departure from China. These articles included limited to watches, cameras, radios, jewelry plus a declaration of the amount of cash you had on you. It is forbidden to bring Chinese currency from British Hong Kong into China. Then finally, we went to the money exchange desk to get our first "yuan" and "jiao".

Between each of the control stations there was a living room with comfortable chairs where our group waited for a few minutes before proceeding to the next station. All of the officials were pleasant, unhurried, and efficient and so much different from their counterparts in many of the Communist Eastern European countries we have visited. It didn't feel like we were entering a Communist country. There was no checking of our reading material nor of our baggage. Our frontier guide then took our group to a train carriage where a group of seats had been reserved for "our Italian friends". We shared this carriage with a Japanese group. Our first guide then wished us a pleasant trip and went back to escort another group of visitors to the frontier.

After the train ride from Hong Kong to the border, I was curious to see what our two-hour train ride from the border to Canton would be like. It was better than I expected. The carriage was neat and clean, and the seats were comfortable with white seat covers. There were four seats facing each other and we had lots of leg room. Each group of two seats could be swiveled 90 degrees to face directly out the window. The small table between the four seats had a white tablecloth and a flower vase on it, along with four mugs for tea. There was a smiling girl in blue pants and blue jacket and long pigtails who was our attendant. She came by to pour tea, compliments of the Chinese railway services. The roadbed was good and the ride smooth. I wondered about the criteria used in defining an undeveloped country. I guess it all depends on what you compare. If, for example, you use the Kowloon-Canton railway line in comparison to the New York-New Haven line, the U.S. would have to be considered the undeveloped country. I don't remember anyone serving me tea at a comfortable seat ten minutes out of Grand Central Station.

The rail line from Soochow to Shanghai was equally good as was the Shanghai-Nanking line. There is also something very charming about the Chinese railway system. They use mostly steam engines which comes with the mournful hoot of a steam train chugging along full speed. This nostalgic sound, and the sight of a long train on a long curve with white smoke pouring out of the engine is a delightful scene which I last remember as a boy in Illinois.

The Chinese countryside through the province of Canton was impressive. The landscape was green, and the fields were orderly and well-tended and looked like neat pictures framed by the geometric irrigation canals. There were no cars on the roads, only bicycles and a few trucks. I saw no agricultural machinery and the plows were pulled by buffalo. Both men and women wearing straw hats were carrying heavy loads balanced on either ends of their bamboo poles.

The land is terraced which also allows the sides of the hills to be utilized for growing crops. We understand that before the revolution the land was divided up into many small and irregular pieces owned in part by the peasants and in part by absentee owners. Efficient farming of the land was difficult. I was surprised to see fewer people working the fields than I had expected and began wondering when we would become aware of the heavy Chinese population.

As our train reached the outskirts of Canton the large population became obvious. The road parallel to the train was now a river of bicycles and the sidewalks were packed with pedestrians. While the crowding I've seen in Lagos, Nigeria produces an antagonistic attitude within the crowds, the impression I had of Canton was one of cordiality and respect for others. That impression continued throughout the rest of China. In any case, it was frightening to step off the train in Canton into a swirling mass of Chinese not speaking a word of their language and not knowing what to do and where to go.

I'm glad our guides had no trouble finding us. Of the three that met us, two were to be with us for the entire trip. Both of the guides spoke Italian well and represented 40% of the Italian speaking guides at the tourist agency. The Chinese tourist agency, LUX was very detailed in numbers, and we were told there were about 400 employees who run the total guide business in the entire country. Of these about 200 speak English, 100 speak Japanese, 20 French, 20 Dutch, 20 German, 7 Spanish, 5 Italian, 3 speak Swedish, 2 speak Greek and 2 speak Portuguese. They don't have any Russian speakers.

Far from being luxurious we found the hotels to be quite adequate. One of the hotels advertised itself as follows: "Pey Win is a high building for service. There are 718 rooms in it. About 1,100 to 1,500 people can be served here. There are single rooms, double rooms, and suites on every floor. The rooms are quiet, clean, beautiful, and comfortable. Visitors can choose from among them. On the 28th floor there is a goldfish pool and the Sun Suites. There is air-conditioning and lifts of high, middle, and low speeds."

I understood better about the flexible capacity of handling from 1,100-1,500 people after I saw our small room which had four other beds in addition to our bed. Fortunately, we didn't have to share our room with other guests. A friend from the Italian company arrived from Canton one evening during an overbooking period. When he finally got a room, he found that he had to share a room with three double beds with six strangers.

In Canton there is a beautiful park and in the area that the French and

British had requisitioned for their exclusive use during the period of the opium wars. When we took our early morning walk in that park, we were surrounded by students that wanted to speak English with us and learn about life in the United States. Lydia and I were in the middle of a forward moving half circle, with students to our left and right, so they could ask us questions and hear our answers. Our mass of students was like a Greek phalanx moving through the park.

On the school front, I was reelected as treasurer of the board of the American school of Milan and our financial structure is strengthening. We have reached $650,000 of our $1,000,000 building fund goal. While total enrollment is near capacity, there is a disturbing drop and the number of American students enrolled went from 270 in 1976 to 190 in 1979. This is a reflection of the sharp drop of the American population in Europe over the past three years.

The reduction of the US expatriate population is disturbing to me. It is bad from a United States-world posture standpoint and will also have a negative impact on the U.S. balance of payments. There is also much more need now to sell American products to pay for our oil imports than before. I have found most Americans sent overseas by their companies to be interesting, intelligent people, and excellent ambassadors for the U.S. The presence of these American citizens within the economic fabric of European countries creates certain ties which cannot be created by U.S. consular and embassy staff. A reduction of this American population in Western Europe will decrease the cohesion between Western Europe and America.

The balance of payment impact is more immediate and striking. Less American equipment and machinery will be purchased for export if the American expatriate population continues decreasing. This is not primarily because the American expatriate is nationalistic and wants to buy American, but that the American expatriate knows the names of American companies that handle certain products, and his European counterpart does not know the names. My experience this year is a typical example. Our Italian company just spent $150,000 to buy a piece of equipment which was exported from America. If I had not been here, this piece of equipment would have been purchased in Europe. When I saw the bids for this steel cutting machine, I asked our purchasing agent if he had asked the company X of Texas to bid. He had never heard of company X. So, he sent a telex to them and asked for a bid. Their bid was the best offer we received, we placed the order with them, and the US balance of payments was helped.

The US tax Reform Act of 1976 has been primarily responsible for the drop in Europe's expatriate population. This tax legislation was influenced by Senator Proxmire who took the position that Americans overseas are primarily wealthy people who are living out of this country to avoid US taxes. There are undoubtedly some in this category, but they must represent less than one tenth of 1% of the Americans overseas. The tax legislation before 1976 was a mild economic encouragement to work overseas as it gave the expatriate certain tax deductions. However, these deductions did not do much more than compensate for the indirect system of taxation existing in many parts of the world. There was a time when the cost of living in Europe and elsewhere was less than in the United States, but the combination of higher European inflation plus dollar devaluations have made the U.S. one of the cheapest countries in the world. Consequently, the expatriate has received a double economic blow, a higher cost of living than in the U.S. plus a higher tax bill than before. The new tax legislation has not only eliminated the minor tax incentives for working overseas but in some cases has become punitive period to maintain their expatriate staff. Many companies went to a policy of tax equalization, assuring the individual the same net pay he would have if he were working in the U.S., but this created a much greater cost to the company than before. Consequently, expatriate staff is being phased out in many countries because American expatriate employees cost too much.

The increased revenues to the U.S. treasury of the new taxes on overseas Americans is infinitesimal. It is significant to note that none of the western European countries tax their citizens when they live and work abroad. This is economic policy established for reasons of national interest. European countries have already been more dependent on export than the U.S. and have found it positive and necessary to have their citizens in foreign markets to promote exports which improve their balance of payments. Write to your congressional representative suggesting that tax legislation be modified to encourage Americans to go overseas to work. I hope all of your letters will cause the tax law to be modified and that in three years we will be back up to our former level of 270 American students in our school.

While we hope to replace the dropping American enrollment with Italians and third country nationals. If the ratio of Italian students becomes too high, the informal language of the school would change from English to Italian. This change could affect the mastery of English for our high school students and their ability to score well on their college boards. Gary is still two years away from high school so there is still time for the impact of your congressional letters to affect him and his College Board scores.

While Gary is approaching high school in two years, our youngest is in kindergarten. Having a child of four, I think of myself often as a young father. Unfortunately, the view one has of oneself is not always reflected in others. Robin and I were at the park one morning with our bicycles. I was a little ahead and a passerby, taken with the cute 4-year-old on a two-wheel bicycle, encouraged her along, "You are doing fine, catch up with Grandfather." I looked around to see who he might be referring to!

While my image of myself is still that of a young father, Robins's image of me is that of Saint George, that is a father with boxing gloves, punching trolls, monsters, and dinosaurs. Books and stories about monsters are very much part of her life now, and I am asked frequently if I can beat up this monster or that troll. It reassures her to know I can beat up the monsters, particularly when it is bedtime. The other day she asked me if I could beat up crocodiles and sharks. I answered no, and she seemed so concerned that I added I could beat up the smaller and middle-sized crocodiles and sharks but not the big ones. Fortunately, she has not started to ask me if I can beat up some of the fathers or grandfathers of the children in her class. Robin got a picture book of dinosaurs for Christmas, and I made the mistake of reading it to her on Christmas night after a heavy dinner. She was very interested in the dinosaurs and their big teeth. At 4:00 in the morning, I was awakened by her crying. I got up and went into her room to see what the matter was.

"I'm afraid."

"What are you afraid of?"

"Crocodiles."

"Well, there are no crocodiles here, please go back to sleep."

"Are you sure no crocodiles can come up here?"

"Yes, Robin. Crocodiles like warm weather and water. It is cold here and the only nearby water is Lake Como. There are no crocodiles in Lake Como."

She was pacified and went back to sleep.

At 4:30 Robin woke me again.

I got out of bed and went in to see what she wanted.

"I am still afraid of the crocodiles. Are you sure there are no crocodiles in Lake Como?"

"I am quite sure. Besides, even if they were, they would not be able to walk up the long steep road from Lake Como to here. Now please go back to sleep."

At 5:00 Robin called again. I got up and went in to see what the problem was for the third time period when I sat down on her bed, she said "I'm not afraid anymore."

Robin's other interest is babies.

"Can't we have another baby now?"

"No, we cannot," answered Lydia.

"I want to have a baby. Can't I have a baby?"

"You have to be a big person, you should be married and have a husband," replied Lydia.

A slight pause.

"Oh," said Robin, "will you take me?"

"Take you where?" asked Lydia

"To where the husbands are!"

Robin's vision must be that every town has a type of corral where husbands are kept, until mothers with their girls come down to pick one out. Do not wrap him up, we will eat him here.

While the image of a father for Robin is a crocodile wrestler, the image of father for the two others includes a baseball coach. Little League has started this year for both boys and girls, and Saturday mornings we go out to the school play field for practice and games. Gary plays third base for the 6th and 7th grade team and is playing a pretty good brand of baseball, while Valeria, with the 3rd to 5th graders, is learning to throw, catch, and swing the bat. It is a particular satisfaction seeing the 3rd and 4th grade girls overcome their fear of the ball. In only a few sessions they pass from a defensive catching position with head turned to one side, wrists stuck together as if handcuffed, to a brave eagerness to clap their hands around the ball. Batting seems to come a bit easier than catching and with the infield in a fluid state, most balls hit are good for at least one base. Conversely, double plays are not unusual with everyone running as the batter swings. Valeria caught a fly ball, and following the screaming instructions of her teammates, ran over to touch second base to put the baserunner out. She did not really understand what it was she had done but was pleased when all the other members of her team treated her as the hero of the day. Scores of 16 to 22 in this age group indicate the amount of running and excitement.

On the academic front, Valeria is an avid reader and has authored a book, with two friends, about pirates. She made and bound 50 copies and sold them all at the spring fair. She has banked the proceeds and takes pride in her growing bank account. She got her banking start with her savings as an actress for a chocolate drink television commercial. She opened her account at the largest savings bank in the world, Cariplo, and the Managing Director of the bank, Mr Nezzo, came down personally to sign her up and receive her money. Valeria may have been the youngest girl to open an account with them and pictures were taken of the ceremony and published in the bank's magazine. She was fascinated by the concept of earning interest.

Gary wanted a savings account so he too could earn interest. While he does not have the initial capital of Valeria, not being as yet a TV actor, he did manage to save up $25 for his initial deposit. He is looking forward to the dollar he will earn at the end of the year in interest. In addition to banking, Boy Scouts and Girl Scouts have taken part of their interest this year. Lydia has participated as one of the Girl Scout excursion

1979: ARE THERE CROCODILES IN LAKE COMO?

leaders and has had both the Girl Scout and Boy Scout troops up to Brunate for a camp out and cookout raw meat burnt on the edges and underdone potatoes. The marshmallows never tasted so good.

Gary, Valeria, and Robin on porch in Brunate

I am learning a lot as an assistant scout master. Trying to explain the meaning of the words in the scout oath and teaching the requirements of Tenderfoot are taxing my abilities. It was enjoyable sitting on the review board and testing the scouts on first aid. To make sure the scouts understood what to do and in what sequence, I sketched an accident for them in which they were the first on the scene. I was a victim who had fallen off a ladder, my ankle was either broken or sprained, my wrist was cut from a piece of broken glass, and I was unconscious, probably in a state of shock. While most of the scouts had studied their first aid, treated me for shock, stopped the bleeding, and bandaged me up, I am afraid I would not have survived the first aid administered by the one that did not pass.

The movement from scouts into the teens carries with it a cautious signaling to the opposite sex. At dinner, the other day Gary was telling Valeria how nice one of the girls in the class had suddenly become.

"Yesterday, she asked me for the answers to the math problems."

"Do you call that being nice?" Valeria asked.

"Of course," said Gary, "before she did not even speak to me!"

Communications between girls in eighth grade increased rapidly this year and a big assist was Gary's birthday party. We asked him what he would like to do at his party and who he would like to invite. We had expected to have a few of the boys of his class over for a soccer game in the park, or maybe take them to a movie and then out for pizza. He surprised us when he said he thought it was time for a dance. We agreed that would be nice.

Then came the trauma of the invitations. "Will the girls come?"

His strategy was admirable. He first called the most influential girl and asked her. She could not come the night he suggested as it was a school night. He came back from the phone defeated. "Now the other girls won't come."

Our suggestion that he have the party on a Friday night, two weeks in the future, gave him new life. He called Jenny again and she said that was fine. He ran around the house jumping in the air. "Whoopee, she can come!"

As he called the other girls one by one, he let it drop that Jenny would also be coming. This seemed to give them the courage and they all accepted. He had Valeria with him beside the phone to give him moral support. Once she wandered off, but he called her back. "Valeria, I need you, please stay with me as I call."

I was impressed with his telephone poise. I remembered the first time I called a girl. I was not only two years older but much less able to handle the situation. I had memorized what I was going to say. I had not counted on a response during my memorized presentation and her reply in the wrong place made me forget what I was supposed to say next. There was an agonizing silence and sweat broke out on my brow. After 30 seconds, which seemed like two hours, the girl came to the rescue and helped the conversation along. I am glad to say that Gary was not a chip off the old block!

The night before the party two of the boys came over to sleep at our house to help Gary fix up the living room. A disk jockey's cockpit was set up in one corner and the lights were covered with colored papers giving purple, green, orange, and blue hues. Foro Buonaparte 44A was turned into the ballroom of the Drake Hotel.

At 6:00 PM the next evening, the first four girls arrived. While they came for grown up activities, the presence reflected 12-year-old interests. We were pleased that the occasional presence of Lydia and me was not inhibiting to them. They mixed very well, and the girls were not standing on one side with the boys on the other. None of them had ever had any dancing lessons but they danced with the routine as if they had just stepped out of the movie Grease. The first dance for the 6th graders turned out to be a remarkable success and they asked when they could have another one. Several dances followed and at the last dance of the year a thank you scroll was presented to Lydia for hosting the parties at our house.

Our trip Sardinia was full of adventure. We rented a villa for the third time on the Costa Dorata, just south of Olbia. A series of large bays and several large islands three to four miles from the coast creates a reasonably protected area. However, if the wind comes up you can get some good-sized waves. We had with us the same rubber boat as before and this time the glue held, and the boat did not come apart. With it we were able to reach the isolated beaches one can only reach from the sea.

Gary, Robin and Valeria in Sardenia

TWENTY

1980: Bulgaria

The Italian economy is in recession which hit very sharply at the end of September. Our sales volume has dropped off 30 percent in one of our product lines. It is hard to reduce labor costs in Italy and the number of employees on the payroll because of Italian labor laws. We are hoping the Italian economy will not get worse in the next six months because we really enjoy the lifestyle of being an American expatriate in Italy.

To offset the sharp drop in business from our local Italian market we are looking to the export market of paint pails to keep the factory employment stable. We have already begun selling our steel container products in Yugoslavia for paints, and in Hungary we are selling our 55-gallon steel drums, with a specially designed plastic lining, for their export of honey.

Bulgaria looks like a good place to expand our sales volume with our machinery producing 55-gallon steel drums. When I think of Bulgaria what comes to mind are roses, wild mushrooms, fresh fruit, and the best yogurt I have ever tasted. This Bulgarian yogurt has the impressive name of Lactobacillus Bulgaricus Streptococcus Thermophiles. In most western European countries where yogurt is made, the process involves adding milk to a small portion of the yogurt yeast of yesterday and the new yogurt grows rapidly in several days. For some unknown reason the production of the tasty Bulgarian yogurt cannot be reproduced outside of Bulgaria using the Bulgarian Lactobacillus as a starter. Consequently, for Bulgarian yogurt lovers, living in major cities of Western Europe, this excellent Bulgarian yogurt could be airfreighted to the local dairy in our 55-gallon drums, at which point it could be repackaged into one quart glass containers in a local dairy facility and distributed through their normal dairy channels.

There is another Bulgarian food product where the Bulgarian production of surplus food could be distributed to other countries in the Soviet Block - tomato paste, as Bulgaria has a tomato surplus. We are working with an Italian agricultural company for designing a 55-gallon steel drum with a special anti-corrosive lining for shipping of tomato paste. We believe Bulgaria could also be the country designated by Moscow as the tomato paste supplier to those communist countries that may have a shortage of tomatoes.

In my trip to Bulgaria, I found it an attractive country with rolling hills, vast fields of roses, good fruit, scenic mountains, good soil, ample fresh water, and a long growing season. Although separated from the Mediterranean Sea by a small strip of Greece, it has more of a Mediterranean than middle European climate. The area of Bulgaria, referred to by the Romans as Thrace and Dacia, suffered under 500 years of Turkish domination which was followed recently by 40 years of a forced "fraternal cooperation" with Russia.

The Turkish domination is looked upon by most of the Bulgarians as their 500 years of dark ages which started at about the time Western Europe began its Renaissance. There is still a strong feeling of animosity towards the Turkish rulers who tried unsuccessfully to stamp out Bulgarian culture, their Greek Orthodox religion and national identity. The Russians and Bulgarians have been common enemies of the Turks for a long time, and it was the Czarist army that helped the Bulgarians drive out the Turks at one time, but they came back. Consequently, there are more historical ties between Bulgaria and Russia than between the other Eastern European satellites and Russia. However, the tie is to Czarist aristocracy and the Orthodox Christian church of Russia rather than to communism. While the Russian communist oppression of Bulgaria has been gentler than the Turkish domination, an independent Bulgaria is a wish nurtured in many a Bulgarian breast.

While Bulgaria is one of the communist countries of Eastern Europe dominated by the Russian Communist party, having traveled to both countries in the last three years, my observations is that the average Bulgarian is much better off than the average Russian. There are more consumer goods in the stores in Sofia than in Moscow. One does not find the long food lines snaking out into the street that we found in Moscow nor empty shelves in the food stores in Bulgaria. The people in the street are better dressed. There is also more animation in Sofia than in Moscow and there are outdoor cafes where people gather. I did not notice any outdoor cafes when I was in Moscow. The people walking the streets of Sofia seem to be talking to each other which was not the case when I was in Moscow, in either 1970 or in 1978.

In spite of the presence of secret police in Sofia, there is still a willingness of Bulgarians to talk to strangers. I had the feeling that most of the Bulgarian young people are pro-western. They like American jazz and western clothes and freedom of free speech. Their greatest wish seems to be to travel to Paris, Rome, London, and especially to the United States.

Regarding the attitude towards politics and particularly communism, one Bulgarian told me – secretly - that in Bulgaria, there are eight million football fans, one communist and two tourists. The one communist he referred to was George Milev, an enthusiastic supporter of Lenin just after the First World War. Mr. Milev was famous for these words,

"September shall be May and a man's life will follow the endless spiral of progress." What exactly does Mr Milev mean?

For these thoughtful and inspiring words along with his support of Lenin, a Bulgarian newspaper in English left in our hotel room, reported that Mr Milev was burned by fascist thugs in 1923 for opposing communism. His place has been taken by Mr Zipkov, who is considered the model Communist. His daughter has the title and government salary of "Chief of Staff", and she has a hairdresser and maid when they travel outside of Bulgaria.

We understand these three state officials love to travel. They seem to spend most of their time traveling first class to Mexico, China, Angola, Finland, Cuba, and Moscow. I believe one reason they travel is to thank the owners of the expensive resorts where they stay for their expressions of solidarity with the Communist cause. They pretend to be selling Bulgarian products to these countries. There was a recent article in the English newspaper published in Sofia, describing how the Bulgarian Communist party and the Russian Communist party are working effectively hand in hand to bring the prosperity of communism to Bulgaria.

There are many posters on walls in the streets of Sofia with pictures of Soviet Premier Brezhnev and President Zipkoff shaking hands while praising the benefits of Communism. It is my impression that most people I meet scoff at the falseness of these advertisements. But as the secret police may be everywhere, the people we met made certain when they talk to strangers they look around before they speak for fear of being identified as an enemy of the people and sent to jail.

The local newspaper in Sofia was the typical Eastern European English paper which contains very little news. Instead, the articles were all about the great economic progress of socialism with pictures of smiling factory workers leaving their shift, carrying their lunch boxes and looking as fresh as when they came to work in the morning. The paper has articles about the great economic progress in Bulgaria since the old reactionary regime was overthrown. The articles include statistics about the increases of productivity, covering the growth of electrical power along with increasing tons of fertilizer. There is no news about Bulgarians speaking up against hypocrisy.

To whom all of this Bulgarian prosperity arrives is not too clear. You don't see it reflected in the standard of living of the average Bulgarians. A toasted sandwich in a standup bar cost one hour of labor. Even a 20-year-old car, like those driven by our high school students in the U.S., is out of reach for 90 % of the population.

Towards the Russians there is a strange ambivalence. On the surface there is a great public demonstration of close ties and fraternal cooperation. As we entered the town of Plovdiv, there were alternate Bulgarian and Russian flags lining the street. Large billboards show Russian and Bulgarian workers joining arms as they march toward a better future. One can imagine stirring music in the background. But underneath there is chafing at the bit, a desire to escape. They know that if they try to break away from Russia the full weight of the Russian army will overwhelm them in a few days. This resignation is a part of the national psyche and a consequence of the 500 years of Turkish domination, where the penalty for opposition was impalement.

At the trade fair, this theme of friendship and cooperation with Russia is played continuously. The Russian exhibit occupies an entire pavilion and as one enters you see four enormous photos of the Soviet Leader Brezhnev and the Bulgarian Leader Zipkoff hugging and smiling at each other. That display could also be called "the four seasons" because in one hugging photo they are both dressed in their winter coats and hats, a second one with their arms around each other is definitely summertime, and the other two pictures of them embracing could easily be of a fall or spring meeting, as both are wearing hats made of beaver or mink.

The machinery and products displayed in the Russian pavilion were unimpressive. They display a large railroad engine, a big machine tool, a few old computers, a scale model of a textile factory and a small dam. This seems to have the objective of showing the Bulgarians what the Russian engineers can accomplish. The message seemed to be that with Bulgaria's close cooperation with Russia, these benefits will also come to Bulgaria. There was no exhibit of a Russian attempt to sell specific consumer articles, or even industrial machinery that may be needed in Bulgaria. In the Russian exhibit there were pretty pictures of attractive old Silk Road cities of Bokhara, Samarkand, and Tashkent. But there were no salespeople there to sign you and your family up for a package tour to any of those fascinating historical places, nor any explanation of how much a tour costs to those wonderful ancient cities. The Cuban and Romanian exhibits seemed to follow the Russian pattern. There were pictures of cooperation between the Russian, Romanian, and Cuban communist party members in smiling hugs with each other but few goods on display for sale.

The exhibits of the communist countries were in stark contrast to those of western countries, where specific products and merchandise were on display with salesmen and engineers on hand to explain the products and provide prices. The Polish exhibit was more market-oriented than the Eastern European section. They did have nice looking consumer goods for sale. There was an attractive section with small sailboats and motorboats. But with the low wage structure in Bulgaria, I would be surprised if there were any Bulgarians who had the money to purchase a sailboat or motorboat made in Poland. We exhibited our steel drums and pails with plastic interiors to preserve Bulgarian food products, such as honey and tomato paste. Our exhibit generated much interest with Bulgarian chemical and food companies, and we developed substantial new business from the trade fair. We also enjoyed the opportunity of talking to some Bulgarian university students vising our stand.

1980: BULGARIA

It would be ludicrous as well as inconceivable to imagine a policeman in Boston coming up to a girl on the street who may have been talking to a French tourist to ask what they had discussed. And advising her she mustn't fraternize with non-Bostonians to avoid the spread of unwholesome political ideas in Boston. It is equally hard to imagine an attractive Bulgarian girl who has grown up under Communism to say "buzz off buddy" to a Bulgarian secret policeman whom she assumed was intruding into her privacy.

While there is a fearful respect by the private Bulgarian citizen towards the police, there is a similar respect in turn from the police to certain strangers who may have high level of political connections from other countries. We are represented in Bulgaria by an Italian company with its office in the capital of Sofia. The manager of that office is Sonja, a Russian woman who is in the unusual position of having three valid passports, Russian, Bulgarian, and Italian as a result of two prior marriages. She is skillful in using the best passport depending upon the occasion, and as Gilbert and Sullivan might say she uses the best passport "to fit the crime". She handles both translations and contracts for us in Bulgaria and is one of the few individuals in Bulgaria who has her own car, and who is not a high Bulgarian government official.

One day our Sales Manager and I were with Sonja in her car driving to an appointment in Plovdiv when we were stopped by a policeman for speeding. This gave us an opportunity to appreciate Sonja's skillful selection of the best of her three passports for the occasion. While I didn't understand what the policeman said, his tone of voice was arrogant and intimidating. He asked to see her documents. When she pulled out her Russian passport, his attitude changed to respect and deference. We were allowed to proceed without a ticket. The policeman added, in a gentle voice, that it would be better if she would please respect the speed limit in Plovdiv. When Sonja comes to Italy, she tells us she uses her Russian and Italian passports, but when she goes to Russia, she uses either her Italian or Bulgarian passport. Sonja has the ability to travel to both east and west, something limited to a tiny fraction of Bulgarians.

When I was in Sofia shortly after the Russian invasion of Afghanistan, I asked Sonja whether she was aware of what was going on there. She said the local newspapers did not write about it, but she had heard something was going on. What she understood was that the Afghan government was having some difficulty with rebels and had requested aid from the Soviet Union. This aid was packaged in a treaty of "Friendship" between the two countries. The Russians answered the call for help from the Afghan government and sent in some Russian soldiers and helicopters to assist the Afghan government to keep order. She understood the rebels had been incited by the Americans working with the Chinese. The attitude of another Bulgarian was, "The Russians were wrong to invade Afghanistan." A third Bulgarian said, "The Russians made a big mistake in Afghanistan." However, for those that did criticize the Russians, I had the feeling that some Bulgarians regard the Afghans as they do the Turks and Turkic people. They probably deserved their problems.

There are some curious contradictions in the attitude of the Bulgarians towards the Russians and the Turks. The Russians dominate the economic and political life in Bulgaria and the general attitude towards the Russians seem to be that of fear, awe and also of sadness, the sadness one would feel towards a large elephant penned up in a zoo and unable to have its freedom. While there are cultural and religious ties between Russians and Bulgarians, there are no such ties between the Russians and the Turks. And yet the Turks now have more liberty and prosperity than the Russians. This is obvious as one sees German cars driving across Bulgaria on their way freely between Turkey and their well-paying manufacturing job in West Berlin.

In West Berlin, the Turkish immigrants earn good wages and with what they earn they can save up enough money to purchase a house or farm when they return to Turkey. This flow of Turks across Bulgaria from Istanbul to West Berlin has created the need for private enterprise on the main motorway between Istanbul and Berlin which caters to that need. And Bulgarian auto mechanics do a good business repairing cars on the road between Berlin and Turkey.

Doing business in Bulgaria is more theatrical than in the west and there is an elaborate procedures and staging. First there is a meeting with the top Bulgarian purchasing agent in his office. Step two is an invitation to a discussion with their technical people. If that goes well in the evening there is a banquet with vodka used as a lubricant to further the technical and economic cooperation between our two countries and the friendships that it brings with it.

The next day a visit is made to the factory and this time, if you are destined to be the successful supplier, you have lunch in the workers meeting room filled with red flags and photos of a smiling face of a "Stakhanovich" hero (a speedy worker) holding a monkey wrench. The final day there is a large banquet starting with vodka and hot peppers. The meal begins at noon, and we finished the last toast at 3:30 in the afternoon. The banquet is anticipated with pleasure by the Bulgarians as it gives them a nice variety of food from their normal fare paid for by their government.

During the dinner, stories are exchanged. One fellow told a charming Bulgarian folk story. The time of this story took place about 600 A.D. after the Romans withdrew and before the Turkish domination of Bulgaria began. Once upon a time there was a brave and wise Bulgarian king was disturbed over the fact that his subjects were getting drunk. He decided that drunkenness was bad, and he banned the growing of grapes and the making of wine. On pain of death all citizens were ordered to pull up and destroy all of their grape vines.

The king then went off to a series of wars. In his travels and between battles he came across a beautiful girl of 18 and wanted to marry her. To provide her with shelter and protection he constructed a comfortable tent for this beautiful girl and left his pet lion to guard her until he returned from battle.

A few days after the king departed, a handsome young man passed by the tent. He saw the lovely girl and fell in love. The youth was so overcome with the girl's beauty and, seeing the big lion guarding her, he realized he must risk fighting the lion to fulfill his love. As he approached, the young man managed to get his arm around the neck of the lion and avoiding the lion's sharp teeth he strangled the beast. Then he and the beautiful young girl fell into each other's arms. But the young man could not stay and so he proceeded on his journey.

When the king's guard came by the tent and saw the strangled lion, he was afraid to tell the king what had happened. Eventually the king found out that a strong man had killed the lion with his bare hands. The king was anxious to find out who in his kingdom was strong enough to kill a lion with only with his bare hands and sent his heralds throughout the land, asking for information about this youth, announcing a pardon for the young man, and a reward to appear before the king.

After three days, the mother of the youth came to the king and said she would provide information as to whom he was and where he was, provided the king gave her his word that there would be no punishment for her or her strong son. The king gave his word along with a bag of gold to the woman. She came back the next day with her son.

Impressed with the strength, appearance and ability of this young man, the king asked the mother how her son developed his strength. The mother answered that she lived in the mountains and had cultivated grapes around her cottage. When she heard the king's order 20 years ago telling all Bulgarians they pull out all of the grape vines in the kingdom, she pulled them out in front of her house, but left a few vines in the back of her cottage and continued to make wine from those grapes. When her boy was born, instead of feeding him milk, she gave him wine to drink. And that is how he grew up to be such a strong young man.

"So," said the king, "if this is what wine produces, I will permit all Bulgarians to plant vines and make and drink their wine again. Perhaps in this way we can produce a stronger race of Bulgarians who will make good soldiers and protect our boundaries against our enemies." From that day forward, Bulgarians started making wine and Bulgaria became one of the best wine-making country in the world.

After this banquet, with much Bulgarian wine consumed and toasts to the king who allowed grapes to grow again in Bulgaria, we signed a protocol agreement for a contract to sell some of our large drums to Bulgaria for them to export their surplus tomato paste to other countries in the communist bloc.

The fair in Plovdiv is about two hours' drive from the Sofia airport by car and about three hours by train. As both Plovdiv and Sofia are stops on the Orient Express from Central Europe to Istanbul, I thought it would be fun to take this segment of the Orient Express. Unusual situations and murders have taken place on the Orient Express in the past and a second-class compartment, holding eight people is comfortable and can provide as interesting a group of travelers as Agatha Christi has described in her play, "Murder on the Orient Express."

I spent the morning walking around the center of this former Turkish city of Plovdiv. In the center of the city was a store for selling railroad tickets. I walked up to the window and was waved off by the clerk. Someone who spoke English told me they were having their morning break and the clerk should return in about 15 minutes. He suggested I wait until the clerk returned to purchase a reserved seat because the trains to Sofia are very crowded and if you don't reserve a seat, you are likely to stand up all the way. So, I waited and waited in line.

While waiting for the clerk to return, I had a chance to speak to a pleasant fellow waiting in line behind me. His name was Fedor and he worked for a company called Balkan Car. His job involved the negotiation and administration in the barter and clearing arrangements of buying and selling used cars with the other communist countries in Europe. I asked him if he could translate for me at the ticket window and also to help me ask for a seat on the 2:30 train to Sofia. He said he was going on the same train and said he would be happy to do this. I asked if they could accept dollars at this window or would I have to go out and make the change at a bank. He made a motion to me to put away my wallet and said with a soft confidential tone, "Don't worry, I'll buy your ticket and make the seat reservation, we can take care of the cost later."

He purchased the tickets and walked out quickly with me following. After about 50 meters he slowed his pace, and I asked how much the ticket cost. I gave him in dollars the price at the official rate of exchange and he was very pleased. I calculated that he made about a 50% profit on that transaction by receiving hard currency - Italian Lira. We would be in the same compartment, and I looked forward to having a chance to speak with him further.

When we got on the train the corridor was packed. It was fortunate I had reserved a seat and got to sit next to this Bulgarian who could speak English. In our eight-seat compartment there were four Bulgarian women of different ages, a colleague of Fedor's from Balkan Car and a tall man sitting next to the window who was Polish, and myself.

Fedor did not seem to be inhibited by these other people in the compartment and we talked frankly for three hours. I learned a lot about the Bulgarian economy, his business, the communist party and its problems, and life in Communist Bulgaria. Regarding his business and work, he described how goods are bartered and prices set between the communist countries. He meets once a year with representatives from Russia, Romania, Bulgaria, Poland, Hungary, Czechoslovakia, and East Germany to establish quantities and prices of used cars. They each present the reasons for an increase of the price of their merchandise, and they argue. Finally, they agree on what is an appropriate price and quantities for the next year.

I asked whether it is the person with the loudest voice or most convincing argument that wins. He said that occasionally the negotiations become harsh, but most of the time they agree on the prices in a friendly way. There is economic interdependence between these countries, and they have the same problems with inflation. The products are divided by country. One country supplies auto motors, another supplies auto components, and a third supplies other products. Hungary for example supplies honey to all Communist bloc countries and Bulgaria supplies tomato paste.

The state companies cannot go bankrupt. There is no boss back home to say, "good job, your efforts helped to make the company additional profit." Conversely, if you are aggressive and harsh, it is more likely there will be a complaint to remove you from the negotiation team, if you make your communist colleagues uncomfortable. Regarding performance and delivery, once the yearly arrangements are made, there are penalties for late delivery. Poor quality is also a problem. When one of the communist partners delivers late or with poor quality, they are forced to go to the West and purchase the replacement products with hard currency.

I was anxious to hear a Bulgarian view of the Polish strikes at the Danzig shipyards. If your communist country is supplying products and your shipments arrive late, can the receiving country collect late penalties from the supplying country? He answered that a strike in a communist country is a new thing, but he believed that the country receiving late products should be entitled to a penalty in hard currency. He added that the current Polish crisis is a complicated situation.

The Polish newspapers have been open about it and there had been considerable bad planning and corruption in Poland. The insiders have been taking advantage of their position. The strikes have brought this issue to the surface. Poland also attempted to industrialize too rapidly and took on large debts from the West to do this. In that process they didn't give enough attention to the consumer side of their economy. The workers got fed up with being the ones to sacrifice so much.

As we continued our discussion, the tall man sitting next to the window across from me, who had been dozing, woke up and began staring at me. His eyes bore through me as if they were X-rays, and I had the feeling his eyes were trying to photograph me. I started talking quieter but as my volume decreased, the attention of this man increased. When he looked straight at me, it seemed as if he trying to read my lips. When he looked straight ahead, showing his fine profile and an expression of ignoring us, his ear seemed to wiggle and grab at my soft words. His glaring was disturbing, and I was curious to know who he was, so I decided to try to draw him into our conversation. The worst that could happen would be a trip to a Bulgarian jail.

So, I asked him in English, if he thought the Polish strikes were good or bad for Poland. He was surprised and raised both eyebrows. Then he answered in very limited English. He answered that he was Polish and lived in Warsaw. He said there was corruption in the Polish government and the strikes were good because it was drawing attention to the Polish leaders taking advantage of their situation. He had been at the Plovdiv trade fair and was interested to hear our discussion. He added that the situation in Poland was very complicated and that the relation between the government and the people had been broken. Some in high positions had been taking advantage of their position for their personal gain. He said the strikes reflected problems of corruption by a few of the communist bosses. I was anxious to have him amplify this part. But his English was spotty, and I couldn't get much more out of him.

He turned to Fedor and asked him if he spoke Russian. Fedor did and they spoke Russian together for a while. His face had a resentful expression as he talked and I managed to pick up such words as Swiss Banks, privileges, corruption, fast cars, luxury food, and factory workers. They talked for about 10 minutes in Russian and then he shrugged his shoulders, sighed, and looked out the window. I think his sigh indicated "What we can do to clean out the swamp in our country".

Fedor was silent for a while, but then turned to me and told me what they had discussed. He said they talked about how Communists in Poland had become corrupt and were using their power to enrich themselves to the disadvantage of all the other Poles. Some of the high-level bureaucrats had built vacation homes in Africa and in the Caribbean and had set up personal bank accounts and ski chalets in Switzerland. The majority of the people had less food than before, but the party members had plenty to eat, along with big cars and many luxury items. It was becoming a swamp and the man indicated that it was time it stopped. Fedor added that this Pole wasn't very communicative and didn't really want to talk. Having been at the trade fair at Plovdiv, he must be an important person in commerce or industry and had been sent by his government. He was probably also a party member and might have felt a conflict of loyalty discussing Polish problems with strangers.

As Fedor raised the point of party membership, I asked him if he was a member of the Bulgarian Communist party. He said he was. He talked freely about how one gets to become a party member and what one does. It sounded like joining an exclusive golf country club. You present your application and credentials, and you are evaluated and passed by other party members. I asked him if this system of "rushing" doesn't tend to make the party a homogenous group of elites from the same educational and social group rather than a cross section of the population, including an appropriate number of blue-collar workers. And if this is the case presently, what would the party membership look like 20 years from now. He said that this was true and that there weren't many new blue-collar workers admitted. This bothered him, as he thought the factory workers should be the base of the party since communism is for the workers. Unfortunately, the workers aren't very interested in the party, nor the extra volunteer work you must do as a party member. He said they were trying to get blue-collar workers to apply but were not having much luck encouraging them.

Fedor told me he spends about one night every 2 weeks at party meetings where discussions are held mostly on local problems. Someone is elected to represent their group at the regional and national meetings which take place every three to six months. I asked him how party policy is formed and to what extent policy comes from the bottom up or imposed from the top down. He said that most policy is imposed from the top down and admitted that this wasn't too good. At the local level the individual party members doesn't have much say about national policy.

One of the things that disturbed Fedor was the lack of care that people had for public property. He said they were starting a program this year to try to change the attitude of people towards public property. He agreed that if more property was private, people would be more careful and would take better care of it. Before we reached Sofia, I had a chance to ask him about the clothing problem and why it was that generally in communist countries the price of clothing is so high with respect to wages. He said it was bad planning and programming. When I suggested that some competition might improve things, he said competition would probably be a good thing, but would be dangerous to the system.

He thought my comments were thought provoking when I asked him what mechanism exists within the party for renewing and updating party philosophy. What made sense to the followers of Karl Marx in 1860, may not make sense in 1960, 1990 or 2020. Bulgaria was already communist when Fedor was born 30 years ago, and he had experienced nothing else. He was intellectually sincere in discussing the party and the system. He seemed well adjusted to the political and economic reality of the country in which he lived, and he did not seem especially frustrated or unhappy about its shortcomings.

I met another Bulgarian at the Trade fair in Plovdiv – Dimitri, a young doctor from Sofia - who had taken a day off to come and see the various exhibits at the trade fair. He told me he liked Italian opera and he had taken a week vacation in Italy the prior year. He could speak some Italian. Dimitri was about 32 and two years out of internship, now practicing medicine at a hospital in Sofia. He was proud of his accomplishment of becoming a doctor as his parents were peasants in a small farm 50 miles from Sofia. He had done well in high school and had gained admittance to medical school in Sofia. He considered himself part of the intellectual elite, doing a highly skilled job. But he was cynical and bitter because he believed something was wrong with the current Bulgarian system which didn't recognize his skills with appropriate compensation. For example, he said waiters in large hotels earned much more than he did, even though not officially. He told me they obtained tips, frequently padded the bills of foreigners, and took some of the restaurant food home.

I was curious about this comment and made a close inspection of my next bill for diner. In total and in dollars the bill was what I would have expected in a good restaurant. But when I went back to the menu and added the prices in Bulgarian Currency of the items I had ordered, I realized I had been overcharged by about 50%. The bill was corrected by the head waiter with many excuses for the error.

In our discussion at our booth at the trade fair, Dimitri was continuously looking around to see if anyone was listening in on our conversation.

As we did not identify any suspicious individual eavesdropping, we had an interesting and honest exchange of ideas. Dimitri told me that there are several people in modest jobs in various government agencies who have a surprisingly high standard of living, including a car, a nice apartment, good clothes, and frequent trips to interesting countries like Italy, France, and Switzerland. Their source of income was unknown, and it seemed a strange coincidence that they are also members of the communist party.

The economic drama of this young unmarried doctor of 32 in Sofia shed light on the bitterness he felt with his monthly cash inflow and outflow. His salary is 150 Leva per month. Of this he pays 50 Leva for one small bedroom in a three-bedroom apartment of another family. He shares their kitchen and bathroom. They prefer he does not share their living room. In his bedroom there is a second bed occupied by another person who also pays 50 Leva per month, and who also shares the kitchen and bathroom. To find an apartment for himself and a wife he may eventually want to marry, but it will be extremely difficult, and he does not see this as being possible in the next five years.

The landlord of Dimitri, on the other hand, who is a member in good standing of the communist party, does pretty well earning 100 Leva income, or two thirds of the monthly salary of a young doctor, for renting out one of his bedrooms to two young doctors who are bachelors. Dimitri told me that the man who owns Dimitri's apartment obtained the funds necessary to purchase this apartment by working overseas for a number of years. He said the price to purchase a similar two-bedroom apartment in Sofia in 1980 was probably $40,000. Dimitri told me his annual salary is equivalent to $2,000, which means an apartment costs 20 times his current salary and it is impossible to get financing. In Italy, by contrast, a worker in our factory in Milan earns the equivalent of about $10,000 per year and a two-bedroom apartment in Milan costs about four years of salary, and some financing is available.

In Sofia, the streetcars are free, but busses cost the equivalent of from five to ten U.S. cents per ride. While this is affordable most young people want independence and wheels. Dimitri would love to have a car, but the price of a small car is about three years of his present salary. Even if someone gave him a small car, he couldn't afford to buy the gas. One gallon of gas represents half a day's pay for Dimitri.

Dimitri described his wardrobe in a similar cynical fashion. A shirt costs him 1 ½ days of pay. A badly made suit is six days of pay. A pair of shoes was about four days of pay. He added that the prices of everything are going up, but the take home pay is not. He feels like he is in an economic vise which is slowly closing and that there is no way to stop it and no way out. The idea of having his own apartment and his own car seems far away.

It was interesting to compare my observations about Bulgaria with a group of American tourists who were on my plane leaving Sofia. They had spent ten days in Bulgaria with a guide and were enthusiastic. They felt the system was not as bad as they had imagined. They heard that some things were positive, such as rent which was only 10% of the monthly salary. These tourists were insulated from the Bulgarian environment, as were Lydia and I when we visited Moscow several years ago. These American tourists didn't have the chance to talk to anyone outside of their group and their guide, who was a member of the Communist party in good standing, filled them full of false economic data.

Tourism is a major source of foreign currency for Bulgaria and tourists come also from other Eastern European countries. For tourists from the west, there is a 50% premium for hard currency exchanged after the first $100 dollars. The only East European Communists countries not under Moscow's thumb is Yugoslavia. Its currency, while not on a par with that of the Common Market, is more convertible than any other currency of the Eastern European countries. Unfortunately, the

Bulgarian currency has no value outside of the communist group of countries.

Having had a substantial exposure to the countries within the Eastern European communist countries of the last few years, it is with a sense of thanksgiving that we send our Christmas greeting, that we had the good fortune to be born and live in the capitalist area of the globe.

On the family side we had important scholastic moves in 1980. Robin graduated from kindergarten and starts serious schoolwork as a first grader. Valeria left the lower school and has passed into junior high and Gary, now an 8th grader, is one step away from high school.

Valeria, Robin, Lydia and David in the Alps

The major events for Lydia this year included the job of costume designer and wardrobe mistress for the high school musical and acting as architect, project engineer and works manager for the development and decoration of some additional rooms we annexed to our Milan apartment. This acquisition of space includes a full room for our newly acquired high powered German washing and drying machine whose impressive vibrations at high frequency threaten to loosen some of the bricks, if not cause our entire floor to disintegrate. This building with 20-foot-high ceiling, was built at the time when Napoleon and his French army occupied Milan. Our location is at the very center of a Roman military outpost at the time Julius Caesar occupied this town at that time called Mediolanum.

At Christmas time we gave Gary a two-man pup tent and he had me sleeping with him outside on top of the snow three days later. Both Valeria and Robin wanted to help Gary and me inaugurate his two-man pup tent and they showed us how we could squeeze all four into the tent. We could put Robin crosswise above our head, in the space where one stores clothes, and Valeria could sleep between Gary and me. We were reluctant as far as Robin was concerned, not so much from a space standpoint, but because Robin is still a thumb sucker and the noise of her sucking her thumb would keep all of us awake.

She promised she wouldn't suck her thumb and we agreed to let her join us. However, she didn't have the chance to show us she could keep her promise because of other events that took place. Lydia dressed Robin up warmly with several layers of pants and sweaters covered by a padded jacket, and she looked as inflated as the Michelin tire man. When we were all settled, with the door zipped up in the 20-degree weather and we had just zipped up in our sleeping bags, Robin said, "I have to vomit." There was a great thrashing about, as Gary and I tried to pull ourselves out of our form fitting sleeping bags to get Robin out before she vomited on our bedding. Once outside in the frigid air she said she didn't have to vomit after all. As we came back into the tent, zipped the door, and zipped ourselves back into our sleeping bags, the claustrophobia must have been too much for Robin. She now found the right words to indicate that maybe sleeping outside all puffed up, four in a two-man pup tent may not have been such a clever idea. She burst out crying, "I want mommy." Out of the sleeping bag, on with the shoes and back into the house I carried Robin and delivered her to Mommy.

After settling back into the tent and into our sleeping bags once more, Valeria announced that she thought it would be better if she went inside and she got up to leave. And she too went back to Mommy. Gary and I stuck it out.

It was cold, the wind was blowing, and my sleeping bag was for summer temperatures. Some blankets took care of keeping the heat in on the top side, but the bottom side was another story. My air mattress had a slow leak and held its air for about two hours. As long as it was inflated, I was warm on the bottom and slept fine. But after about an hour and a half some bone would encounter the frozen ground. I realized things were not going to get any better and I should do something before all my body heat was drained out through whose two bones. So, I had to crawl out of my warm bag and huff and puff to blow it back up again. My night consisted of 4 one and a half hour naps.

This winter camping experience was followed by two Boy Scout outings in the spring. In the first campout we had the opportunity of testing the waterproof quality of this new tent. We found a fine place on the banks of the Po River for the first camp out and, with threatening skies, managed to get our tents up before the rain started. A friendly farmer gave us some dry wood and with a roaring hot fire from his wood, we managed to dry out and warm up.

The cooking merit badge, involving cooking outside without utensils, was an objective reached. Tomatoes, peppers, onions, and meat were impaled on wooden spears and sour dough was wrapped around smaller sticks. Those sticks and spears were laid across a trench fire.

It is a skillful scout who manages to turn his stick with sufficient frequency to make an edible meal and yet keep the pieces from falling into the fire. When it is dark, you are cold, and a thin mist is falling on the back of your neck, a mouth full of bread, even half burnt and half dough, is most welcome. The alternate, crisp and raw pieces of shish kebab remaining on the spears were also wolfed down with relish and warmed us. The tent held up well that night as the drizzle turned into a heavy rain. Except for one boy who slept all night in contact with the wall of his tent, which soaked his sleeping bag, we emerged dry the next morning.

After crawling out of a warm sleeping bag into a cold moist and foggy day, there is no greater pleasure than having your front side warmed before a fire and then having your back side warmed. Seeing steam pouring out from your damp pants, as you heat the pants and your legs inside of them in front of the fire, adds to this pleasure. I really appreciated the comfort of our apartment and a warm bath when we returned to Milan.

The second Boy Scout camp out was without rain, but we had winds instead. We found a very scenic camp site in a saddle at the beginning of the Alps. However, due to its location, we were in the path of alternating winds. During the day a warm wind blew uphill from the valley and at night it reversed itself by howling downhill into the valleys passing over our tents and causing a loud flapping of the canvas. This gave the boys the impression we were perched on a ridge of the Himalayas.

Valeria, also a scout, had her Girl Scout troop campout in the spring. We had four tents full of girls, camped among the trees at our summer place in the village of Brunate above Lake Como. The fire building skills of the Girl Scouts was very good and their outdoor cooking, supervised by Lydia in the background was first class.

The three children in Brunate

1980: BULGARIA

Gary, Robin, Lydia and David during Brunate winter

Lydia worked with the Girl Scouts this year and took on a major responsibility for the costumes of the high school musical, "The Boy Friend," a musical which takes place in the 1920's and has a change of costume for each act. Lydia designed a wonderful mixture of 70 flapper costumes with the help of the students and other mothers. The performances were colorful, well done, and well received.

For our home leave we enjoyed a visit to Princeton, New Jersey, with the Myslik family, friends from Milan, and had a balloon ride. Our balloon ride started one very clear day at 6:00 AM. The balloon was similar to the kind used in the movie "80 days around the world." The edge of the wicker basket in which we were standing reached only to my belt and, rising slowly above tree level, I was surprised not to have a feeling of acrophobia, even when we reached 1,000 feet above the ground. The balloon is pushed by only the wind and the only means of control is up or down, piloted by the licensed balloon pilot. The detail of the landscape is beautiful as you float slowly above the ground. We saw many deer running through the fields and woods. As you coast along silently, the only noise is an occasional bark of a dog below.

It takes a lot of skill to land a balloon in the proper place. The pilot must plan the downward movement, gliding to clear any telephone poles or electric transmission lines and landing in an open field upwind of the next bank of trees. Our pilot made several practice landings fine, but when we came down for our final landing, we had a bit of trouble. The wind started blowing harder and our balloon overshot the field our pilot had identified.

When our basket hit the ground, gently, the wind pulled the upper part of the balloon ahead and tipped us in the basket at a 45-degree angle. In this position our basket was dragged along the ground and our pilot warned us not to get out until we came to a complete stop. The wind tipped us even further over and we were almost horizontal to the ground. Lydia and Valeria found themselves on the bottom of the basket hanging on to the ropes, almost lying down.

I was above them suspended from the rigging like a sailor on an 18th century ship with my legs dangling down. Every time we came to a stop, and thought we could get out, a new gust of wind bumped us further ahead. Two hundred meters ahead were some bushes and just beyond was a bank of trees. The wind kept bumping us ahead towards the bushes and as we got closer, I recognized them as tall blackberry brambles. We were almost stopped before we reached these thorns but at the last moment a fresh gust of wind blew us into the middle of the thorns.

The task of extricating ourselves, and the balloon, from these seven feet tall thorny arms was like trying to free oneself from the center of a swarm of octopi. No sooner did I get a part of nylon fabric of the balloon free from one bramble than I would discover another branch of spines catching ahold of my sweater. Reaching to liberate my sweater from the attachment of the nearby thorn bush the liberated balloon would be blown ahead to a different thorn bush while we and the basket changed positions from almost horizontal to the ground returning to a 45-degree angle. Then into the grasp of the next blackberry thorn bush went the balloon and my pants.

Half an hour later, alternating from freeing ourselves and the balloon from several different spiny brambles, we emerged on the other side of this wild blackberry thorn. Nevertheless, this floating over the country just above the treetops was a delightful experience. Valeria would like to do it again.

Conclusion of my 20 wonderful years of working and living in Italy

I look back on our wonderful 20 years living in beautiful Italy and recall with great pleasure and gratitude the many adventures experienced over this period of time. Our Milan apartment in the center of the historical area of the city of Milan two blocks from the Sforza Castle was a perfect launchpad for trips within Italy and around the world. In Milan, we thoroughly enjoyed introducing our children to the rich musical offering of grand opera and ballet at the La Scala opera house which was a 15-minute walk from our apartment. We were lucky to obtain a five-person family box for ten grand operas and ballets every year which we enjoyed for 20 opera seasons. Living within a three-to-five-hour drive to the nearby Italian-French, Italian-Swiss and Italian-Austrian Alps made our annual winter ski vacation and occasional weekend winter trips possible. We explored up and down the Italian boot as well as its islands, absorbing its long and rich history, first as a couple and then as a family. Lydia has been able to accompany me on several business trips to interesting places like Moscow, Budapest, Nigeria, Israel, and Saudi Arabia.

As the 1970s came to a close and the 1980s began, we began thinking

CONCLUSION OF MY 20 WONDERFUL YEARS OF WORKING AND LIVING IN ITALY

it was probably time to transplant our family back to the United States. We had several reasons for this decision. First, while the education at the American School of Milan (ASM) was excellent and our children were thriving, we wanted them to experience everyday life in the United States to better prepare them for an American university experience. With ASM the size of a small U.S. public elementary school, we knew that it could not offer the variety of courses and extracurricular activity that were available in the U.S. and began looking in the Boston area for excellent public schools for all three children – elementary school for Robin, middle school for Valeria and high school for Gary. We settled on Lexington, Massachusetts.

Another reason was the alarming rise of the communist Red Brigade in Italy. This group started their terrorist campaign with the murder of the Attorney General of Genoa in 1974 followed by the Editor of the newspaper La Stampa shortly after. Then they murdered five bodyguards of the Italian Prime Minister Moro, kidnapped him, and eventually murdered him before negotiations had been completed to define a ransom price for his release. The Italian Press reported that from 1975 to 1980 there have been 100 political murders in northern Italy. Their targets were not only Italian as American managers of large American manufacturing companies were also considered to be targets of the Red Brigade. For protection, one of my good friends and colleague in Milan was driven to work in a large car with steel plates on its sides and with an armed bodyguard in the company car.

Finally, it seemed that Italy was forging a path to becoming a socialist country. In the 1980 national Italian elections, the Socialists and Communists together won 45% of the votes. Had any of the minor Italian parties, each with 2% or 3% of the votes in the following election joined a center-left coalition, an agreement could follow for a majority communist/socialist government and eventually the communists could take power in Italy. As I experienced in my travels to many Eastern European countries, the Middle East, Asia, and Africa, many of these countries are ruled by a small kleptocracy. After seeing what happened in Eastern Europe when the communists took power, we would not want to experience a similar shift in the politics and culture of Italy.

Between the ongoing recession, inflation and terrorist threat in Italy, Lydia and I agreed that these factors were strong enough for us to pack up and move the family to the United States. We started in Lexington, Massachusetts and moved to Newton, Massachusetts a year later. I started out with a high-tech company in Boston and eventually branched out on my own as a financial consultant for startup companies and real estate appraiser. Our adventures in the United States will be the subject of my next book.

CPSIA information can be obtained
at www.ICGtesting.com
Printed in the USA
LVHW020339211122
733501LV00021B/1417